Accessible, lively and timely, this book makes bodies visible in youth sociology. Coffey's analysis of body work by young people draws effortlessly on the insights of Deleuze, Guattari and Spinoza to disrupt accepted understandings of youth. Using vivid examples, she shows how young people engaging in body work both produce and resist gendered inequalities and health risks. Coffey issues a challenge to 'embody' youth studies – and the broader field of sociology. Reading this book is a must.

Johanna Wyn, *Director, Youth Research Centre, the University of Melbourne*

Julia Coffey's materialist approach places the body and its capacities at the forefront of analysis in youth studies research. It documents the body work of contemporary young people, ranging from cosmetic surgery and fitness classes to sexting, football and tattoos. A must-read book for youth work students and professionals alike!

Nick J. Fox, *Professor of Sociology, University of Sheffield*

In this truly innovative and ground breaking contribution to the study of embodied experience Coffey invites us to rethink the role of the body in the study of youth. Drawing upon advancements in new materialist thought, a framework for understanding the body as a set of dynamic, relational processes and affective engagements is offered as a corrective to established approaches which cast the young body as a site where risk and social problems are managed. Throughout the analysis this reorientation makes way for more complex, contradictory and open ended explorations of the interconnections between bodies, gender, health and youth. This non-reductive reading of body work practices sets the tone for new research agendas and will surely inspire further theoretical and methodological advances in the study of embodied experience across a wide a variety social contexts.

Shelley Budgeon, *Senior Lecturer in Sociology, University of Birmingham*

Body Work

The rise of the health, beauty and fitness industries in recent years has led to an increased focus on the body. Body image, gender and health are issues of long-standing concern in sociology, but a specific theoretical and empirical focus on the body has been largely missing from the field of youth studies. This book explores young people's understandings of their bodies in the context of gender and health ideals, consumer culture, individualisation and image.

Body Work examines the body in youth studies. It explores paradoxical aspects of gendered body work practices, highlighting the contradiction in men's increased participation in these industries as consumers alongside the re-emphasis of their gendered difference. It explores the key ways in which the ideal body is currently achieved, via muscularising practices, slimming regimes and cosmetic procedures. Coffey investigates the concept of 'health' and how it is inextricably linked both to the bodily performance of gender ideals and an increased public emphasis on individual management and responsibility in the pursuit of a 'healthy' body.

This book's conceptual framework places it at the forefront of theoretical work concerning bodies, affect and images, particularly in its development of Deleuzian research. It will appeal to a wide range of scholars and students in the fields of youth studies, education, sociology, gender studies, cultural studies, affect and body studies.

Julia Coffey is a lecturer in the School of Humanities and Social Science at the University of Newcastle, Australia.

Youth, Young Adulthood and Society Series
Series editor: Andy Furlong, University of Glasgow, UK
Andy.Furlong@glasgow.ac.uk

The *Youth, Young Adulthood and Society series* brings together social scientists from many disciplines to present research monographs and collections, seeking to further research into youth in our changing societies around the world today. The books in this series advance the field of youth studies by presenting original, exciting research, with strongly theoretically- and empirically-grounded analysis.

Published:

Body Work
Youth, gender and health
Julia Coffey

Young People and the Aesthetics of Health Promotion
Beyond reason, rationality and risk
Kerry Montero and Peter Kelly

The Subcultural Imagination
Theory, research and reflexivity in contemporary youth cultures
Edited by Shane Blackman and Michelle Kempson

Forthcoming:

Young People in the Labour Market
Past, present, future
Andy Furlong, John Goodwin, Sarah Hadfield, Stuart Hall, Kevin Lowden and Henrietta O'Connor

Youth, Class and Culture
Steven Threadgold

Spaces of Youth
Identities, inequalities and social change
David Farrugia

Rethinking Young People's Marginalisation
Beyond neo-liberal futures?
Perri Campbell, Lyn Harrison, Chris Hickey and Peter Kelly

Muslim Youth in the Diaspora
Challenging extremism through popular culture
Pam Nilan

Body Work
Youth, gender and health

Julia Coffey

LONDON AND NEW YORK

First published 2016
by Routledge
2 Park Square, Milton Park, Abingdon, Oxon OX14 4RN

and by Routledge
711 Third Avenue, New York, NY 10017

First issued in paperback 2018

Routledge is an imprint of the Taylor & Francis Group, an informa business

© 2016 Julia Coffey

The right of Julia Coffey to be identified as author of this work has been asserted by him/her in accordance with sections 77 and 78 of the Copyright, Designs and Patents Act 1988.

All rights reserved. No part of this book may be reprinted or reproduced or utilised in any form or by any electronic, mechanical, or other means, now known or hereafter invented, including photocopying and recording, or in any information storage or retrieval system, without permission in writing from the publishers.

Trademark notice: Product or corporate names may be trademarks or registered trademarks, and are used only for identification and explanation without intent to infringe.

British Library Cataloguing in Publication Data
A catalogue record for this book is available from the British Library

Library of Congress Cataloging in Publication Data
Names: Coffey, Julia, author.
Title: Body work : youth, gender and health / Julia Coffey.
Description: Abingdon, Oxon ; NewYork, NY : Routledge, 2016. | Series: Youth, young adulthood and society
Identifiers: LCCN 2015036967| ISBN 9781138911512 (hardback) | ISBN 9781315692609 (e-book)
Subjects: LCSH: Human body–Social aspects. | Youth. | Body image. | Identity (Psychology) | Sex role. | Health behavior.
Classification: LCC HM636 .C64 2016 | DDC 306.4/613–dc23
LC record available at http://lccn.loc.gov/2015036967

ISBN 13: 978-1-138-59284-1 (pbk)
ISBN 13: 978-1-138-91151-2 (hbk)

Typeset in Times New Roman
by Taylor & Francis Books

 Printed in the United Kingdom
by Henry Ling Limited

Contents

Acknowledgement   viii

1 Introduction to youth sociology and the body   1

2 Theorising the body   17

3 Researching the body   42

4 Assembling gender: body work, identities and the body   72

5 Health, affect and embodiment   98

6 'Buff culture', cosmetic surgery and bodily limits   121

7 Conclusion: embodying youth studies   143

Index   159

Acknowledgement

This project has involved the support, encouragement and advice of many people over many years. Thank you to my Ph.D. supervisors and mentors, Professor Johanna Wyn, Professor Timothy Marjoribanks and Associate Professor Helen Cahill; your generosity and encouragement will stay with me always. I also want to thank my colleagues at the Youth Research Centre, University of Melbourne and more recently Pam Nilan, David Farrugia and Steve Threadgold at the University of Newcastle for their comments and advice in drafting this book. Thank you to my parents and sister Rachel, who have always supported and encouraged me in everything I do. Finally, thank you to my partner, Aaron, for everything.

1 Introduction to youth sociology and the body

Introduction

This book develops an embodied approach to youth sociology. Body image, gender and health are issues of long-standing concern in sociology and youth studies, however a focus on the body, both theoretically and empirically, has been largely absent. This book draws upon data from a qualitative study which explored young people's understandings of bodies and body work practices in the context of gender and health ideals, consumer culture, individualisation and image. It maps the implications of the social context in which the body is becoming an increasing area of attention and concern. 'Body work' is introduced to theorise the dynamic process by which bodies and societies shape each other. This concept is developed from feminist sociological approaches to the body drawn from Deleuze, Guattari and Spinoza as an active, productive force which operates in relation to broader socio-historical–cultural contexts. Body work is explored through a focus on *body work practices* as a way of studying how the body is lived and produced in relation to gender, image, health and appearance. It speaks to a conceptualisation of the body as assembling through connections.

In this chapter, I will first map the approaches to the body that have been developed in sociology to address the body, theoretically and empirically. I will then locate the concept of 'body work' as I am developing it in relation to other sociological discussions of body work and the relations between the body and the social. I will then consider the way the body has largely remained an absent presence in youth studies, arguing that the concept of body work enables a theoretically grounded approach to the empirical study of young people and the body.

The body and society

The body represents a key problematic in both popular and academic discussions. In contemporary Western societies such as Australia, the body tends to be understood as an 'object' to be worked on, as a way of improving one's

2 Introduction to youth sociology and the body

appearance and self-image, and by extension, one's life. The body in this sense is understood in sociology as shaped by social norms related to gendered, classed and raced ideals, and broader structures such as the labour market and the demands of late capitalist consumer societies. The body is seen as both the consuming entity and the product. The body is *the* mode by which the individual and the social collide. For these reasons, the dynamics of the body and its relations with society has been a core issue in academic discussions in sociology, philosophy, cultural studies and gender studies. How to understand the dynamics by which the body is shaped by and contributes to the shaping of social context? If the body is understood as primarily influenced by the social forces that surrounds it, this sets us up well to critique the inequalities beyond a person's control that shapes experiences, opportunities and lives. If we are at the mercy of social forces beyond our control, how then do we account for the instances of social change which occur unexpectedly, or 'despite the odds'?

We all engage with the social world differently, which means the dynamics of social influence affect us differently. Such questions have led to intense debate in sociology and feminist philosophy surrounding the body's role for understanding the dynamics of inequality. Early gender theorists highlighted that the body is the product of social inequalities, rather than the basis for it. This political move was important because the female body was for so long considered to be 'naturally' inferior to the male body, and this bodily difference was used to legitimate the exclusion of women from public life as the 'household' was rationalised as a woman's 'natural' place. Similarly, eighteenth-century biological determinist perspectives which saw racial and class differences as inherent and 'natural' in the body were used to hold the white, upper-class European male's body as the 'human' norm by which all others were judged as lacking. This 'standard' was legitimated by the rise in modern 'science' through fields such as phrenology and social Darwinism, and formed the basis of some of the most appalling atrocities in human history including genocide and slavery. Raced, gendered and classed differences were enshrined by these fields as the fields themselves were constituted, including those of biology, genetics and psychology. Because human differences (inferiorities) were seen as bodily, hierarchies of dominance were by implication 'natural' and inevitable. The involvement of fields of science, medicine and technology in the naturalisation of inequality and discrimination is a continuing critique made by sociologists and other fields of social science. At each stage, the body has been the battleground of these debates.

The body and embodiment are now key areas of social inquiry. Where it was once an 'absent presence' in sociology (Turner 1984; Shilling 2003), in recent decades the body has become a central area of social theory and study throughout the social sciences and humanities as well as in science and technology. The 'absent presence' thesis is that the body tended to be implicitly 'present' in all studies of social patterns and human behaviour, it was conspicuously 'absent' from specific attention, discussion or analysis. The body

Introduction to youth sociology and the body 3

and human physicality is implicitly part of almost all sociological study (for example, in relation to identity, governance, power, social action, etc.); however, as sociologists of the body argued, the body was seen as extraneous to these processes, relegated as a lesser concern. The relegation of the body is rooted in dominant Western philosophy, particularly the work of Descartes, and the core dualism of mind/body. Feminist philosophers in particular have been highly critical of the impact of the mind/body dualism and its role in sustaining philosophical inequalities between men and women, as maleness (and masculinity) is associated with the mind, reason, logic and order; while femaleness (and femininity) is associated with the body and the passions, irrationality and disorder (Grosz 1994). Finding ways to theorise bodies beyond dualisms has been a central tenet of much post-structural feminist work, and has also contributed to recent sociological approaches to the body empirically. This concern has led to different approaches being sought to think through some of the most important sociological problems, including the relations between people and social structures and processes associated with how individuals negotiate 'structure' and 'agency'. Here, Deleuzian understandings of bodies as processes (not entities) which are constantly shifting and being redefined based on their relations with other bodies and forces in the world, have been proposed as offering a way of conceptualising bodies beyond the most problematic dualisms in both feminist and sociological theory (Grosz 1994; Budgeon 2003; Coleman 2009).

The body is shaped in relation to social, historical and structural contexts which surround it and in which people live. However, just as these contexts are dynamic and ever-changing, so too is the body. The body is more than an object upon which culture and society is written. The body is a social and biological organism, and its complexities and potentialities are still not well understood. We need a theoretical approach to the body that does justice to the complexities of living and the social world. We need a framework which approaches both the body and the social as dynamic, contextual and complex.

This book mobilises an approach to bodies informed by Deleuzian, feminist and sociological insights to open alternative, more complex understandings of bodies, youth, gender and health. The book demonstrates the potential for innovative conceptual tools for the study of youth. The main objective of the book is to demonstrate an embodied approach to youth, developed from innovations in feminist sociological thought based on the concepts of Deleuze, Guattari and Spinoza. The book aims to build on a rapidly growing area of sociological empirical research which develops these concepts for sociological inquiry. This is the first overt attempt to develop and mobilise these concepts in the sociology of youth. As such, the book aims to push the boundaries of sociological research on the body and body work practices, setting the agenda for a different way of thinking about bodies and the relationship between bodies and society in youth studies.

4   *Introduction to youth sociology and the body*

Body work

I develop the term 'body work' to theorise the dynamic process by which bodies and societies shape each other. This concept is developed from feminist sociological approaches to the body drawn from Deleuze, Guattari and Spinoza as an active, productive force which operates in relation to broader socio-historical–cultural contexts. The term body work entails a consideration of the body beyond the individual only, including the range of relations between bodies and the social world and the complex engagements which mediate 'what a body can do'. The term is used to denote a particular theoretical approach to the body as *in process*. Body work highlights a focus on process and practice in relations between the body and the social. In the study I discuss throughout this book, body work was studied through a focus on *body work practices* as a way of studying how the body is lived and produced in relation to gender, image, health and appearance. In the study, body work practices included any activities aimed at modifying or maintaining the body's appearance, including dieting and exercise (commonly understood as 'health' practices), particularly related to the presentation of self. Body work practices were explored in the context of gender and health ideals, consumer culture, individualisation and image, I argue that a focus on body work as productive, affective engagements can enable more complex understandings of bodies, youth, gender and health.

In contemporary sociology, body shape and physical control are understood as increasingly central to people's sense of identity. The concept of body work addresses this area of study. Conceptually, it also aims to contribute to non-dualist sociological understandings of the body. Elsewhere in sociology, the term 'body work' has been defined in general terms as the practices or 'work' one performs on one's own body (Gimlin 2007). Gimlin identifies the different forms of body work as (1) the work performed on one's own body; (2) paid labour carried out on the bodies of others; (3) the management of embodied emotional experience and display; and (4) the production or modification of bodies through work (2007: 353). 'Body work' can also refer to all forms of bodily labour such as in caring and welfare industries and domestic labour (Shilling 2011: 336). Recent work by Mears has also developed the term 'aesthetic labour', distinct from body work, to describe 'the practice of screening, managing, and controlling workers on the basis of their physical appearance' (Mears 2014: 1330). In contrast, I use the term 'body work practices' to describe work performed on one's own body that connects to aesthetic modifications or maintenance of the body. These practices are important because they entail an understanding of the body as an active force which is produced by these practices and broader relations with other matter, forces, discourses and affects, all of which comprise 'what a body can do'.

Other approaches which have focused on the dynamics of bodily display and identity have been conceptualised in sociological approaches (Giddens 1991; Shilling 2003) as part of the 'body project' associated with the modern,

Introduction to youth sociology and the body 5

Western individual's 'project' of self-identity. Giddens (1991) and Shilling (2003) have proposed that work on the body is aligned with a range of other work on the 'self' which, along the lines of psychological models of development, enables an individual's self-identity to be 'accomplished' (Shilling 2003). The focus on body work practices is in some ways similar to Giddens's (1991) 'body projects' and Crossley's (2005) 'reflexive body techniques', since all three terms describe the ways that individuals, in the current neo-liberal context, monitor, maintain and modify their bodies and 'selves'. This focus on body work practices, however, differs significantly in terms of the ontology underpinning the conceptualisation of bodies and the social. This is discussed further in Chapter 2. Unlike the term body 'project', which suggests that the body and identity can be at some point completed, 'body work' emphasises that the relations between bodies and the social are processural and ongoing.

The body in youth studies

The body has been identified as a central area of theoretical attention in sociology since the 1990s, but a comprehensive theoretical and empirical approach to the body in youth studies has been missing.

While a significant range of work in youth studies has explored young lives in relation to gender, class, race and ethnicity, sexualities and popular culture, the body has tended to be studied indirectly through these broader themes rather than being the focus of study per se (Frost 2001). For example, in studies of how young people negotiate transitions from school to work, or are implicated in class or gender relations, the bodies of young people are obviously inherently involved, yet they remain invisible. The embodied dynamics of young people's experiences tend not to be foregrounded, with most accounts focusing on the cognitive in descriptions of young people's lives; in their thoughts, descriptions and perspectives on a range of issues. The non-rational or sensate aspects of experience or individuality are often latent, or are not the key focus of analysis.

One of the most pervasive approaches that youth studies scholars must battle with is the contemporary discourses of adolescent brain development. Kelly (2015) argues the developmental model of young people primarily understood in relation to their not yet fully formed brains is reductive and creates a very limited understanding of young people's lives, essentially conflating all of the complexity of experience and consciousness to just 'one organ in the body'. This has the significant implication of effectively 'stripping young people of their bodies, gender, histories and contexts' (Kelly 2015: 618). A focus on the dynamics of embodiment can be understood as one primary way of developing a critique of reductive understandings of youth, and a way of pursuing understandings which embrace complexity and ambivalence as a strategy of resistance to the homogenising influences of neo-liberalism.

A focus on embodiment entails a specific intention to place the body – and embodied experience – at the forefront of analysis. This approach also aims to

6 Introduction to youth sociology and the body

highlight the active relations between bodies and the world. This focus on the body's potential and lived experience can assist in moving beyond previous approaches in which the body is invisible or rendered inferior to the mind in a binary logic. More than this, beginning to 'think through the body' can open up a way of exploring the ways the body is implicated in the complexities and tensions in young people's lives. However, theoretical approaches to 'the body' have a complex history in terms of philosophy. The body brings significant 'baggage' that needs to be addressed and acknowledged if we are to understand its current significance in sociological theory and research. I develop this in depth in Chapter 2, and in the chapters that follow.

Youth, 'risk' and the body

The young body is the implicit focus of discussion in areas of health, illness and risk. The focus on young people's bodies is problematic conceptually, however, as a specific focus on corporeality is obsured beyond the body being seen as an 'object' to be managed. Young people's bodies tend to be seen as the sites of 'problems', such as those related to health, for example the 'risks' related to growing figures of childhood and youth obesity (Lupton 2013a), binge drinking (Nairn et al. 2006; Katainen and Rolando 2014), sexuality (Paechter 2011; Renold et al. 2015) and sexting (Albury and Crawford 2012; Rice and Watson 2016), and body image and eating disorders (for a discussion, see Coffey and Watson 2015; Coffey et al. 2016).

The 'youth at risk' discourse frames public discussions of youth in a range of interconnected ways, primarily around concerns that young people are not 'transitioning' successfully through traditional pathways from education to employment (Wyn and Woodman 2006). This concern for youth who are marginalised by traditional education and employment trajectories then turns to other related issues associated with unemployment and 'idleness', including poor mental health outcomes, substance use, crime and delinquency, and teenage pregnancy (Kelly 2001; Harris 2004; te Riele 2006). Developmental markers and health status work to separate 'normal' youth from those deemed as needing intervention. Typically, the successful completion of normative developmental objectives in health and risk are a key focus in youth health policy. As many youth studies scholars have pointed out, however, this approach fails to appreciate the complex interactions of factors related to class, gender, race, ethnicity and ability (White and Wyn 2008). The emphasis placed on health and meeting normative goals also reveals anxiety about particular dangers young bodies pose to society in the present and in future adulthood. In countries such as Australia, the UK and USA this has centred around so-called lifestyle (and by implication preventable) health issues such obesity, mental illness, eating disorders, and alcohol (particularly binge drinking) and other drug use. As Kelly (2001: 24) has argued, the 'youth at-risk' discourse, drawn primarily from developmental psychological

Introduction to youth sociology and the body 7

approaches, potentially encompasses all youthful behaviours and dispositions and thus places all young people as 'at risk'.

This also occurs in a broader context of the individualisation and responsibilisation of risks that Beck (1992) describes as characteristic of the 'risk society'. Beck theorises that broad economic and social shifts that have occurred in late modern societies such as Europe, the USA and Australia have led to a situation where individuals are compelled to be responsible for creating their own trajectories and biographies. This context is vastly different from previous generations and the relatively stable patterns of work and family which characterised industrial societies (Beck 1992). As numerous youth studies scholars have argued, following Beck's work, the individual management of structural risks is a central feature of contemporary society. There is a pernicious underside to the 'risk society', in that risks are understood as able to be managed by the individual, regardless of structural or institutional inequalities. Although the 'relations of inequality' including class and gender have remained more or less the same, structural risks related to these inequalities are recast as individual risks. Those who fail to manage these risks thus bear the full weight of responsibility, regardless of the structural inequities which are beyond the realm of 'choice'. Many of the key risks which young people are understood as being particularly susceptible to relate to concerns of sexualisation, and the bodily management and responsibility of such risks (see Chapter 3).

The dominant understandings of young people's bodies tend to be drawn from developmental psychological perspectives which position young people primarily in terms of their susceptibility to risk. As Kelly (2001) has argued, this view is used to justify a range of attempts to regulate young people's behaviour, or more accurately, to compel young people to regulate their own behaviour and bodies. The 'at risk' approach to youth has been widely criticised in the youth studies literature as a 'deficit approach' (Kelly 2001; Wyn and Woodman 2006) which further marginalises those young people who are more vulnerable as a result of structural inequalities (te Riele 2006), as well as being a simplistic, reductive and normalising framework which is ill-equipped to offer a comprehensive understanding of the complexity and ambiguity which characterises young people's contemporary lives (Kelly 2015).

Body image

The body and body 'image' of young people is seen as a major social problem affecting young people's well-being (Grogan and Wainwright 1996; Grogan 2008). Images of bodies are everywhere in consumer culture. Online and printed news media run stories about celebrities' bodies almost every day, highlighting their transformations, lamenting their imperfections, and detailing everyday people's 'battles' with their bodies. Crucially, body image is an issue associated in particular with the experience of youth. Body image continues to be an issue of primary concern for young people, and it has been

8   *Introduction to youth sociology and the body*

ranked in the top three issues of most concern for young Australians aged 15–24 for the past five years consecutively (Mission Australia 2014). The term 'body image' however tends to focus primarily on the psychological and individual aspects rather than social, historical or cultural contexts which frame experience. For this reason particularly, a term such as 'body work' is needed to capture the social processes which shape the body's relations with the world.

Literature relating to body image in particular is drawn from psychological perspectives in which the primary focus is to bolster individual resilience to harmful images (Coleman 2008). As Davis (1995) has argued, understandings of body image and body dysmorphic disorder which present people as having 'faulty image-reading practices' or 'disordered eating' patterns tend to pathologise sufferers without adequately addressing the sociocultural context in which these images are produced and consumed. More certainly needs to be achieved to adequately understand body image concerns beyond a focus on the individual's brain and thought patterns. The physical body has largely been obscured by explanations which have privileged the cerebral, in both empirical and conceptual approaches to youth.

A focus on the body and embodiment is needed to broaden our understandings of some of the most important issues for young people. It is particularly important to expand the discussion of body image concerns beyond psychological frameworks of understanding, given the emphatially social nature of body image and the widespread concern young people themselves have for this and other body-related issues including sexuality.

Health, gender and consumer culture

A focus on the body is crucial in youth studies, not least because the body is more prominent than ever in contemporary life. Themes of gender, health and consumer culture are key to understanding the current popular and sociological concern surrounding the body.

The contemporary rise of health, beauty and fitness industries is aligned with an increase in attention to the body, body work and 'body image'. The health, beauty and fitness industries are highly profitable in Australia, and continue to grow and change rapidly (Australian Centre for Retail Studies 2005; Australian Bureau of Statistics 2009). In 2004, health and beauty retailing in Australia amounted to $8,821 million, up 13 per cent on 2003 (Australian Centre for Retail Studies 2005: 3). The health and fitness industry has seen a significant increase in demand for personal training and gym memberships, and the increase in fitness club openings and sales of fitness programmes (Australian Bureau of Statistics 2009). Between 2001 and 2005 the number of fitness centres in Australia rose by 24 per cent, and the operating profit of fitness centres in this same period rose by 89 per cent (Australian Bureau of Statistics 2009). More recently, the health and fitness industry has continued to grow 4.8 per cent between 2009 and 2014, with

Introduction to youth sociology and the body 9

revenue increasing 1.4 per cent each year. In 2013, revenue grew by 1.4 per cent to $1.31 billion. The growth of these industries has occurred against the broader social and cultural context in wealthy, advanced, liberal, post-industrial countries such as Australia. This context includes the development of new technologies such as health tracking (Lupton 2013b), social media platforms and the new forms of image-sharing they afford (Tiidenberg and Gómez Cruz 2015) and the broader call by neo-liberal governments and public health initiatives for citizens to take responsibility for their own health (Ouellette and Hay 2008).

Crawford uses the term 'healthism', defined as the primary preoccupation with personal health as the achievement and definition of well-being, to describe the ways that solutions to health 'rest within the individual's determination' (Crawford 1980: 368). Health and working on the body are promoted as consumer choices; 'choices' essential to general well-being and success and the 'quest to fulfil themselves' (Rose 1996: 162). In this domain of consumption, 'individuals will want to be healthy, experts will instruct them on how to be so, and entrepreneurs will exploit and enhance this market for health. Health will be ensured through a combination of the market, expertise and a regulated economy' (Rose 1996: 162).

Health is also interlaced through the bodily performance of gender ideals. As well as being strongly gendered, health ideals are central in the increasing public emphasis on individual management and responsibility of the body towards an image of 'health'. In the context of increased individualisation of health and emphasis on individual responsibility for managing health 'risks', health is increasingly understood as an image or as visible through the body's appearance. The practices aimed at crafting the 'healthy' body and self-responsible citizen are also strongly delineated by gender (Moore 2010). Though men are now argued to be suffering the 'dubious equality' as consumers of health, fitness and cosmetic products (Featherstone 1982), the idealised physical dimensions of the body are gendered in ways which link with traditional gendered hierarchies and inequalities (Moore 2010). The idealised 'healthy' woman's body in this context remains slender (Bordo 2003), while the idealised man's body is toned and muscular (Crossley 2006). The gendered physicalities of these 'ideal' bodies are telling, and relate to a range of underlying assumptions around men's 'natural' physical strength and prowess, and women's 'natural daintiness', as one participant in this research put it. The rise in men's concern for the body can be understood as linked to their increasing participation in consumption practices around the body (Featherstone 2010), yet the sorts of practices both women and men undertake in this context are as strongly geared towards emphasising gender differences as ever. Moore (2010) argues that traditional ideas about gender also underpin the particular attitude to the body found in contemporary health promotion. The body consciousness and self-awareness demanded in new paradigms of health are attributes that have historically been associated with femininity (Moore 2010: 112). The increase in health, beauty and fitness industries is

10 *Introduction to youth sociology and the body*

aligned with an increase in attention to the body, and 'body image' for both women and men. This book discusses a range of problematic implications associated with the connotation of health as an idealised (gendered) image.

The examples of body work, health and gender described in the book detail the complexities, contradictions and ambivalences in the ways the body is experienced by participants. The book explores the paradoxical aspects of gendered body image and body work practices, highlighting the contradictions in men's increased participation in these industries as consumers and the re-emphasising of gendered difference. The book explores the key ways in which this is currently undertaken through work on the body via muscularising practices which are increasingly engaged in by young men, and slimming and cosmetic procedures such as breast implants engaged in by young women in the study. Participants' descriptions of bodies and experiences necessitated finding an approach to the body which was able to do justice to the complexities they described. I found binaries of structure and agency, or regulation and liberation, for example, wholly inadequate for understanding the dynamics and negotiations of their bodies in relation to social forces. Their accounts spoke to more than the dominant discourses of health or gender; other dimensions like the way the body feels was described as crucial in motivating action (affect) and difference. Further, the individuality of their responses made it difficult to generalise about what the 'impacts' or effects of particular body work practices were, such that it was insufficient to describe practices like jogging or cosmetic surgery as being one-dimensionally oppressive or positive. For example, for participants like Victoria, jogging was described as exhilarating and giving her a 'rush'; whereas for Gillian it was related as the 'only way' she can allow herself to 'not feel bad' about herself (see Chapters 5 and 6). Similarly, though Kate and Isabelle had both had breast implant surgery, this practice had a different set of implications for their lives. For Kate, it enabled her to live more 'fully' and to 'just enjoy life without stressing all the time', whereas Isabelle described planning on having 'everything done' in the future but wondered 'when will it stop?'. Drawing on feminist developments of Deleuzian, Guattarian and Spinozan concepts and perspectives of the body affords attention to these complexities and nuances of social life. Such a perspective approaches the body as produced through its relations with social forces such as health and gender in unpredictable and dynamic ways. The concept of affect, for example, draws attention to the embodied sensations which mediate action. This can help to explain why different people have different responses to the same practice, such as cosmetic surgery: it has an impact on their possibilities for living differently because the *affects* related to the practice differ.

Similarly, drawing on this feminist, Deleuzo-Guattarian perspective I aim to show how body work practices can be understood not simply as the effects of gender or health discourses (Markula 2006). Instead, gender and health can be understood as assemblages which produce bodies through the dynamic processes of their engagement. Such a perspective is needed to do justice to

Introduction to youth sociology and the body 11

the complex and non-binary nature in how gender is embodied and lived, while also paying careful attention to the dynamics of power and territorialisations which also comprise and produce the assemblages. Participants described their experiences of their bodies related to gender and health in complex, paradoxical and ambiguous ways. Kate and Jason both explained that they 'get caught up in' wanting to physically resemble the dominant images of gender; Paul, Steph and Gillian explained the complex embodied sensations associated with exercise, health and happiness, with Steph for example saying she would 'get fit so that [she] could be happy'; and Ben and Isabelle portrayed how body work practices can become crucial to their sense of self. Examples showed that the intensity of affects related to practices can limit the range of possibilities available for how the body can be experienced, and these cannot necessarily be known in advance.

Gender and health assemblages produce bodies. The body's capacities for living and action are produced through their engagements, which means they assemble differently for different people, and in different contexts. The examples throughout this book show the need to attend to the complexities and specificities of micro context.

As this book will explore, the body is a key area of feminist and sociological study due in part to the centrality of the body in consumer culture as well as for the study of identities and inequalities. Exploring how people live their bodies and explain their practices of body work is crucial for understanding the processes and connections between societal forces and bodies. This has important implications for sociology that will be considered throughout the book.

There are three implications in particular of this specific approach to the body. The first relates to a focus on the body and its potential to enable nuanced, more complex analysis of the dynamics between bodies and the social which can unsettle some of the most dominant and limiting understandings of youth (e.g. risk discourses). Second, this perspective assists in the denaturalisation of bodily inequalities, showing the ways in which hierarchies emerge through processes rather than being based in any natural 'essence'. Third, this approach speaks to a range of theoretical and empirical implications associated with the use of post-human, new materialist feminist theoretical approaches to the body which are developing in feminist sociology and cultural studies. I return to each of these key points in the final chapter of the book.

Chapter outlines

Chapter 2, 'Theorising the body', introduces key conceptual debates in sociology relating to the interplay between the body and society. I situate the body in recent debates surrounding 'structure and agency' in youth studies, and suggest this debate is indicative of broader issues related to the lack of an expressed focus on the body in this field. I introduce Bourdieu and Foucault's

12 *Introduction to youth sociology and the body*

perspectives on the body, and trace key feminist theoretical debates and innovations stemming from critiques of the mind/body binary and the political move to separate sex (natural) from gender (socially constructed). I argue that these innovations in feminist sociology are productive for understanding the body and for re-theorising structure and agency in sociology and youth studies. Stemming from this, I then introduce a Deleuzo-Guattarian understanding of the body and the key concepts that are used throughout the book: assemblage, affect and becoming. I explore the implications of this approach to the body for theorising gender and health, two major themes which emerged from the study of young people's body work practices.

Chapter 3, 'Researching the body' charts the diverse array of social contexts in which the body has been theorised and studied across the fields of youth, gender and feminist studies and sociology. I consider the ways the body has been present or absent in the dominant strands of research in youth studies in 'transitions' and 'cultures' perspectives. A focus on the body can add much-needed nuance and richness in studying the diverse and complex dynamics between young people's lives and the production of sociality. It can also be useful in disrupting and critiquing dominant knowledge 'about' youth, for example, in concerns around 'risky' practices which often implicitly centre on the body. I draw on studies of 'sexting' to show how a focus on the body assists in highlighting the limitations of media risk discourses for understanding young people's engagements with the practice. I then discuss the studies central to the research on body work relating in particular to gender, sexuality and health, as well as the analytical implications associated with some studies of 'agency' in relation to beauty practices. The primary study of youth and body work is introduced, alongside a discussion of the methodological issues associated with embodying youth studies research.

Chapter 4, 'Assembling gender: body work, identities and the body' explores the current emphasis on the body's (gendered) appearance and the context in which body image is an increasing issue of concern for young people. Data from young people's discussions of body work, gender and identity sheds light on the ways body work practices are central in how gender is performed, produced and negotiated materially in the broader context of prevailing neo-liberal discourses of individualistic health and well-being. While contemporary young femininity is performed in 'spectacular' ways (McRobbie 2009), the increasing visibility of particularly muscular young men's bodies can be seen as sharing elements of spectacularity based on bodily differences which also serve to emphasise gender differences as 'natural'. A Deleuzo-Guattarian understanding of the body, developed further by feminist philosophers and sociologists and, more recently, new materialist perspectives are used to assist analysis of the complex and contradictory ways gender assemblages are produced through the body in body work practices. This analysis contributes to a focus on how the body's possibilities assemble in relation to both individual, micro factors as well as broader factors including social context.

Introduction to youth sociology and the body   13

Chapter 5, 'Health, affect and embodiment' explores the context in which young people are encouraged to be responsible for their own health and well-being through body work. Drawing on interview data on young people's body work practices, this chapter unpacks the complex ways 'health' is conceptualised and embodied in relation to social life. Health was described in interviews as a set of practices, activities or performances that involve the body and have social dimensions. Health is commonly understood to entail a state of being that can be attained through a series of practices such as diet and exercise. However, the experience of 'health' is not the straightforward result of undertaking 'healthy' practices, and these practices require negotiation. One participant described the potential for health to become 'dangerous' such as through under-eating or over-exercising. The chapter draws on concepts of assemblage, affect and becoming to explore the complex and contradictory ways health is produced, understood and lived by young people.

Chapter 6, 'Buff culture, cosmetic surgery and bodily limits' extends the discussions of health and gender in the previous chapters to explore the ways that two key assemblages, health and gender, through body work practices, produce the body's possibilities in relation to more 'intensive engagements' with body work practices such as intensive weights training and cosmetic surgical procedures. These examples further complicate the simplistic discourses of health, gender and image (such as in the 'look good, feel good' adage). Concepts of affect, becoming and territorialisation are used as tools useful for analysing the ways that bodies, body work practices, affects and relations work together to produce the body's possibilities for action. Rather than reducing the body to its functions, Deleuze and Guattari make the question of what a body can do constitutive, refiguring the body as 'the sum of its capacities' (Buchanan 1997: 75). The more a body is opened to difference and multiple possibilities for affect, the more force it has; the more it can do. The implications of this theoretical perspective on the body are consolidated and extended in this chapter through the focus on 'bodily limits'. This analysis aims to show that the ways the body is assembled in relation to these practices is profoundly complex. Understanding the body as being continually produced through shifting affects, relations and engagements can enable the profoundly complex and often unpredictable dynamics of the body's relationships with the social to be more fully explored.

The final chapter, 'Embodying youth studies', returns to the key implications relating to the particular conceptual approach to theorising and researching the body discussed throughout the book. Feminist–Deleuzo-Guattarian understandings of bodies highlight processes and relations as crucial, and argue that studying these dimensions shows the contingent and often unpredictable ways in which bodies and other assemblages are produced. I consider the two main implications in particular that result from this specific approach to the body, and what these can contribute to youth studies or sociological accounts of the body more broadly. These include embracing complexity to disrupt reductive understandings of youth; and the denaturalisation of bodily

14 *Introduction to youth sociology and the body*

inequalities. Following this, I return to the key concepts used throughout the book and what they bring to our understandings of gender and health in relation to the body. I then discuss some of the current developments in feminist approaches aiming to 'embody' theory and methods including new materialist and post-human perspectives drawn from Barad and Braidotti, and the potential for feminist politics and critique. Efforts to embody youth studies will come with a range of challenges and potential. However, the key focal points in the field such as critiquing inequalities and the interplay between young lives and social context can only be enriched by a focus on the body and embodiment.

References

Albury, K. and Crawford, K. (2012). Sexting, Consent and Young People's Ethics: Beyond Megan's Story. *Continuum*, 26(3), 463–473. doi: 10.1080/10304312.2012.665840

Australian Centre for Retail Studies (2005). Australian Health and Beauty Report (B. a. E. Department, Trans.) *ACRS Secondary Research Report*Monash University.

Australian Bureau of Statistics (2009). Feature Article 2: Health and Fitness Centres and Gymnasia, 4156.0.55.001 *Perspectives on Sport, May 2009* Canberra: www.abs.gov.au/AUSSTATS/abs@.nsf/Lookup/4156.0.55.001Feature+Article2May%202009

Beck, U. (1992). *Risk Society*. London: Sage.

Bordo, S. (2003). *Unbearable Weight: Feminism, Western Culture and the Body* (10th anniversary edn). Berkeley: University of California Press.

Buchanan, I. (1997). The Problem of the Body in Deleuze and Guattari, or, What Can a Body Do? *Body and Society*, 3(3), 73–91.

Budgeon, S. (2003). Identity as an Embodied Event. *Body and Society*, 9(1), 35–55.

Coffey, J., Budgeon, S. and Cahill, H. (2016). Introduction: Learning Bodies: The Body in Youth and Childhood Studies. In J. Coffey, S. Budgeon and H. Cahill (eds), *Learning Bodies: The Body in Youth and Childhood Studies*. New York: Springer.

Coffey, J. and Watson, J. (2015). Bodies: Corporeality and Embodiment in Childhood and Youth Studies. In J. Wyn and H. Cahill (eds), *Handbook of Children and Youth Studies*. New York: Springer.

Coleman, R. (2008). The Becoming of Bodies: Girls, Media Effects and Body Image. *Feminist Media Studies*, 8(2), 163–178.

Coleman, R. (2009). *The Becoming of Bodies: Girls, Images, Experience*. Manchester and New York: Manchester University Press.

Crawford, R. (1980). Healthism and the Medicalisation of Everyday Life. *International Journal of Health Services*, 10(3), 365–388.

Crossley, N. (2005). Mapping Reflexive Body Techniques. *Body and Society*, 11(1), 1–35.

Crossley, N. (2006). In the Gym: Motives, Meaning and Moral Careers. *Body and Society*, 12(3), 23–50.

Davis, K. (1995). *Reshaping the Female Body*. New York: Routledge.

Featherstone, M. (1982). The Body in Consumer Culture. *Theory, Culture and Society*, 1, 18–33.

Featherstone, M. (2010). Body, Image and Affect in Consumer Culture. *Body and Society*, 16(1), 193–221.

Giddens, A. (1991). *Modernity and Self-Identity: Self and Society in the Late Modern Age*. Stanford, CA: Stanford University Press.

Gimlin, D. (2007). What Is 'Body Work'? A Review of the Literature. *Sociology Compass*, 1(1), 353–370. doi: 10.1111/j.1751–9020.2007.00015.x

Grogan, S. (2008). *Body Image: Understanding Body Dissatisfaction in Men, Women and Children*. London: Routledge.

Grogan, S. and Wainwright, N. (1996). Growing up in the Culture of Slenderness: Girls' Experiences of Body Dissatisfaction. *Women's Studies International Forum*, 19, 667–673.

Grosz, E. (1994). *Volatile Bodies: Towards a Corporeal Feminism*. St Leonards: Allen & Unwin.

Harris, A. (2004). *Future Girl: Young Women in the Twenty-First Century*. New York: Routledge.

Katainen, A., and Rolando, S. (2014). Adolescents' Understandings of Binge Drinking in Southern and Northern European Contexts – Cultural Variations of 'Controlled Loss of Control'. *Journal of Youth Studies*, 18(2), 151–166. doi: 10.1080/13676261.2014.933200

Kelly, P. (2001). Youth at Risk: Processes of Individualisation and Responsibilisation in the Risk Society. *Discourse*, 22(1), 23–33.

Kelly, P. (2015). Zygmunt Bauman's Challenge for Critical Youth Studies. In P. Kelly and A. Kamp (eds), *A Critical Youth Studies for the 21st Century*. Leiden and Boston: Brill.

Lupton, D. (2013a). *Fat*. London: Routledge.

Lupton, D. (2013b). Quantifying the Body: Monitoring and Measuring Health in the Age of Health Technologies. *Critical Public Health*, 23(4), 393–403. doi: 10.1080/09581596.2013.794931

McRobbie, A. (2009). *The Aftermath of Feminism: Gender, Culture and Social Change*. London: Sage.

Markula, P. (2006). Deleuze and the Body without Organs. *Journal of Sport and Social Issues*, 30(1), 29–44. doi: 10.1177/0193723505282469

Mears, A. (2014). Aesthetic Labor for the Sociologies of Work, Gender, and Beauty. *Sociology Compass*, 8(12), 1330–1343.

Mission Australia (2014). *Youth Survey*. Mission Australia.

Moore, S. (2010). Is the Healthy Body Gendered? Toward a Feminist Critique of the New Paradigm of Health. *Body and Society*, 16(2), 95–118.

Nairn, K., Higgins, J., Thompson, B., Anderson, M. and Fu, N. (2006). 'It's Just Like the Teenage Stereotype, You Go Out and Drink and Stuff': Hearing from Young People Who Don't Drink. *Journal of Youth Studies*, 9(3), 287–304. doi: 10.1080/13676260600805655

Ouellette, L. and Hay, J. (2008). Makeover Television, Governmentality and the Good Citizen. *Continuum: Journal of Media and Cultural Studies*, 22(4), 471–484.

Paechter, C. (2011). Bodies, Identities and Performances: Reconfiguring the Language of Gender and Schooling. *Gender and Education*, 24(2), 229–241. doi: 10.1080/09540253.2011.606210

Renold, E., Ringrose, J. and Egan, D. (eds) (2015). *Children, Sexuality and Sexualisation*. London: Palgrave Macmillan.

Rice, C. and Watson, E. (2016). Girls and Sexting: The Missing Story of Sexual Subjectivity in a Sexualized and Digitally-Mediated World. In J. Coffey, S. Budgeon and H. Cahill (eds), *Learning Bodies: The Body in Youth and Childhood Studies*. New York: Springer.

16 *Introduction to youth sociology and the body*

Rose, N. (1996). *Inventing Our Selves: Psychology, Power and Personhood*. Cambridge: Cambridge University Press.

Shilling, C. (2003). *The Body and Social Theory* (2nd edn). London: Sage.

Shilling, C. (2011). Afterword: Body Work and the Sociological Tradition. *Sociology of Health and Illness*, 33(2), 336–340. doi: 10.1111/j.1467–9566.2010.01309.x

Riele, te K. (2006). Youth 'at Risk': Further Marginalizing the Marginalized? *Journal of Education Policy*, 21(2), 129–145. doi: 10.1080/02680930500499968

Tiidenberg, K. and Gómez Cruz, E. (2015). Selfies, Image and the Re-making of the Body. *Body and Society*. doi: 10.1177/1357034x15592465

Turner, B. (1984). *The Body and Society: Explorations in Social Theory*. Oxford: Blackwell.

White, R. and Wyn, J. (2008). *Youth and Society* (2nd edn). Oxford: Oxford University Press.

Wyn, J. and Woodman, D. (2006). Generation, Youth and Social Change in Australia. *Journal of Youth Studies*, 9(5), 495–514. doi: 10.1080/13676260600805713

2 Theorising the body

The body and society

Theories of the body matter in sociology because they concern the dynamics of stasis and change between people and the world we live in. Theories of the body are about the interplay between the micro and the macro; individuals and structures; bodies and societies. If we want to understand the reasons and mechanisms by which both inequalities and social changes occur, our questions will centre on the dynamics between large-scale social processes and the individual, micro actions carried out by people and other actors. For this, we need a theory of society, and a theory of action for the people who comprise a society. Sociology has historically been very good at theorising the ways that social structures shape people's lives; analysing the hierarchies and inequalities which sustain social systems of power. Theories of gender, race and class have been pivotal in exposing the decidedly constructed nature of systems of dominance which are held in place only by the prevailing norms and ideals of a particular society, which means that they can be changed for the better. Sociology has also shown that the dominant systems in societies are inherently changeable, and vary significantly not only over time but across different geographical and cultural lines. Sociology has been less adept in exploring the mechanisms of this change. We know change occurs in the world and social formations around us; we can see it, measure it, feel it. But explaining *how* it occurs is a much more nebulous process, and one that the traditional, positivist and structuralist approaches which founded sociology are arguably ill-equipped to address. As I argue in this book, theories of the body which approach it as in an active, dynamic relationship with the social and as *productive* can give us an expanded understanding of both individual and social formations. To begin with, I briefly introduce the ways in which classical sociology has approached the body, and its links with philosophical understandings of the body.

A range of traditions in classical sociology have focused on the relationship between the body and society over the past century. Norbert Elias's (1939) analysis of the ways the body has been involved in civilising processes, which changed greatly over time, provided one of the first examinations of the body

18 *Theorising the body*

in society. Erving Goffman's (1969) theorisations of the body, social interaction and presentation of self have also contributed significantly to sociology. Through the work of Elias, Goffman and feminist theorists, the body (rightfully) became important to studies in sociology as it was seen to be not merely a natural, self-evident 'thing' in the world, but as intrinsically implicated in processes of acting upon (and being acted upon by) societal and structural forces. However, even in studies or theories which focused on the body in classical sociology, it tended to appear as an absent presence, rather than as central as an area of sustained investigation (Shilling 2012). Sociology's concern for the structure and function of societies and the role of human action necessitated addressing the role of human embodiment. For example, Marx (1997) understood the bodies of workers as a crucial component in capitalist regimes of production; Durkheim (1976) understood the body as fundamental to the functioning of collectives and groups through rituals such as scarring and tattooing. Shilling argues that despite many accounts of the body being underdeveloped, they can still be useful for understanding contemporary issues relating to the body, though the treatment of the body in such work needs to be carefully interrogated. Though the work of Marx and Durkheim and other classical sociology cannot be accused of being 'disembodied', it does tend to suffer from 'the dual approach that sociology traditionally adopted to the body' (Shilling 2012: 13). This 'dual approach' is the tendency to focus on explaining how society acts on the body and gives it meaning, rather than the specific, embodied characteristics of bodies which create social meanings in-of-themselves (Shilling 2012: 14). Further, functionalist approaches such as Durkheim's tend to view the human body as largely constrained and produced by social structures, or as Blackman (2008) puts it, 'pawns within ideological processes' rather than capable of change. To clarify: few sociologists would argue that bodies are simply the passive receptors of social meaning, but what is at issue is that the focus has tended to be on the character of societies to mould bodies, rather than the other way around. This example points to a central theme in sociological theory: the interplay between social structures and human agency.

A key aspect of sociological understandings of the body is that it is a social rather than purely natural entity. Feminist sociological theoretical developments in the 1980s highlighted the need to explore and understand human physicality beyond explanations provided by the natural sciences. To this end, Haraway (1991: 10) argues 'Neither our personal bodies nor our social bodies may be seen as natural, in the sense of existing outside the self-creating process called human labour'. The tensions associated with structure and agency arise from the understanding that human bodies are social. The human body and social relations are often used as evidence for either side that humans are structured or determined, or agentic and capable of change. This leads to debates about the extent to which bodies are at the mercy of social structures which implicate them in the reproduction of inequalities, or whether change and creativity is implicit in bodies or social relations. Theorisations of the

Theorising the body 19

body's relationship with society often hinge on the dynamics of structure and agency.

Structure, agency and the body in youth studies

The key debates about structure and agency relate to the extent to which and dynamics by which bodies, humans or agents create or are created by the social. Within youth studies, discussions about agency have become essential to some of the most significant conceptual debates currently driving the field. Agency is fundamental to one of the most substantial macro-theoretical debates in contemporary youth sociology: the relationship between individualisation (Beck 1992) and contemporary youth inequalities. Beck's (1992) individualisation thesis describes the ways in which significant social changes and the fragmentation of collective class cultures have led to conditions in which young people must fashion individualised and reflexive identities. As Coffey and Farrugia (2014) discuss, debates in youth studies have centred on the extent to which this theoretical perspective acknowledges the continuing role of social structures in shaping young people's lives and trajectories. Woodman (2009) argues that Beck is portrayed as a theorist of agency by some (notably Brannen and Nilsen 2005; Lehmann 2004), while Bourdieu (1990) is drawn upon to re-emphasise the role of social structures (a situation that Woodman (2009), Threadgold (2010) and Farrugia (2013) have argued is based on a misreading of both Beck and Bourdieu). In empirical work in this field, an emphasis on social structure is used to demonstrate instances of social reproduction, or examples in which young people are constrained by social conditions not of their making or choosing; while an emphasis on individual agency is mobilised to present examples of creative resistance or social change. Agency and structure are also drawn upon in discussions relating to social media use, sexting and selfies, and participation in feminism online in an effort to understand the contradictory conditions of postfeminism and neoliberalism in which young femininities are formed. As Harris and Dobson (2015) have shown, agency often seems to be associated with activity and action against passivity or victimhood; a subject position which young women are increasingly reluctant to claim against the broader cultural narratives of choice and empowerment.

There is often confusion about just what agency is exactly: is it an individual property residing in all bodies that can be stifled by structures, or somehow 'unlocked' or let loose? Is agency a necessary dimension of subjectivity or 'the human condition'? In relation to these debates, Coffey and Farrugia (2014) have argued that there are significant conceptual problems associated with discussions of structure and agency in youth studies and that agency needs to be more rigorously theorised. The ways in which Bourdieu, Foucault and feminist approaches conceptualise the body's relationship with society is discussed below. The implications of these theorists' understandings

20 *Theorising the body*

of the body are then discussed in relation to recent agency/structure debates as an area of contention in contemporary youth studies.

Bourdieu's theory of the body

Bourdieu's concepts of habitus, field and capital aim to show that the way social life is structured profoundly affects individuals and their potential for change; and that the body is inextricably part of these processes. The 'habitus' can be understood as 'embodied, socialised subjectivity', expressing the process of how individuals 'become themselves and the ways in which those individuals engage in practices' (Webb *et al.* 2002: 11). Fields are 'structured contexts which shape and produce these practices and processes' of the habitus (McLeod 2005: 14) and Bourdieu describes that the habitus and field's interactions are akin to 'learning to rules of the game' (Bourdieu and Wacquant 1992). Capital refers to economic valuables in the social order, as well as cultural capital, symbolic capital and physical capital; all of which are involved in power relationships and social dominance or inequality. 'Symbolic violence', Bourdieu asserts, 'accomplishes itself through an act of cognition and of misrecognition that lies beyond – or beneath – the controls of consciousness and will' (Bourdieu and Wacquant 1992: 171–2). Symbolic violence occurs when a discourse is so established in society that it is unquestioned and taken for granted. Bourdieu (2001: 55) has argued that the biological body, ascribed with masculinity or femininity 'induces a somatisation of the relation of domination', and that the domination of women was the most profound example of symbolic violence.

In relation to gender in particular, however, Bourdieu's theories of the body and the process by which gender norms are reproduced have been strongly critiqued. Beverley Skeggs argues that as it stands, Bourdieu's model offers a limited understanding of changes or dynamics within sex and gender. She argues that his theory of the gendered habitus offers 'no potential to move beyond traditional gender divisions ... because it is locked within that which produces it [the gendered habitus]' (Skeggs 2004: 27). Skeggs (2004: 30) further argues that Bourdieu's concepts need to be developed to enable the framework of the embodied habitus to account for the 'ambiguities and contradictions' in the way people engage with the social, because in most of his work, 'the focus is on order and structure' rather than ambivalence (see also Adkins 2004). While, as Woodman and Threadgold (2015) argue, Bourdieu's theories should not be dismissed as 'deterministic', further conceptual work is needed to explore the dimensions of experience and action beyond the 'well organised habitus' (Skeggs 2004). Woodman and Threadgold (2015) suggest that notions of the 'split' habitus and hysteresis may be productive for further developing the less consistent aspects of habitus. Further development of these concepts is needed to account for the ambivalent and contradictory aspects of identity such as those Skeggs identifies.

Foucault's theory of the body

Michel Foucault's concepts of the body have been widely used and critiqued. Foucault (1979, 1980, 1982) understands the body as a site of discourse and power, and as an object of discipline and control. Foucault's conceptualisations regarding the body and its relation to structural powers (which operate as discourses) provide a way of understanding the ways that the body is controlled and disciplined for the purposes of social order. Foucault's extensive work on the relationship between knowledge and power helps to explain the way power operates to 'subjugate individuals' (1982: 212). Foucault (1980: 52) argues, 'it is not possible for power to be exercised without knowledge, it is impossible for knowledge not to engender power'. The materiality of power operates on the very bodies of individuals for the purpose of creating the kind of body the current (consumer, neoliberal) society needs (1980: 55–8).

Foucault's concept of biopower, or power over life, theorises the process by which the minutiae of the body's activities in everyday life link with large-scale organisations of power (Dreyfus and Rabinow 1983). He positions claims of a 'right to life, to one's body, to health, to the satisfactions of one's needs' work within the model of biopower and 'control by stimulation: "Get undressed – but be slim, good-looking, tanned!"' (Foucault 1980: 57). Rose (2007: 54) argues the perspective of biopower can be used to examine the ways that authorities have attempted to govern bodily conduct and populations. Foucault's focus on the body coincided with feminist inquiry into the politics of personal life (Sawicki 1991: 95). Feminist writers such as Susan Bordo (2003) and Sandra Bartky (1990) extended and critiqued Foucault's concepts of disciplinary power and the body to discuss the ways women's bodies particularly are more greatly affected by these disciplinary processes through required beauty and health regimes. From this perspective, while Foucault does focus on the micro-aspects of bodily activities, his focus is more on the workings of power on the body than the potential of bodies to alter or respond to power (Dreyfus and Rabinow 1983: 85). Elizabeth Grosz's critique of Foucault's perspective on the body is more forthright: 'Foucault takes the body as a resistant yet fundamentally passive inertia whose internal features and forces are of little interest to the functioning of power' (Grosz 1994: 146). In Foucault's theorisations, then, we are largely left with a body 'largely deprived of causal powers' (Lash 1984: 5), susceptible to normalising and reactive forces (Lash 1984: 7).

Feminist approaches to the body

The body is central to feminist theory in a range of disciplines including sociology, cultural studies and philosophy for a number of reasons. Historically, women have been understood both in philosophy and the natural sciences as 'biologically' and mentally inferior to men, stemming from their physicality as women. Clearly, the body is centrally implicated in the feminist

22 *Theorising the body*

critique of gendered inequalities because of the ways in which such inequalities have been said to be *naturalised* by the body. If women are 'naturally' inferior, so the logic goes, then so too are gendered inequalities and nothing can be done to change this argument of naturalised inequality. Decades of feminist theory and activism have challenged this. Feminist theorists have set about 'wresting notions of corporeality away from the constraints which have polarized and opposed it to mind, the mental or the conceptual, not to mention away from the confines of a biology that is considered universal, innate, fundamentally nonhistorical' (Grosz 1994: 187). Contemporary feminist philosophy and theory, through frameworks of embodiment and a focus on materiality, has set about deconstructing or unhooking the body from naturalistic, dualistic and binaristic frameworks (Budgeon 2003), as well as from psychoanalytic theories which define the female body primarily as a 'lack' (Butler 1993). As this section discusses, the challenges of theorising the body as matter (and as sexed and gendered) are indicative of broader challenges of theorising the negotiations of structure and agency, and of the relationship between bodies and society. Beginning with a discussion on feminist perspectives on the body, sex and gender, this section discusses Judith Butler's theories of bodies and subjectification and consequent theories of agency, and other feminist work which has extended and rethought some of Butler's concepts and ontology.

The relationship between the body and gender has been widely debated by feminist sociologists (R. Connell 1987; R. W. Connell 1995, 2009; Davis 1995; Oakley 1972; Witz 2000) and feminist philosophers (Butler 1993; Gatens 1988; Grosz 1994; Young 2005). Much feminist theory on the body has been concerned with showing the ways that women's and men's bodily differences have served as excuses for structural inequality (Young 2005: 4). Social constructivist feminists have sought to dispel bodily differences as a basis of inequality, arguing that it is the discourses of gender that create inequality, not the bodies of men and women themselves (Budgeon 2003). As such, the term 'gender', as distinct from 'sex', was intended to challenge the idea that 'biology is destiny' (Young 2005: 13). These critiques led to sex being understood as separate from gender. There are some further conceptual issues with this, however. Witz (2000) argues that the sex/gender distinction has led either to the body being absent in accounts of gender, or of the body being 'valorised' above gender and social processes. In other words, the binary of natural/ social still lies as a key tension at the centre of body theory. Witz (2000: 10) argues it is important to make the body central in feminist sociology, however we must do so without 'overwhelming the sociality of gender by over-discursivising bodies or (re)embedding the totality of the meaning of bodies'. Witz proposes then that a feminist sociology that is able to incorporate attention to the lived experience of the body as well as the social dimensions of gender could be achieved through paying attention to the operations and underlying politics of embodiment, corporeality and sociality. It is important to pay attention to the materiality and historicity of the body as sexed, gendered, raced and

Theorising the body 23

embodied, but also to recognise the salience of social structures such as gender for conceptualising inequalities. Feminist theorists, along with post-colonial theorists (Mohanty, 1997) have been leaders in recognising the significance of the body for understanding intersecting social inequalities. Further feminist work (Grosz 1994) has also been crucial in conceptualising the body, sex and gender in problematising the mind/body dualism.

Feminist approaches in particular highlight that it is crucial to look for ways to negotiate and move beyond the core dualism that frames the body: the mind/body dualism. This stems from the philosopher Descartes, who theorised that the mind was completely separate to (and superior to) the body, and crucial to 'being': 'I think therefore I am'. This dualism is particularly problematic for feminism because the mind (and logic, reason, order) has traditionally been associated with the masculine, while the body has been devalued as its feminine opposite (symbolising disorder and excess) (Butler 1990; Grosz 1994; Bray and Colebrook 1998; Braidotti 2011). The founding system of binaries has haunted the body, and much feminist work has exposed the epistemological and ontological problems that accompany dualist understandings of the body (Grosz 1994; Budgeon 2003; Coleman 2009). This feminist post-structural work has enabled an understanding that the 'rational subject' is an illusion, constituted through the mind/body dualism in particular (Davies and Gannon 2005: 320). Most importantly, feminism has drawn attention to the ways that dualistic thought aids in the construction and maintenance of gender divisions and inequality, since Cartesian dualisms are implicitly hierarchical. Grosz, among many others (Butler 1993; Bordo 2003; Braidotti 2011), has critiqued the sorts of dualistic thought that extends from Cartesian philosophy, arguing that the social devaluation of the body has gone hand in hand with the oppression of women (Grosz 1994: 10). As Budgeon has argued

> It is this founding system of binaries which has served to negate the feminine and locate women outside the realm of the subject. As a consequence, the feminine, (and the female body) has historically been constituted as that which must be defined, directed and controlled through the application of disembodied, objective, masculine knowledge.
>
> (2003: 39)

The issues sketched above show that the epistemologies, or underlying theoretical perspectives of knowledge, are crucial in basing our understandings of the interplay between bodies and social inequalities. We need to give careful thought to the epistemologies of the body and the social which underpin the conceptual approaches we use to avoid theoretical pitfalls such as dualist or disembodied understandings of the body, as this has significant implications for how to understand the social.

Deconstructing binaries such as mind/body, which underpin so many other constructed oppositions (such as subject/object, materiality/representation) is

24 Theorising the body

a crucial ongoing task for feminist empirical and theoretical studies of the body. Following from the critique of dualist thought introduced in Chapter 1 in relation to the philosophical heritage of the mind/body binary for socio-logical theory, the following discussion of the materiality/representation binary is unpacked to demonstrate how a non-dualist approach to the female body for example can be enacted.

Materiality and representation

The ways that the female body is represented has also been a focus of feminist critique. According to Bray and Colebrook argue, in much feminist theory, 'the female body is considered as that which has been belied, distorted, and imagined by a male representational logic' (1998: 35). What they mean is that feminist theory has called attention to the ways that female bodies are typi-cally understood through masculinist or patriarchal frameworks or standards. While this position is useful for critiquing the knowledge and power systems that organise thoughts and norms, they argue that there is a problem in the philosophical argument that 'representation intervenes to objectify, alienate, and dehumanize the body'. Bray and Colebrook argue such a view of repre-sentation unintentionally recreates a dualism in which the body is passive or overcoded, similar to Durkheim's view of the body as 'culturally inscribed', by an 'an all-pervasive, repressive, and dichotomous phallic logic' (Bray and Colebrook 1998: 37). Where gender is understood as a 'cultural construction', this approach often fails to think of the body as anything other than an effect of non-corporeal factors (Bray and Colebrook 1998: 41).

A further issue with gender and 'representation' is the near invisibility of critical attention to the representations of male bodies (Gill *et al.* 2005; Bell and McNaughton 2007). Where men's bodies and experiences are not ana-lysed in their cultural and historical contexts, men are left as 'universal sub-jects' and patriarchy or gender inequality is made to seem static, rather than under constant renegotiation (Bell and McNaughton 2007).

Bray and Colebrook insist that conceptualisations in which the body is theorised as merely an effect of representation, or an effect of image con-sumption (in the case of popular psychological understandings of female body image, for example) are inadequate, yet these often underlie theorisations of the body. This is not to say that the body is not strongly influenced by media images; for many, media images and other cultural norms relating to gender are powerful mediators of embodiment. However, what Bray and Colebrook are arguing is that the epistemology underlying the materiality/representation binary is telling only part of the story. They, along with other feminist sociologists and philosophers, have drawn on the work of Deleuze and Guat-tari in an effort to develop conceptual frameworks able to understand the complexity and ambiguity inherent in relations between bodies and the social.

A key way that debates about the relationship between bodies and the social world in sociology are played out is through arguments around the

Theorising the body 25

roles of structure and agency. As I have discussed in the above examples, the ambiguity relating to the conceptual work done by the term 'agency' in youth studies as discussed above is emblematic of similar issues associated with the concept in other fields of sociology, particularly related to gender and feminist sociology.

(Re)theorising structure and agency

Conceptualisations of agency are interwoven with other key terms and concepts including subjectivity, power and the body. Butler, along with Foucault, has argued that agency cannot be understood as separate from the process by which the subject is formed. In other words, if we want to understand what agency is, we must first understand how people come to be part of their societies and have identities. Butler argues that people and particular identities are created through discourses, and that 'the constituted character of the subject is the very precondition of its agency' (Butler 1995: 46). The character of the subject is formed through a process which is not always predictable. A person's identity is not fully constrained or known in advance based on social structures. This perspective is in significant contrast with functionalist perspectives such as Durkheim's above who approaches bodies and subjects as primarily socially and culturally inscribed, meaning passively determined.

As in Butler's understanding of agency, Bourdieu's concept of the habitus (Bourdieu 1977) describes the way in which identities and actions are shaped by social structures. However, post-structuralist and postmodern approaches understand identities and bodies as formed in ongoing processes rather than being determined or known from the outset. Though Bourdieu is generally understood as a theorist of social reproduction and social structure (Shilling 2012), his account of the body through the concept of habitus gives a useful framework for understanding embodiment particularly in relation to social inequalities such as social class. McNay (1999, 2000) has argued that the concept of habitus can be understood as a kind of embodied potentiality, or 'structured improvisation' of practice as Bourdieu termed it. If social reproduction occurs, according to Bourdieu, it is because bodies tend to be oriented towards certain dispositions. Importantly, this perspective is not deterministic. Although the potential for agency or change is included as a possibility in the concept of habitus, Bourdieu arguably focuses more on the processes by which social patterns are reproduced than on processes of unpredictability or change in the formation of habitus.

Theories of agency described by Rose (1996) and Coleman (2009) are drawn from the philosophies of Gilles Deleuze and Felix Guattari. This perspective affords more attention to change and unpredictability in the relationship between bodies and the social world than the theorists above. Rose argues that 'agency is no doubt a "force", but it is a force that arises not from any essential properties of "the subject" but out of the ways in which humans have been-assembled-together' (1996: 188). This understanding of agency has

26 *Theorising the body*

much in common with Barad's (2007) theory of agential realism, in which agency is re-theorised as the 'intra-active' process of assembling human and non-human bodies through relations and forces. This perspective on agency informs an array of feminist 'new materialist' theory and scholarship.

The task of thinking through the relationship between embodied subjectivities and the diverse forms of power that structure the contemporary social world lead Rose (1996) and Coleman (2009) to draw on the Deleuzian metaphor of 'the fold' to theorise agency and subjectification. This sees processes of connections between bodies and the world as occurring through points of overlap, or 'folding' of each into the other:

> subjectification is always a matter of folding. The human is neither an actor essentially prepossessed of agency, nor a passive product or puppet of cultural forces; agency is produced in the course of practices under a whole variety of more or less onerous, explicit, punitive or seductive, disciplinary or passional constraints and relations of force. Our own 'agency' then is resultant of the ontology we have folded into ourselves in the course of our history and our practices.
>
> (Rose 1996: 189)

According to Rose, force is that which is folded (1996: 189). Folding produces the effects of subjectification – but the relations of folding (and of subjectification) are processual rather than passive or deterministic. Through this process, bodies 'become through relations which are neither random nor inevitable but which assemble through the intensity of experience. These experiences can neither be located in structures nor agents but rather are folded through bodies in particular ways' (Coleman 2009: 212).

The concepts of Deleuze and Guattari have been increasingly drawn upon in feminist sociology and sociology more broadly in an effort to move beyond some of the key conceptual impasses which have concerned theories of structure and agency, and the body and society. Below, I introduce the key theoretical perspectives of the body introduced by Deleuze and Guattari and the concepts which have been developed and mobilised by feminist philosophers, sociologists and social theorists for social analysis.

Introduction to Deleuze and Guattari's theory of the body

As the above sections have detailed, a range of scholarly work in education and social sciences has theorised the relationship and interplay between the body and the social in an effort to understand the significance of the body in everyday life. Deleuze and Guattari (1987) contribute a particular perspective of the body which is useful for sociological analysis. In the work of Deleuze, Guattari and Spinoza, the body is understood as an active productive force which operates in relation to broader socio-historical–cultural contexts. A body is not a physical entity only, but is rather a 'relationship of forces' which

Theorising the body 27

connects to other forces, including social relations such as those central to this book: gender, consumer culture and health discourses. The body from this perspective is not only the fleshy, physical body, but refers to what Rose describes as 'regimes of corporeality'. Rose argues that 'rather than speak[ing] of "the body", we need to analyse just how a particular body-regime has been produced' (Rose 1996: 184). He insists that 'a body' in Deleuze's work is *more than* the physical, fleshy body and that "the body" is far less unified, far less "material" than we think' (Rose 1996: 184). Instead, it is the linkages, connections, affects and engagements which create a body. This is about seeing a body as not limited by its fleshy boundaries of the skin, and looking for the ways that a body links up with the inside and outside:

> Consider what diverse machinations a body is capable of: the bravery of a warrior in battle, the tenderness or violence of a lover, the endurance of the political prisoner under torture, the transformations effected by the practices of yoga, the experience of voodoo death, the capacities of trances to render organs capable of withstanding burning or recovering from wounds. These are not properties of 'the body' but machinations of the 'thought body' whose elements, organs, forces, energies, passions, dreads are assembled through connections with words, dreams, techniques, chants, habits, judgments, weapons, tools, groups.
>
> (Rose 1996: 185)

Braidotti provides another way of expressing this distinction between a Deleuzian approach to 'a body' and 'the body':

> The 'body' is to be understood as neither a biological nor a sociological category, but rather as a point of overlap between the physical, the material, the symbolic, and the material social conditions
>
> (Braidotti 1994: 161, cited in Rose 1996: 201)

Similarly, Budgeon's description of the body as 'an event' also sought to move away from a perspective which limits analysis to the physical, fleshy body only to instead highlight an understanding of bodies as 'multiplicities that are never just found but made and remade' (Budgeon 2003: 50). What Deleuze's approach to the body amounts to is a perspective which prioritises the connections rather than stability or 'being' of the body. Deleuze conceptualises the body in terms of what a body can do; the capacities, capabilities, and transformations that may be possible (Grosz 1994; Budgeon 2003; Coleman 2009). This approach entails a significant shift in how the body is approached from the outset, since, as we have seen above, approaches in social theory such as Bourdieu tend to begin from the premise that social structures affect physical bodies (though not in deterministic ways). In relation to the discussion of structure and agency above, a Deleuzian approach to bodies involves shifting focus from the distinctions of structure and agency to the relations

28 *Theorising the body*

between bodies which constitute those bodies. This consideration of bodies and the social extends beyond questions of either agency or constraint, to explore the ways in which both change and stasis are mutually implicated in a body's relationship with the social world. This perspective shifts to instead focus on what bodies can do or what bodies are capable of, and provides a profoundly different set of possibilities for conceptual and empirical work.

Key concepts: assemblage, affect and becoming

Although social and cultural forces are undoubtedly central to practices of body work and embodiment, Deleuzian analysis starts from a very different premise in which the affects and capacities of bodies are foregrounded in exploring the practices, meanings and experiences of the body. The key concepts introduced in this section are assemblage, affect and becoming.

In much of Deleuze and Guattari's work, the body, as a set of forces that connects with other forces, is termed an 'assemblage'. Deleuze and Guattari write that assemblages emerge from the contestation between the relations and affects and the body's own creative desire and sense-making capacities (1984: 9 ff). As Fox describes, 'assemblages emerge from the process of inter-action between a body's myriad relations and affects' (Fox 2011: 364). The elements which go towards creating the assemblage can 'be material, psychic, social or abstract/philosophical' (Fox 2011: 364). Deleuze and Guattari (1987) refer to assemblages through the metaphor of 'machine' to describe how assemblages are produced through relations between a body and other entities. The assemblage can be understood as comprising the range of relations that people engage in and connect with including norms, discourses, ideals and practices which are dynamic and change over time. In other words, the assemblage can be understood as the outcome of the embodied process of encounter. This 'outcome' however is dynamic rather than a 'set state of being' and will also 'vary from person to person' (Fox 2011: 364). Assemblages are 'always processual: they are about doing, not being'.

Potts describes assemblages as developing 'a kind of chaotic network of habitual and non-habitual connections, always in flux, always reassembling in different ways' (Potts 2004: 9). In other words, assemblages may resemble what we understand to be relatively stable norms of ways of being (gendered practices, for example); however, the concept of assemblage highlights the ways things form in contestation, and in relation to myriad other aspects. Human bodies (which too can be understood as assemblages rather than strictly whole, unified entities) engage with other assemblages, and in this process, the conditions for further engagement and possibility are generated.

Seeing the body as an assemblage conceptualises the body as a relationship in connection with numerous other forces. From this perspective the body is not a prior, unitary entity, but 'merely a particular relationship capable of being affected in particular ways' (Rose 1996: 184). Affect is a cornerstone of

Theorising the body   29

Deleuze and Guattari's Spinozan-influenced conceptualisation of the body, and how it 'works' (or what it does) with/in society. The concept of affect is critical for understanding what Deleuze and Guattari mean when asking 'what can a body do?' If the assemblage can be understood as the outcome of a body's relations and engagements, affect can be understood as the intensity which guides those engagements towards particular outcomes and directions.

'Affect' is a burgeoning area in the field of body-studies in sociology. This concept understands bodies as entangled processes that are 'defined by their capacities to affect and be affected' (Blackman and Venn 2010: 9). Fox and Ward define affect 'not in the sense of an emotional reaction, but simply as something which affects something else' (2008: 1008), following Deleuze and Guattari's definition (see Deleuze and Guattari 1987: xvi, 257). The concept of affect as it is used in *A Thousand Plateaus* is based on Spinoza's concept *affectus*. It is defined simply as 'an ability to affect and be affected' (Massumi 1987: xvi):

> [Affect] is a prepersonal intensity corresponding to the passage from one experiential state of the body to another and implying an augmentation or diminution in that body's capacity to act. Spinoza's affection is each such state considered as an encounter between the affected body and a second, affecting, body.

From a practical perspective, affect can refer to the psychological, emotional and physical connections a body has: with other people (lovers, friends, colleagues, fellow commuters); abstract ideas (literature, film, music); activities (such as through body work practices of jogging, weights training, aerobics or walking) and social assemblages (including gender, race, class and dominant discourses of health) (Fox and Ward 2008). There are numerous other examples that could be used to describe how affect works as a process. Hickey-Moody and Malins (2007) describe affect as a process involving an 'unconscious set of assumptions that motivate an embodied response to a woman in a hijab, or a person with a disability', for example. In the context of the research informing this book, affects relating to the body's gendered appearance motivate numerous participants' embodied responses. Isabelle, for example, described feeling 'yuck' if she goes to a shopping centre when she doesn't have her hair and make-up done: 'I don't make eye contact with people ... I feel like people are staring at me and I get panicky, like I can't breathe and I have to go home'. As discussed in Chapter 4, these embodied responses can be intensive, and guide further action; in Isabelle's case, the necessity of wearing make-up and attending to very strict regimes of feminine bodily presentation in order to feel 'nice' and to look 'normal'.

Affective relations are not confined to human interactions. Crucially, the process of relations and affects is 'dynamic, ongoing and dialogical' because bodies are never fixed or given (Fox and Ward 2008: 1009). Deleuze's position is that we are produced by affects, rather than in possession of affects. The

30 *Theorising the body*

affect a person experiences is what connects individual practice and feeling to social meanings, since it is a body's 'capacity for affecting and being affected that defines a body' (Deleuze 1992: 625). Affect, then, is crucial in bodily encounters, and links closely to another of Deleuze's key concepts: becoming. If assemblage can be understood as the outcome of a body's engagements, becoming is the *process* by which the engagement occurs.

'Becoming' can be understood as the processes of connection in a body's affective relations with other bodies, entities, structures, discourses, spaces, images, etc. The concept 'becoming' is closely associated with assemblage (Phillips 2006). Deleuze's (1992) framework of becoming refers to the process of connections and relations that forms (and re-forms) the assemblage. Rather than asking 'what are bodies', or questioning the *being* of bodies, Deleuze (1992) asks 'what can a body do?'. Or, what does the process of engagements that occurs in the (ongoing) formation of an assemblage make possible or impossible? This process of engagement, and (indeterminate) orientation towards action, can be understood as becoming. If assemblage is what is formed through engagement, becoming is the orientation which drives the 'assembling'. To study becoming is to study the micro-processes of change that occur through affect and relations. Bodies are thus understood in the context of the connections and relations that are formed and their potential for becoming.

What Coleman terms 'the becoming of bodies' refers to the conviction that 'bodies must be conceived of as processes continually moving, rather than as discrete, autonomous elements' (2009: 1). Deleuze's ontology of becoming dissolves the gap between subject and object, materiality and representation, and questions of cause and effect relating to the body in the social world, because Deleuze conceives of bodies not as discrete, independent entities but, rather, as constituted through their relations with other bodies and things. As Coleman (2009: 49) argues, 'a Deleuzian account would understand bodies not as a bounded subject that is separate from images (for example) but rather would see the connections between humans and images as constituting a body'. The term 'becoming', then, can be used as a way of understanding the ways that bodies are experienced, affected, affecting and ultimately lived.

The concepts introduced here all relate to the underpinning perspective of a body as composed by engagements, relations and forces. Put simply, affect can be understood as the intensity which guides engagement; becoming is the process of engagement that is mobilised through affect; and assemblage is the ultimate (though potentially fleeting) outcome of the engagement.

The concepts introduced in this section have introduced the ways that a Deleuzo-Guattarian approach theorises bodies and their relations with the social. The entirety of their philosophy cannot be engaged with here, but it is intended that these concepts will enable a Deleuzo-Guattarian approach to the body to be developed throughout the book.

Deleuze and Guattari (1994) argue that the aim of philosophy is to create and enable concepts which allow something new to be thought or felt.

Theorising the body 31

Hickey-Moody and Malins (2007: 2) explain that for Deleuze and Guattari, the question of a theory or concept is not whether or not it is 'true', but whether it works, and whether it 'opens up the range of possibilities in a given situation'. I argue that these concepts and theories of Deleuze and Guattari along with others such as Barad and Bray and Colebrook work in relation to the body in youth studies namely because they enable a retheorisation of the body and the social beyond dualistic frameworks as an ongoing process. They understand bodies as formed but not determined by the relations or forces connected or engaged with.

This potential for generation and change is a central tenet of the ontology of Deleuzian theory, which has particular implications for how human and other bodies are conceptualised. Rather than understanding the human body as a biological, stable or natural entity, Deleuze conceptualises it as 'a physiological and social institution, a relationship, an intense capacity that is sensed ... it is a site where forces engage with each other' (Goodchild 1997: 43).

From this perspective, the current social, cultural and economic contexts form the 'unstable assemblages in which humans are caught up', and affect what the body can and cannot do (Rose 1996: 184). The body as a 'relationship of forces' connects to other forces, including social relations such as gender, consumer culture and health discourses. These engagements are productive because they shape what happens next – action, change, stasis – or what a body can do.

These concepts have been developed and 'applied' in burgeoning areas of research in sociology and education in particular. The implications of these concepts for the key themes of the book, health and gender, are considered below.

'Doing' gender: molar assemblages and becoming

Gender can be understood as an assemblage (or 'machine' in the following examples) which is central to the current organisation of societies. Deleuze and Guattari refer to social structures and institutions such as the state, gender, class and other dominating and normalising forces (including discourse) that operate on binary logic as 'binary machines'. Deleuze and Parnet have argued that the binary machine 'overcodes society, [is] that which organises dominant utterances and the established order of a society, the dominant languages and knowledge, conformist actions and feelings, the segments which prevail over the others' (2002: 129). Dominant and established orders are termed 'molar'. The 'molar' is 'something that is well-defined, massive and governing – such as large structures or identity categories' (Jackson 2010: 581). The relations of affect that mediate becomings are termed 'molecular'. Becoming 'is movement through a unique event that produces experimentation and change' (Jackson 2010: 581), and such change is conceptualised as 'molecular'. Social identities such as man/woman, rational/irrational, masculine/feminine, mind/body, adult/child are products of the binary machine, and

32 *Theorising the body*

categories which Deleuze and Guattari (1987) seek to extricate from binarism through their theorisation of becoming. A Deleuzian framework is interested in looking at the ways powerful social systems of thought such as gender are already always being undermined and reorganised.

Deleuze and Guattari suggest that the production of difference and change is imminent within molar segments (and binary machines), power and assemblages are inherently unstable, and have a 'molecular underside' that is always at work concurrently. This comes back to their theory of assemblage, as developing in unpredictable and interdeterminate ways due to the 'shifting fields of connection' (Currier 2003: 336). Accordingly assemblages including binary machines (for example, gender) and power are inherently unstable and susceptible to change. Although 'our lives are made in these segments' of power and normalising discourse, 'something always escapes' (Deleuze and Guattari 1987: 195). Deleuze and Guattari specify, 'from the point of view of micropolitics, a society is defined by its lines of flight, which are molecular. There is always something that flows or flees, that escapes the binary organizations' (1987: 216). The point is not that everything is flexible and unpredictable all the time; rather, that the potential for change is imminent and happens in micro ways. As Colebrook argues, 'the only constant in time, the only same, is the power of not remaining the same' (Colebrook 2002: 60).

The perspective of gender as an assemblage attends to the discursive, performative and regulative aspects of normative gender categories, and also to the affective, embodied, sensate and unpredictable dimensions as it is lived. Rose draws on Butler's (1990) concept of gender as a performative 'doing' to argue that gender is a verb in more ways than in 'linguistic utterance, citations, conventions'; that 'gendering ... is a matter of meticulous and continually repeated prescription of the deportment, appearance, speech, thought, passion, will, intellect in which persons are assembled by being connected up not only with vocabularies but also with regimes of comportment' (Rose 1996: 186). Rose insists that these aspects are crucial to understanding the 'technics' by which the body-regime is assembled. In this sense, comprising these multiple and unstable binary elements, gender can be understood as an assemblage which intersects with produces, and is produced *by* bodies.

This framework positions gender as a current, but not eternal point of differentiation between bodies which affect the ways bodies are lived. Our regime of corporeality (Rose 1996) results from the assemblages we are caught up in, which currently differentiates the body by sex and race, defines what it can and cannot do. The body is a practical relationship and is capable of being affected in numerous other ways, which are not known in advance. Gender is important to understandings of the body because gender is involved in the assemblage that the body enters into relations with. Gender is one of the main elements of the social assemblage that bodies (as 'relationships') connect with. The affective relations that result from these connections mediate the body's capacities, or limits, towards action. In this way, gender is

Theorising the body 33

crucial to the body's affective relations and capacities. In Coleman's words, gender 'constitutes bodies ... Gender is one of the ways in which the affective capacities of bodies become organised and produced' (2009: 142).

The concept of assemblage can also be used to describe the ways gender relations operate, through a 'functional collection of connections' (see Currier 2003), including discourses, norms, ideals, institutions, bodies, affects and practices. An assemblage is 'always collective, [and] brings into play within us and outside us populations, multiplicities, territories, becomings, affects, events' (Deleuze and Parnet 2002: 51). Assemblages are functional because they create the conditions for orientation towards action; this is what is meant by describing assemblages as 'active'. Understanding gender as an assemblage sees it as a functional, active arrangement of connections which operates as only a temporary articulation rather than an essential identity category. This is not to say that gender as an assemblage is benign and neutral; gender is certainly cut-across by power and operates in many instances as a binary machine insofar as it is a dominant organising principle of current social and bodily arrangements. What the perspective of gender as an assemblage contributes conceptually, however, is that the current dominance of current arrangements has *no essential or originary basis.*

Following Fox, assemblages can be understood as 'elaborated from disparate elements that can be material, psychic, social and abstract/philosophical' (Fox 2011: 364). Fox gives an example of this through delineating elements of an 'eating assemblage, [composed of] (in no particular order), at least: Mouth – food – energy – appetite' (Fox 2011: 364).

What might a relational gender assemblage look like/be composed of?

At least (in no order):

the (sexed) body – bodily presentation – body work – discourses – norms – ideals – images – performance – expectations – sexuality

Deleuze and Guattari's concepts have been drawn on by a number of feminist authors to assist theorisations of bodies and gender. One key reason this perspective is seen to hold promise relates to Deleuze and Guattari's insistence on there being no essential or biological basis for current dominant relations of power and resulting inequalities. Instead, they draw focus to recognising positive potential and affirmation of difference. For these reasons, this approach can add important dimensions to analysis of the embodiments and negotiations of gender in everyday life in order to better understand these ambivalent, less coherent experiences of the embodied self (Coleman 2009).

Feminist critiques of Deleuzian perspectives on gender

It is important to recognise the tensions between Deleuze and Guattari's work and aspects of feminist theory that centre on the body. Deleuze is regarded by some as having dubious feminist credentials (Braidotti, 2011). Whilst some

34 *Theorising the body*

have welcomed the potential for feminism in Deleuze's work to move beyond the dichotomy of man/woman, masculine/feminine (Markula 2006; Coleman 2009), shifting focus away from the sexed and gendered body is seen by others as problematic as it is seen to 'take the specificity of women away from women' (Driscoll 2002: 21). Many of these concerns have centred in particular on the concept of 'becoming woman' (see Grosz 1994: 162–3). One of the main reasons for this is that Deleuze and Guattari's 'becoming woman' does not refer to a woman as 'defined by her form, endowed with organs and functions, and assigned as a subject' (Deleuze and Guattari 1987: 275). Denying the materiality and specificity of a woman's body is seen as problematic as it is taken to have the impact of neutralising and depoliticising women's particular struggles against gendered inequality (Jardine 1984; Irigaray 1985; Grosz 1994). From Deleuze and Guattari's perspective, gender, along with structures and institutions such as the state, class, race and other dominant categories, is a normalising force that operates on binary logic as a binary machine. They do not focus explicitly on the characteristics of binary machines, but are more concerned with 'what escapes' these machines (Deleuze and Guattari 1987: 216). Braidotti argues that Deleuze should not be read as advocating the destruction of gender, and that it is important instead to pay attention to the 'processes of undoing, recomposing and shifting the grounds for the constitution of sexed and gendered subjectivities' (Braidotti 2011: 279). Armstrong argues that we need to understand Deleuze and Guattari (1987) as privileging those forms of resistance to subjectification which are creative of new possibilities of life (Armstrong 2002: 49). Deleuze and Guattari's (1987: 5) insistence on non-binarised forms of thought compels them to look beyond 'woman' as a subject or essentialist identity category, to think through new possibilities, not entirely separate from gender, and not bound by its dualism either.

These tensions are indicative of broader struggles in feminist and gender theory to conceptualise gender in relation to the body, and in relation to the potential for broader social change. This tension between wanting to highlight the material conditions of gender inequality yet avoiding essentialist frameworks in which women's bodies are the continuing basis for inequality can be likened to the tensions between frameworks of structure and agency in theorising the potential for change and the strength of the status quo in sociology. Indeed, it is this appeal to the body as potential, rather than reverting to a view of the body locked in dualism which is the key appeal for many feminists drawing on Deleuze and Guattari's theories and concepts (see Grosz 1994; Colebrook 2000). Deleuze and Guattari's insistence on non-binarised forms of thought drives the concept of becoming-woman which means thinking beyond the boundaries of the body-as-flesh and subjectivity, to think through new possibilities, not entirely separate from gender, but not bound by its dualism. For those concerned with the philosophical problems of dualistic thought and what it means for the way we conceive of bodies and lived experience, Deleuze and Guattari's approach holds promise and possibility.

Theorising the body   35

Drawing on Deleuze to theorise gender differs significantly from a Bourdieusian framework, described earlier in the chapter in Skeggs's criticisms. Skeggs argues that Bourdieu's concept of the habitus is 'cannot encompass all the practices between gender and sexuality, the contradictions, plays, experimentations, swappings, ambiguities and passings both within gender and between gender and sexuality' (2004: 27). In this sense, Bourdieu and Deleuze can be seen as at opposite ends of the scale in terms of theorising stasis and change in relation to the body. Bourdieu's habitus gives a clear account of the stability of subjectivity and social relations, which is useful in highlighting the ways in which inequalities repeat over time and can be very hard to shift. While Bourdieu's concept of habitus does include elements of 'improvisation', this aspect of his theory was less developed than the aspects geared towards accounting for the stability of the habitus. Deleuze, on the other hand, is oriented towards the inherent instability he sees at the core of even the most seemingly monolithic binary organisations, such as gender. The point is that both perspectives are relevant and useful, depending on what particular ends the concepts are put to use. In wanting to more carefully theorise the body, it is my perspective that a more developed understanding of the potentiality of the body can lead to expanded understandings of the theoretical tensions (such as between structure and agency) that have polarised and stifled sociological debate. Rather than the focus being on privileging or relegating one theorist or another, placing focus on the work each theorist makes possible (and impossible) can lead to more fruitful discussions and can assist us in advancing our conceptual tools.

Examples in later chapters of the book will show the ways gender is performed and produced in relation to gender as a complex relational assemblage. Gendered embodiments are not simply the reproductions of dualist gender formations; rather, gender is engaged, negotiated and produced continually through affects and relations (micro-politics). This approach to gender as continually produced through affects, relations and doings enables the ambiguities and complexities of gender to be explored, including the bodily and sensate dimensions beyond the discursive. The point is not to show that gender is endlessly fluid or loose, but rather that it is actively produced in ways that can be both restrictive and creative, often simultaneously. It is important to pay attention to these complexities and nuances to develop fuller understandings of how gender, health and other key social arrangements assemble.

Health in postmodernity: what can a body do?

A Deleuzo-Guattarian approach to the body seeks to understand health 'as a function of encounters between bodies, between forces and between practices' (Duff 2014: 186), moving beyond 'human nature' as the prime ontological category of analysis to also explore the ways in which matter, affect, biology, technology, politics and other forces are crucial in 'assembling' what we understand as human and natural (Rose 2007). As introduced above, to

36 *Theorising the body*

describe the body as an assemblage places attention on a body's engagements and connections, including discourses, affects, ideals, norms, practices, institutions and other bodies and objects.

The current social, cultural and economic contexts form the 'unstable assemblages in which humans are caught up', and affect what the body can and cannot do (Rose 1996: 184). Dominant discourses of health, for example, and its links with consumer culture and broader individualised responsibility comprise aspects of the health assemblage, and are thus key forces affecting the body. Fox (2011) describes the ill-health assemblage as comprising 'the myriad physical, psychological and social relations and affects that surround a body during an episode of ill-health' (2011: 367). At its simplest, the assemblage could include: 'Organ – virus – immune system – symptoms' (Fox 2011: 367); extending out to include the spaces of the doctor's surgery, hospital, substances of medications, and so on. Fox's point in describing an ill-health assemblage thus is to show that 'ill-health is shaped by these relations' (2011: 367). This perspective can assist in analysing the ways in which broader ideologies of health and individualism, as part of the health assemblage, currently affect a body's range of potentials. Analysing the specific practices and events that form understandings of health and bodies enables an analysis of what bodies can do, how they connect, affect and are affected in the context of the unstable assemblages that form them.

This approach to the theme of health can contribute to opening more complex understandings of the dynamics by which health is embodied. Deleuzian concepts, such as understanding health as an assemblage attends to the discursive aspects of health, and also aims to move beyond a focus on 'health discourses' only to also consider the intensities and sensations which accompany the physical and embodied dimensions of 'health'. In so doing, the analysis aims to add further impetus to approaches aimed at disrupting simplistic associations between 'health' and normative 'image' or appearance (Featherstone 2010).

In Chapter 5 for example, health is shown to be experienced and conceptualised in highly complex ways by participants in the study. Health was described in relation to 'doses' or in relation to 'boundaries' rather than being a state of being that can be simply achieved. Clare, for example, described 'health' as having the potential to 'become dangerous', and shows the complexity of health not as 'innate' or natural but generated through the body's encounters. It is important to interrogate the ways health assemblages such as those described here are cut across by a range of different normalising forces, such as gender, class, race and ethnicity and ability.

This analysis complicates any straightforwardly causal link between the experience of 'health' as the result of undertaking 'healthy' practices. Unsettling this link can assist in challenging the pervasiveness of 'look good, feel good' logic of consumer culture which currently dominates popular approaches to health and the body in advanced liberal societies such as Australia. It is clear from participants' examples that 'health' is not simply produced from

Theorising the body 37

activities broadly considered to lead to the experience of health, such as through eating 'healthy' food or exercising for fitness, as discursive analyses would show. Rather, a focus on the extra-discursive aspects of 'health' – as embodied processes of engagement and negotiation rather than concrete 'states' that can be unproblematically obtained through supposed healthy practices – enables a broader understanding of the nexus between health, bodies and the social.

New materialist and 'vitalist' perspectives, influenced by Deleuze, Guattari and other 'post-human' scholars have contributed to efforts to rethink the 'healthy' body beyond binaristic frameworks.

New material perspectives are aimed at giving particular attention to matter as a way of moving beyond the dualist approaches which underpin numerous philosophical perspectives. Many of its core aspects are drawn from, Deleuzian and Spinozist concepts (van der Tuin and Dolphijn 2010) such as those described in the section above. The new materialist perspective has the following central components, as laid out by Fox and Alldred (2014: 5):

> This approach is predicated upon three propositions: that we should look not at what entities are, but at their material effects – what they do; that all matter has an 'agential' capacity to affect, rather than being merely the inert clay moulded by human agency, consciousness and imagination; and that this focus on the materiality of effects (rather than things) allows thoughts, desires, ideas and abstractions to be considered alongside the 'hard' matter of bodies.

Dismantling the distinction between nature and culture in understanding human life is a central tenet of new materialist perspectives, which aims to show 'how cultured humans are always already in nature, and how nature is necessarily cultured' (van der Tuin and Dolphijn 2010: 154). The 'natural body' has a privileged relation with health (Keane 2009). Duff (2014) and Fox (2012), among others, have aimed to develop understandings of health and the body from new materialist perspectives beyond the nature/culture binary to focus on the ways matter is assembled.

This perspective sees health and illness as emergent properties which come about as the outcomes of relations between bodies and other objects, settings, etc. Health and illness come about through particular conditions of engagement, rather than emerging from organs or bodies themselves. This perspective sees health and illness as assemblages in which 'organs are but one element, and neither biology nor the social is privileged over the other' (Fox 2011: 361).

Conclusion: embodying theory

Theories of the body are concerned with the interplay between the micro and the macro; individuals and structures; bodies and societies. The dynamics by

38 *Theorising the body*

which social change occurs and entrenched inequalities recur are often produced through the same processes. Both need to be studied in relation to large-scale social processes as well as the individual, micro-actions carried out by people and other actors. Concepts need to be able to engage with the ways things both change and stay the same in dynamic relations. Historically, the debates in sociology centring on the dynamics between individuals and social structures, as well as how the processes of social changes and recurring inequalities occur, have centred around structure and agency. Within youth studies, discussions about agency have become essential to some of the most significant conceptual debates currently driving the field. The question of how to theorise the body sits against the dynamics of micro–macro, social change–continuing inequality, structure–agency. How can the body be understood both in context of the social world which produces it, and as an unpredictable, vital force in itself?

To engage with this question, this chapter has explored perspectives of the body and society developed by Bourdieu, Foucault and recent feminist approaches. Theories of agency described by Rose (1996), Barad (2007) and Coleman (2009) were connected with Deleuze and Guattari's theories of the body, and afford more attention to change and unpredictability in the relationship between bodies and the social world. The potential for generation and change is a central tenet of the ontology of Deleuzian theory, which has particular implications for how human and other bodies are conceptualised. This perspective was developed in reference to gender and health in particular, as these are key themes of the book. The promise of a feminist Deleuzian perspective of the body lies in the attention it affords to the complexities and nuances of social life to enable fuller understandings of how gender, health and other key social arrangements assemble.

References

Adkins, L. (2004). Reflexivity: Freedom or habit of gender? *Sociological Review*, 52, 191–210. doi: 10.1111/j.1467–1954X.2005.00531.x

Armstrong, A. (2002). Agency reconfigured: narrative continuities and connective transformations. *Contretemps: An Online Journal of Philosophy*, 3, 42–53.

Barad, K. (2007). *Meeting the Universe Halfway: Quantum Physics and the Entanglement of Matter and Meaning.* Durham and London: Duke University Press.

Bartky, S. (1990). *Femininity and Domination: Studies in the Phenomenology of Oppression.* New York: Routledge.

Beck, U. (1992). *Risk Society.* London: Sage.

Bell, K., and McNaughton, D. (2007). Feminism and the Invisible Fat Man. *Body and Society*, 13(1), 107–131.

Blackman, L. (2008). *The Body: The Key Concepts.* New York: Berg.

Blackman, L. and Venn, C. (2010). Affect. *Body and Society*, 16(1), 7–28.

Bordo, S. (2003). *Unbearable Weight: feminism, Western culture and the body* (10th anniversary edn). Berkeley: University of California Press.

Theorising the body 39

Bourdieu, P. (1977). *Outline of a Theory of Practice* (R. Nice, trans.). Cambridge: Cambridge University Press.

Bourdieu, P. (1990). *The Logic of Practice* (R. Nice, trans.). Cambridge: Polity.

Bourdieu, P. (2001). *Masculine Domination*. Cambridge: Polity.

Bourdieu, P. and Wacquant, L. (1992). *An Invitation to Reflexive Sociology*. Chicago, IL: University of Chicago Press.

Braidotti, R. (2011). *Nomadic Subjects: Embodiment and Sexual Difference in Contemporary Feminist Theory* (2nd edn). New York: Columbia University Press.

Brannen, J. and Nilsen, A. (2005). Individualisation, choice and structure: a discussion of current trends in sociological analysis. *Sociological Review*, 53(3), 412–428. doi: 10.1111/j.1467–1954X.2005.00559.x

Bray, A. and Colebrook, C. (1998). The Haunted Flesh: Corporeal Feminism and the Politics of (Dis)embodiment. *Signs: Journal of Women in Culture and Society*, 24(1), 35.

Budgeon, S. (2003). Identity as an Embodied Event. *Body and Society*, 9(1), 35–55.

Butler, J. (1990). *Gender Trouble*. New York: Routledge.

Butler, J. (1993). *Bodies that Matter: on the Discursive Limits of 'Sex'*. London: Routledge.

Butler, J. (1995). Contingent Foundations. In S. Benhabib, J. Butler, D. Cornell and N. Fraser (eds), *Feminist Contentions: A Philosophical Exchange*. New York: Routledge.

Coffey, J. and Farrugia, D. (2014). Unpacking the Black Box: The Problem of Agency in the Sociology of Youth. *Journal of Youth Studies*, 17(4).

Colebrook, C. (2000). From radical representations to corporeal becomings: The feminist philosophy of Lloyd, Grosz. *Hypatia*, 15(2), 76.

Colebrook, C. (2002). *Gilles Deleuze*. London: Routledge.

Coleman, R. (2009). *The Becoming of Bodies: Girls, Images, Experience*. Manchester and New York: Manchester University Press.

Connell, R. (1987). *Gender and Power: Society, the Person and Personal Politics*. Cambridge: Polity Press.

Connell, R. W. (1995). *Masculinities*. St Leonards: Allen & Unwin.

Connell, R. W. (2009). *Gender* (2nd edn). Cambridge: Polity Press.

Currier, D. (2003). Feminist Technological Futures. *Feminist Theory*, 4(3), 321–338. doi: 10.1177/14647001030043005

Davies, B. and Gannon, S. (2005). Feminism/Poststructuralism. In B. Somekh and C. Lewin (eds), *Research Methods in the Social Sciences* (pp. 318–325). London: Sage.

Davis, K. (1995). *Reshaping the Female Body*. New York: Routledge.

Deleuze, G. (1992). Ethology: Spinoza and Us. In J. Crary and S. Kwinter (eds), *Incorporations*. New York: Zone.

Deleuze, G. and Guattari, F. (1984). *Anti-Oedipus: Capitalism and Schizophrenia* (R. Hurley, M. Seem and H. Lane, trans.). London: Athalone Press.

Deleuze, G. and Guattari, F. (1987). *A Thousand Plateaus: Capitalism and Schizophrenia* (B. Massumi, trans.). Edinburgh: Edinburgh University Press.

Deleuze, G. and Guattari, F. (1994). *What Is Philosophy?* New York: Columbia University Press.

Deleuze, G. and Parnet, C. (2002). *Dialogues II* (H. Tomlinson and B. Habberjam, trans. 2nd edn). New York: Columbia University Press.

Dreyfus, H. L. and Rabinow, P. (eds). (1983). *Michel Foucault: Beyond Structuralism and Hermeneutics*. Chicago, IL: University of Chicago Press.

Driscoll, C. (2002). *Girls: Feminine Adolescence in Popular Culture and Cultural Theory*. New York: Columbia University Press.

40 Theorising the body

Duff, C. (2014). *Assemblages of Health*. New York: Springer.

Durkheim, E. (1976). *The Elementary Forms of the Religious Life*. New York: Routledge.

Elias, N. (1939). *The Civilising Process: The History of Manners*. Oxford: Basil Blackwell.

Farrugia, D. (2013). The Reflexive Subject: Towards a Theory of Reflexivity as Practical Intelligibility. *Current Sociology*, 61(3), 283–300. doi: 10.1177/0011392113478713

Featherstone, M. (2010). Body, Image and Affect in Consumer Culture. *Body and Society*, 16(1), 193–221.

Foucault, M. (1979). *The History of Sexuality* (R. Hurley, trans. Vol. 1). London: Allen Lane.

Foucault, M. (1980). Two Lectures. In C. Gordon (Ed.), *Power / Knowledge: Selected Interviews and Other Writings 1972–1977*. New York: Pantheon.

Foucault, M. (1982). Afterword: The Subject and Power. In H. L. Dreyfus and P. Rabinow (eds), *Michel Foucault: Beyond Structuralism and Hermeneutics* (2nd edn). Chicago, IL: University of Chicago Press.

Fox, N. J. (2011). The Ill-Health Assemblage: Beyond the Body-With-Organs. *Health Sociology Review*, 20(4), 359–371. doi: 10.5172/hesr.2011.20.4.359

Fox, N. J. (2012). *The Body*. Cambridge: Polity.

Fox, N. J. and Alldred, P. (2014). The research-assemblage: a new materialist approach to social inquiry. Paper presented at the BSA Annual Conference, Leeds.

Fox, N. J. and Ward, K. J. (2008). What Are Health Identities and How May We Study Them? *Sociology of Health and Illness*, 30(7), 1007–1021.

Gatens, M. (1988). Towards a Feminist Philosophy of the Body. In C. Pateman and E. Gross (eds), *Crossing Boundaries: Feminism and the Critique of Knowledges*. Sydney: Allen & Unwin.

Gill, R., Henwood, K. and McLean, C. (2005). Body Projects and the Regulation of Normative Masculinity. *Body and Society*, 11(1), 37–62.

Goffman, E. (1969). *The Presentation of Self in Everyday Life*. Harmondsworth: Penguin.

Goodchild, P. (1997). Deleuzean Ethics. *Theory, Culture and Society*, 14(2), 39–50. doi: 10.1177/026327697014002005

Grosz, E. (1994). *Volatile Bodies: Towards a Corporeal Feminism*. St Leonards: Allen & Unwin.

Haraway, D. (1991). *Simians, Cyborgs, and Women: The Reinvention of Nature*. New York: Routledge.

Harris, A. and Dobson, A. S. (2015). *Theorizing agency in post-girlpower times*. London and New York: Continuum 1–12. doi: 10.1080/10304312.2015.1022955

Hickey-Moody, A. and Malins, P. (eds). (2007). *Deleuzian Encounters: Studies in Contemporary Social Issues*. New York: Palgrave Macmillan.

Irigaray, L. (1985). *This Sex Which Is Not One*. Ithaca, NY: Cornell University.

Jackson, A. Y. (2010). Deleuze and the Girl. *International Journal of Qualitative Studies in Education (QSE)*, 23(5), 579–587.

Jardine, A. (1984). Woman in Limbo: Deleuze and His (Br)others. *SubStance*, 13(3).

Keane, H. (2009). Sport, Health and Steroids: Paradox, Contradiction or Ethical Self-formation? In A. Broom and P. Tovey (eds), *Men's Health: Body, Identity And Social Context*. New York: Wiley.

Lash, S. (1984). Genealogy and the Body: Foucault/Deleuze/Nietzsche. *Theory, Culture and Society*, 2(2), 1–17. doi: 10.1177/0263276484002002003

Theorising the body 41

Lehmann, W. (2004). 'For Some Reason, I Get a Little Scared': Structure, Agency, and Risk in School–Work Transitions. *Journal of Youth Studies, 7*(4), 379–396. doi: 10.1080/1367626042000315185

McLeod, J. (2005). Feminists Re-reading Bourdieu: Old Debates and New Questions about Gender Habitus and Gender Change. *Theory and Research in Education,* 3(3), 11–30.

McNay, L. (1999). Gender, Habitus and the Field: Pierre Bourdieu and the Limits of Reflexivity. *Theory, Culture and Society,* 16(1), 95–117.

McNay, L. (2000). *Gender and Agency: Reconfiguring the Subject in Feminist and Social Theory.* Cambridge: Polity.

Markula, P. (2006). Deleuze and the Body without Organs. *Journal of Sport and Social Issues,* 30(1), 29–44. doi: 10.1177/0193723505282469

Marx, K. (1997). *Writings of the Young Marx on Philosophy and Society* (L. D. Easton and K. H. Guddat eds). New York: Doubleday.

Massumi, B. (1987). Translator's Foreword: pleasures of philosophy (B. Massumi, trans.) *A Thousand Plateaus: Capitalism and Schizophrenia.* London: Athlone Press.

Mohanty, C. T. (1997). Under western eyes: feminist scholarship and colonial discourses . In A. McClintock, A. Mufti, and E. Shohat (eds), *Dangerous liaisons: Gender, nation and postcolonial perspectives* (pp. 255–277). Minneapolis: University of Minneapolis Press.

Oakley, A. (1972). *Sex, Gender and Society.* London: Temple Smith.

Phillips, J. (2006). Agencement/Assemblage. *Theory, Culture and Society,* 23(2–3), 108–109. doi: 10.1177/0263276406602300219

Potts, A. (2004). Deleuze on Viagra (Or, What Can a 'Viagra-Body' Do?). *Body and Society,* 10(1), 17–36. doi: 10.1177/1357034x04041759

Rose, N. (1996). *Inventing Our Selves: Psychology, Power and Personhood.* Cambridge: Cambridge University Press.

Rose, N. (2007). *The Politics of Life Itself: Biomedicine, Power, and Subjectivity in the Twenty-First Century.* Princeton, NJ: Princeton University Press.

Sawicki, J. (1991). *Disciplining Foucault: Feminism, Power and the Body.* New York: Routledge.

Shilling, C. (2003). *The Body and Social Theory* (2nd edn). London: Sage.

Skeggs, B. (2004). *Class, Self, Culture.* London and New York: Routledge.

Threadgold, S. (2010). Should I Pitch My Tent in the Middle Ground? On 'Middling Tendency', Beck and Inequality in Youth Sociology. *Journal of Youth Studies,* 14(4), 381–393. doi: 10.1080/13676261.2010.538042

van der Tuin, I. and Dolphijn, R. (2010). The Transversality of New Materialism. *Women: A Cultural Review,* 21(2), 153–171. doi: 10.1080/09574042.2010.488377

Webb, J., Schirato, T., and Danaher, G. (2002). *Understanding Bourdieu.* Sydney: Allen & Unwin.

Witz, A. (2000). Whose Body Matters? Feminist Sociology and the Corporeal Turn in Sociology and Feminism. *Body and Society,* 6(2), 1–24.

Woodman, D. (2009). The Mysterious Case of the Pervasive Choice Biography: Ulrich Beck, Structure/Agency, and the Middling State of Theory in the Sociology of Youth. *Journal of Youth Studies,* 12(3), 243–256. doi: 10.1080/13676260902807227

Woodman, D. and Threadgold, S. (2015). Critical Youth Studies in an Individualised and Globalised World: Making the Most of Bourdieu and Beck. In P. Kelly and A. Kamp (eds), *A Critical Youth Studies for the 21st Century.* Leiden and Boston: Brill.

Young, I. M. (2005). *Throwing Like a Girl: Phenomenology of Feminine Bodily Comportment, Motility and Spatiality* (2nd edn). Oxford: Oxford University Press.

3 Researching the body

The body in youth studies research

Broadly speaking, the body has not been a key focus of study or research in youth studies to date. The body has been something of an absent presence in the key strands which currently dominate youth research; that is, youth transitions and youth cultures perspectives. These perspectives and the ways in which studies of the body are emerging within them are explored first in this chapter, before discussing some key studies which have been undertaken in 'youth studies'. Studies of body work relating to gender and health are discussed, followed by a consideration of some of the key methodological tensions associated with the body in empirical research.

Youth transitions research

'Transitions' has been a dominant theme in youth sociology. This perspective encapsulates a number of empirical interests in youth research, in particular young people's (increasingly prolonged) transitions to adulthood in relation to changing contexts of education and employment (Côté 2002; Bynner 2005; Côté and Bynner 2008; Sanders and Munford 2008; Sanders and Munford 2013). Numerous youth studies scholars however have been critical of an approach to youth that is primarily interested in their capacity to transition out of youth for a number of reasons. The dominance of the transitions model has been argued to devalue the importance of youth in its own right by idealising adulthood; assume a simplistic linear model of development; and depend on economistic models of youth which view young people primarily in terms of their ability to contribute capital and labour through employment (Wyn and Woodman 2006; ; Woodman and Wyn 2015). Wyn and Woodman argue 'current approaches inevitably identify education, work and family patterns of young people's lives as evidence of their faulty, failed transitions, measured against the standard of the previous generation' (2006: 495). Woodman and Wyn (2015) suggest a 'generations' approach can offer a more nuanced conceptualisation of youth which places biography, social context

Researching the body 43

and the state at the centre of analysis. They argue that these factors are crucial for understanding the processes of social change and inequalities, and in the processes by which young people form identities. France and Roberts (2014) have critiqued Wyn and Woodman's generations approach and have pointed out a range of work in youth studies which attends to the political and structural contexts of youth transitions beyond economistic frameworks. One of the central issues in 'transitions' debates relates to tensions between exploring macro social systems (such as 'transition' patterns of large cohorts) and the micro-dimensions in which these patterns play out in young people's lives. The embodied dimensions of such micro-social practices have not yet been developed in the focus on youth transitions. As both Woodman and Wyn (2015) and France and Roberts (2014) argue, it is crucial to attend to both the macro- and micro-processes which shape the lives and experiences of young people. The body, as I argue in this book, is one particular dimension of focus that could add much to understandings of the interrelationships between the macro- and micro-processes of social practices.

Youth cultures research

The body's importance for understanding cultural practices has not always been recognised in cultural studies (Featherstone 2010). While the physical body had previously been absent in the bulk of studies of youth cultures and subcultures it is growing as a key area of focus. Earlier studies of youth tended to take the body as self-evident in cultural or subcultural practices, without subjecting it to theoretical or conceptual analysis. However, recent work in youth cultural studies has begun to emphasise the importance of embodiment for understanding additional dimensions of youth cultures. Bennett and Robards's edited collection *Mediated Youth Cultures* (2014) includes a section on 'bodies spaces and places', which explores the significance of bodily representations on the internet, for example, in relation to space and place.

Driver's ethnographic study is one particularly significant example of an embodied approach to youth (sub)cultures research. He studied the embodied, affective and sensory aspects of young men's participation in hardcore music and draws upon the theoretical frames of Bourdieu and Deleuze to argue that identity and subcultures are emergent; that is, both come into being continually through the embodied practices of participants (Driver 2011: 987–8). Similarly, Sharp and Nilan explore the importance of embodied dimensions of art and music and how these are relevant for young women 'becoming queer punx' in the masculinist space of the hard core scene in Australia (2014). Driver and Bennett have also recently begun to theorise the ways in which music scenes can be further understood as embodied spaces (Driver and Bennett 2014). Hodkinson (2012) cautions that we should 'ensure that enthusiasm to study the affective and the sensual does not result in the reduction of subculture to the specifics of spectacular emotional or bodily

44 *Researching the body*

experience'. He argues that while it is important to look at the immediate and embodied sensations of the dance floor, for example, there is more to understand about these practices than sheer experience itself. This is undoubtedly so. However, given that there has certainly been an overemphasis on cerebral aspects of subcultures such as consciousness at the expense of the body (Driver 2011), it is important to retain a focus on these additional embodied dimensions in youth cultures and subcultures research.

Youth, gender and the body

Gender has been thoroughly examined in empirical studies of young women, and more recently, young men, across a range of disciplines including cultural studies, education, gender studies and feminist studies. Young femininities have received significant empirical and theoretical attention, notably through the work of Harris (2004), Aapola *et al.* (2005), Driscoll (2002) and McRobbie (2001, 2004, 2007, 2015), Gill and Scharff (2011), Hauge (2009) S. Jackson (2015) Ringrose (2013) Renold and Ringrose (2008). Likewise, young masculinities is a focal point of study through the work of Willis (1977) Connell (1995); Frosh *et al.* (2002), Mac an Ghaill (1994) and Kenway *et al.* (2006), among others. Nayak and Kehily's (2006, 2008a) ethnographic study of young people's displays of gender embodiment in Britain examined the ways that gender is regulated, performed and embodied in school-based cultures. While the body and embodiment have not always been the explicit focus in studies of gender and youth in the past, the body is a growing focus in youth research (Coffey and Watson 2015; Coffey *et al.* 2016). The body is becoming a particular focus in youth research on gender and sexualities, which is discussed in detail in the next section.

Numerous other studies have also explored the ways gender intersects with other dimensions of identity, inequality and embodiment in the lives of young people in relation to class (Skeggs 1997; Walkerdine *et al.* 2001), poverty (Frost 2003), race, ethnicity, and the invisibility of whiteness (Bird 2008; Nayak 2003; Unterhalter *et al.* 2004), dis/ability (Addlakha 2008; Gibson *et al.* 2013; Priestly 1998); sexuality (Bay-Cheng 2003; Allen 2008; Ringrose 2011a; and Mphaphuli 2015), consumption (Brown 2008; Frost 2003; Hollands 2002) and place (D. Farrugia *et al.* 2015; Nayak 2003, 2006). Nayak's (2003) study of race and ethnicity in the UK, for example, picks apart the complexities and 'multiple interconnections' between race, gender, sexuality and social class. Ethnicity, along with gender and class, plays an important role in youth cultures. Nayak (2003) argues that 'zones of bodily consumption' including sport, music, hairstyles and fashion are examples of young peoples' experimentation with 'a new corporeal canvas'. The prime mode in which the body is most explicitly the target of focus in youth research, however, relates to concerns over 'bodily risks'; in particular, those related to sexualisation and 'sexting'.

Sexualisation and 'sexting'

Sexualisation is a crucial and growing area of research concerning the body in youth studies. Feminist studies in Australia, New Zealand and the United Kingdom have critiqued consumer society's demand for young women to embody hypersexualised modes of femininity (Harris 2004; Gill 2007; McRobbie 2007; Renold and Ringrose 2008; Dobson 2013; S. Jackson 2015; Retallack *et al.* 2016). Images of girls' bodies proliferate in Western visual media, regulating 'what it is to be a sexual subject' and providing a 'technology of sexiness' (Gill 2008: 53). Paradoxically, there is a paucity of information regarding positive sexual embodiment (Coffey *et al.* 2016). The key message is that girls are 'being sexualised by sexualised media' (S. Jackson 2014) and must therefore be better informed through such campaigns in order to avoid the narratives of shame and regret that are depicted as the result of sending an explicit image.

The increasing sexualisation of culture and bodies has been theorised in relation to post-feminist discourse in which feminism is obsolete as gender equality has been achieved (Retallack *et al.* 2016; Ringrose *et al.* 2013). In post-feminist understandings, young women's 'self-objectification' is represented as a mode of empowerment rather than oppression, and as a way of gaining pleasure and value (Ringrose *et al.* 2013). This 'postfeminist media culture' of sexiness through bodily display increasingly extends to young men's bodies too (Gill *et al.* 2005; Manago 2013; Siibak 2010), particularly through new digital technologies and social networking (Harvey *et al.* 2013). However, the 'normalisation' of sexiness through visual display, enabled by digital media technologies has led to a generalised moral outrage, exemplified through moral panic surrounding 'sexting'.[1]

This concern has spread to legal and law enforcement agencies, as well as education and health policy agencies who have been enlisted to address what has been termed the 'teen sexting epidemic' (Ringrose *et al.* 2013). The sexualisation of children and young girls (or tweens) and the harmful effects of 'sexting' and accessing sexual content on the internet are overwhelmingly discussed in relation to notions of 'risk' and harm. Education campaigns focus on equipping young women in particular with the knowledge and skills to navigate the ill-effects of sexting (which are variously described as linked with damaging self-esteem and even leading to depression or suicide). One high-profile public campaign warning young people of the dangers of sexting in Australia was 'Megan's Story'. The clip shows a young women taking a photo of her breasts under her school uniform and sending it to a boy in her class, who instantaneously sends the photo to others in the class, including her male teacher. Albury and Crawford (2012) discuss this example in the context of the disparities between the legal penalties and official responses to sexting, and the responses to sexting by young people themselves. They argue that the 'current legal and policy responses to sexting have failed to account for the range of meanings that young people themselves might apply to the

46 *Researching the body*

practice' (Albury and Crawford 2012: 464). The UK-based short film *Exposed* runs on a similar narrative as 'Megan's Story', and depicts a 'girl putting herself at risk by sending explicit photos to her boyfriend' (Ringrose *et al.* 2013). As well as failing to locate the practice of sexting in relation to the actual experiences and strategies of negotiation used by young people themselves around the consumption and engagement with such images, Ringrose *et al.* argue that the film presents an entirely uncritical view of the gendered dynamics of blame and shame which underpin the sharing of images without consent:

> ['Exposed'] does not scrutinise the cultural sexism that normalises the coercive, unauthorised showing and distribution of images of girls' body parts. The implicit message in this and other anti-sexting narratives is that inherent responsibility for sexting gone wrong therefore lies with the body in the image rather than, for instance, the agents of distribution.
>
> (2013: 307)

This analysis contributes an important analysis of the specific meanings of bodies and body parts mediated through digital image-sharing beyond discourses of risk only, to explore the complex, affective and embodied processes which contribute to the currency of images linked to gender relations. This disrupts the media risk discourse of sexting as a problem of 'under-aged girls lacking vigilance in their uses of social media, by sending images of their bodies to boys, and boys as predatory and over-sexed', refocusing attention on the socially mediated meanings of gender and the body (Ringrose and Harvey 2015).

A range of research has aimed to critique and unsettle the media risk discourse in a number of ways: by exploring the perspectives and understandings young people themselves have of sexting and 'sexualised media' (Albury and Crawford 2012; S. Jackson 2014); through exploring the ways masculinities are constructed and embodied through digital media technologies and the sharing and hoarding of sexual images as capital (Harvey *et al.* 2013); through exploring the ways young women perform contradictory femininities in relation to (hetero)sexuality (Renold and Ringrose 2011); and through placing a specific focus on image content and the meanings associated with particular body parts (Ringrose and Harvey 2015). In relation to sexting narratives in particular, Ringrose and Harvey question the ways in which girls' and boys' bodies and body parts are constructed differently and carry different social meanings. They ask, 'How are images of girls' breasts surveilled and owned by others? Why can images of girls' bodies be used to sexually shame them? How do images of "six packs", "pecks" and "bits" work differently than "boobs"?' (2015: 205) Ringrose and Harvey argue that 'affective intensities' associated with images of girls' bodies and moral discourses of reward and shame serve to materialise gender differences which regulate girls' sexuality. These studies which focus on image content along with the discourses and representations prevalent in the mainstream under-standings of 'sexting' provide important insights into young people's negotiations of digital social media and images, as well as a strong critique of the implicit sexism and regulation of young women's bodies and sexualities in particular. These critical perspectives of the media risk discourse in relation to sexting enable a more detailed, critical perspective on new technologies of social media and the implications of bodily display in the lives and worlds of young people. As Renold and Ringrose argue, in academic and mainstream analysis, we need to go beyond the tendencies to fix girls as 'objectified, innocent victims' in sexualisation/sexting theses, or as agentic, savvy navigators of a 'toxic' sexual culture, to instead explore how these themes obscure the 'messy realities of lived sexual subjectivities and how girls may be positioned in these ways simultaneously' (2011: 392).

Studies of body work practices

While there is a significant range of work in youth studies that has explored young women's and men's lives in relation to gender, class categories, race and ethnicity, sexualities and popular culture, the body and appearance are generally studied indirectly in relation to these broader themes (Frost 2001). The majority of scholarship on 'body work' and body modification does not focus on youth specifically. Frost's (2001, 2003, 2005) work is some of the first scholarship in the specific field of youth studies which places a sustained focus on the body and body appearance practices in relation to social processes and the production of identity (see also: Wright *et al.* 2006; Karupiah 2012). Frost argues that context in which the body and appearance has come to matter more for both young women and men is related to the mass changes related to consumption and identification under late capitalism, particularly in the West (Frost 2003: 54). In these conditions, 'the body for both boys and girls is a basis of judgment and differentiation' (p. 60). Damage can be inflicted on boys and girls in relation to their appearance – bodies – along gender lines, but also related to disability, class and race. Young people's 'bodies – how they adjust and adorn them – may leave them subject to humiliation and isolation, as well as identification and inclusion' (Frost 2003: 67). As a result, Frost argues that 'the most important structural inequality in relation to consumer-based image production' relates to poverty and socio-economic inequality as these factors exclude young people from participating in consumption practices.

The body and body work practices have been studied more extensively in broader sociological studies in relation to gender and health. Studies of the body, gender and body work by Crossley (2004, 2005, 2007), Davis (1995, 2003) and Spitzak (1990) have undertaken empirical research of men and women's embodied experiences in relation to body projects of modification/maintenance. Studies involving the embodied experiences of participants often do not foreground gender as related to the participants' embodied

48 *Researching the body*

experiences; or focus solely on masculinity (Monaghan 1999, 2001b; Gill *et al.* 2000, 2005; Watson 2000;); or femininity (Spitzack 1990; Spitzack 1994; Davis 1995; Markula 1995). Studies that deal with the embodied experiences of gender of both men and women are relatively scarce (although exceptions are Nettleton and Watson 1998; J. Hargreaves and Vertinsky 2007). Furthermore, although these studies deal extensively with the bodies of men or women separately (and very occasionally both), few studies focus on body work and men and women together (see Coffey 2013a, 2013b, 2014). These studies usually focus on one related aspect of body work, such as fitness or work at the gym (Markula 1995; Crossley 2005) or broader concepts of health (Watson 2000).

Numerous studies have explored particular practices of body work, such as bodybuilding, cosmetic surgery, 'beauty work' and health practices, and the discourses of health and gender that are involved in these practices. Studies which focus explicitly on more than one practice of body work include those by Gill *et al.* (2000, 2005), Gimlin (2002) and Crossley (2006). Gill *et al.* (2005) for example explored young, healthy (predominantly British) male adults' experiences of embodiment in undertaking body projects, mainly on the broad topic of body modification. Other studies of body work practices draw upon Foucault's 'disciplined body' to discuss gender and inequality (Bartky 1990; Spitzack 1990; Spitzack 1994; Markula 1995); Bourdieu's concepts of physical capital and habitus related to gender relations in snowboarding (H. A. Thorpe 2009; H. Thorpe 2011); and analyse the cultural contexts and discourses surrounding health practices (Crawford 2006; Lupton 2012, 2013; Leahy 2014; Mears 2014).

Studies of exercise and 'health' in consumer culture

Numerous studies have used textual analysis of 'health' and 'fitness' discourses surrounding body work or 'body projects' through analysing the content of magazines. Dworkin and Wachs (2009) provide a detailed discussion of discourses of health and fitness, and their implications for gender, class and race. Through content and textual analysis of men's and women's health magazines in America over a period of ten years, Dworkin and Wachs analyse 'how a discourse of health is used to validate relational gender and engagement in consumer culture, and how healthism legitimates neoliberalism and consumerism' (2009: 24). Lloyd (1996) also uses content analysis of women's health and fitness magazines in America but focuses specifically on aerobics to critique the way aerobics intersects with dominant norms of femininity, namely beauty and the 'tyranny of slenderness'. Similarly, Duncan (1994) undertakes a Foucaultian analysis of American fitness magazine *Shape* to explore the 'self-conscious body monitoring in women' encouraged by this text (1994: 49). These studies do not research the perspectives of those who consume health and fitness magazines, but their findings and discussions are relevant to analyses of the social contexts of body work.

Researching the body 49

Many studies of 'fitness' practices locate body practices in the current neo-liberal consumer context. Numerous studies focus on women's embodied experiences of body work practices including aerobics (Markula 1995; Lloyd 1996), Pilates (Markula 2006, 2011), jogging (Allen-Collinson 2011), swimming (McMahon 2011) and yoga (Lea 2009: 269) for example. An edited collection by Kennedy and Markula (2011) entitled *Women and Exercise: The Body, Health and Consumerism* draws together studies on diverse practices of body work undertaken by women, such as striptease aerobics (McIntyre 2011), martial arts (Aikido) (Lokman 2011); as well as the experiences of stigmatisation of large women's experiences of exercise at the gym (Groven *et al.* 2011; Mansfield 2011; Rich *et al.* 2011), health promotion for older women of diverse ethnic backgrounds (Wray 2011) and the nexus between gender, ageing and exercise (Pike 2011). Hargreaves's (2007) study of the ways the bodies of Muslim women in sport are experienced and mediated through different ideological interpretations of Islam in a Western, modern context is another important study of the negotiation of femininities through the body and health and exercise practices.

Studies of men's 'fitness' have a narrower focus on practices associated with muscularity and hegemonic masculinity through weights training at the gym (Crossley 2005, 2006; Olivardia *et al.* 2004) and on boxing (Wacquant 1995, 2005) and bodybuilding (Bridges 2009; Lee *et al.* 2009; Monaghan 1999, 2001a, 2002; Atkinson and Monaghan 2014). Bridges's (2009) study of male bodybuilders in Britain examined the ways that masculinity and gender capital is connected with the sport of bodybuilding. He also uses qualitative methods including participant observation, interviews with 23 men, and a grounded theory approach to the data. Monaghan's (1999, 2001) work on the embodied experiences of British (predominantly male) bodybuilders also uses in-depth interviews to explore the connections between bodybuilding, consumer culture imperatives, health and fitness discourses and bodily regimes. Monaghan (2001) has argued that very little is known about people's experience of health, particularly 'vibrant health' and physicality.

There have been far fewer studies focusing on the body in men's experiences of gender than women's. Gill *et al.* (2000, 2005) focus on British men's embodied identities through their practices of body modification, including working out at a gym, body piercing and tattooing through individual life-history interviews and small focus groups. They examined the ways that hegemonic and normative masculinity was regulated and negotiated by men through working on the 'look' of their bodies, and the prevalence of discourses of individualism and masculinity in the ways the men discussed their embodied identities and experiences of their bodies (Gill *et al.* 2005: 60). Connell's *Masculinities* used life-history interviews to explore the experiences of a group of Australian men in the context of broad social and economic changes, and how patterns of gender are being renegotiated or reinscribed.

As the above sections show, the body has been studied in relation to a diverse array of social contexts and themes across youth, gender and feminist

50 *Researching the body*

studies and sociology more broadly. While the body has not previously comprised a key area of focus in youth studies, the body has been a focal point in numerous sociological studies relating in particular to gender, sexuality and health. The way the body is theorised in these studies is similarly diverse, and is drawn from social constructionist, structuralist, phenomenological and post-structural traditions. The next section returns to the theme of 'agency' introduced in the previous chapter to consider the way in which theories of the body's relationship with the social are mobilised in empirical studies relating to young bodies.

Studies of body work and agency

'Agency' is a concept that is widely used in empirical studies in fields of sociology, and youth, gender and feminist studies; particularly in those studies concerning the body. Agency is often used in sociological analysis as a taken-for-granted element of an individual's being, where an agent, possessing an intrinsic 'agency', is understood as imbued with the power to act in ways other than dominant 'structures' impel (Coffey and Farrugia 2014). However, as discussed in the previous section, agency, where it is theorised as an 'essential property of the subject' can lead to ontological problems in analysis of the relationship between the body and the social.

A recent example of debate surrounding the theorisation of 'agency' in feminist and youth sociology can be seen in the exchanges between Duits and van Zoonen and Gill relating to the article 'Headscarves and Porno-Chic: Disciplining Girls' Bodies in the European Multicultural Society' (Duits and van Zoonen 2006). In this article, Duits and van Zoonen argue that whether wearing a headscarf or 'porno-chic' clothing (such as 'visible G-strings'), girls' bodies are submitted to the meta-narratives of the dominant discourse, which define their everyday practices as inappropriate regardless of how the girls wearing a headscarf or 'porno-chic' clothing define it. Duits and van Zoonen argue that in the process of debates about both headscarves and porno-chic, 'girls are denied their agency and autonomy' (2006: 104). Duits and van Zoonen's (2006) central argument is that feminist analysis should be aimed at 'giving girls a voice' to enable them to exercise their 'agency' relating to their clothing choices.

Gill's (2007) response raises numerous theoretical difficulties implicit in Duits and van Zoonen's treatment of the terms 'agency', 'autonomy' and 'choice' from a feminist perspective. Gill asks 'how well such terms serve contemporary feminism' in regard to their analytical purchase for the complex lived experience of girls' and young women's lives in a postfeminist, neo-liberal society (Gill 2007: 72). Gill argues that a focus on the autonomous choices made by girls remains complicit with, rather than critical of, post-feminist and neo-liberal discourses: 'Duits and van Zoonen's young women are constructed as unconstrained and freely choosing' (Gill 2007: 74). In this

Researching the body 51

way, Duits and van Zoonen conflate agency with autonomous choice, rather than interrogating the 'powerful interests at work in promoting particular products and practices' associated with the fashion, cosmetic and health industries (Gill 2007: 75).

The issues raised by Gill here are emblematic of the theoretical tension between structure and agency in a broad range of sociological and feminist empirical work. This tension holds that people (subjects) are neither 'cultural dopes' nor 'free agents' (Davis 1995), but that 'we are all enmeshed in matrices of power' (Gill 2007: 77). The difficultly here is explaining the processes through which both agency and structure are brought to bear on the individual, since such explanations usually remain caught up in dualistic understandings of bodies and society, framing them in terms of liberation/repression or subjectification/objectification (see Budgeon 2003). For example, Kennedy and Markula (2011) problematise the constructivist feminist argument that listening to the voices of women is a form of resistance to oppressive social forces. They argue that this perspective assumes a binary between those forces and women's bodies whose practices, voices and experiences are 'endorsed as more authentic representations of femininity than media representations' (Kennedy and Markula 2011: 11). As discussed in the previous chapter, the view that representation intervenes and organises the body is problematic because this presupposes a prior 'authentic' body which is then passively overcoded (Bray and Colebrook 1998).

Kwan and Trautner's (2009) study of women's 'beauty work' further illustrates the ways that agency can be mobilised in analysis and lead to dualistic understandings of the relationship between the body and the social. Kwan and Trautner discuss numerous and wide-ranging empirical studies of women's practices of 'beauty work', including those related to their hair, make-up, body hair, body size and shape, clothing and nails. Kwan and Trautner (2009) argue that women are held accountable for these appearance norms, which are aligned with cultural representations of beauty in contemporary Western societies which are largely homogeneous and emphasise a feminine ideal of slenderness and firmness. These are valid critiques of the cultural representations of femininity. However, it rests on a model of 'passive inscription' of social norms on women's bodies. They argue that these dominant norms of femininity are 'transmitted by the mass media and other visual images', and rather simply inscribe power and social relations on women's bodies 'as a text' (Bartky 1990; Kwan and Trautner 2009). This leads Kwan and Trautner to argue that women who participate in beauty practices and body modification 'can be thought of as "cultural dopes", passively adopting hegemonic beauty norms, who would require "consciousness-raising" to inform them as to how their practices are complicit in larger systems of domination' (2009: 63). Alternatively, they argue, it is possible to understand women as 'active agents' who participate in these practices to 'reap certain rewards and avoid stigma', as in through Davis's (1995) study of women who undergo cosmetic surgery to alleviate suffering (Kwan and Trautner 2009: 63).

52 *Researching the body*

Either way, Kwan and Trautner argue that beauty work practices reinforce hegemonic ideals which sustain and reproduce the social order (2009: 63).

As a result, their analysis is based on an ontological understanding of the female body as fundamentally overdetermined by patriarchy as the 'victim' of representation and beauty practices, since even in women's capacity as 'agents' they remain bound in repressive and constraining representations of femininity. Budgeon argues that the mind/body binary underlies critiques of the ways women's bodies are 'represented', because such understandings reinforce that 'women's bodies can only ever be outside of representation, and within current representational practices women's bodies can only be negated' (2003: 41). We need a more nuanced approach to understanding the relationship between women's bodies and the social, because 'bodies are never just objects but part of a process of negotiating and renegotiating self-identity' (Budgeon 2003: 45).

Coleman too argues that there has been significant recent feminist empirical work on the relations between young women's bodies and images in the media, but much of this is underpinned implicitly by an oppositional model of body/image, subject/object (2008, 2009). For example, feminist studies of body dissatisfaction of young women in relation to media images (Grogan and Wainwright 1996) often maps women's bodies and media images through subject/object relations and tensions in representation and structure/agency. Kwan and Trautner's (2009) article exemplifies the issues associated with such an approach.

Rather than seeing the body as primarily an 'object' upon which culture writes meanings, Budgeon (2003) and Coleman (2009), following insights from Deleuze and Guattari's theorisation of bodies, propose that it is the connection and processes between bodies and the world that affect how bodies are experienced, and how they may be lived. This involves a shift from a concern for 'being' to 'becoming', and for the different connections that are always in process between bodies and the world.

Deleuze and Guattari and studies of the body

Empirical work which uses Deleuzian theory explicitly in methodology and analysis is relatively new in sociological studies of the body, though it is beginning to proliferate. In the section below, I explore some of the studies of identity, gender, the body and body work which have utilised Deleuzian theory in the methodology and analysis. The collection edited by Coleman and Ringrose (2013), and key studies by Budgeon (2003), Hickey-Moody (2007), Fox and Ward (2008), Fox and Alldred (2016) Coleman (2009), Jackson (2010), and Renold and Ringrose (2008, 2011; Ringrose 2011b, 2013) in particular have developed feminist sociological approaches to understanding young bodies drawn from Deleuze and Guattari's concepts. The studies described below relate specifically to the core themes of this book, in

Researching the body 53

Deleuzian feminist approaches to understanding youth, gender and health through the body.

Budgeon (2003) explored the ways young women produce identities through the body. Budgeon interviewed 33 young women across five sites in a city in northern England to explore the complex relations between embodiment and identity through their bodies and broader everyday lives. She argues for a way of thinking about bodies and identity which moves beyond a concern for what the body means towards a concern for what the body can do and how it becomes through a multiplicity of connections with other bodies (Budgeon 2003: 51). Budgeon shows that bodies can be understood as more than the effects of representational practices, conceptualising embodied selves as processes or 'events' of becoming.

Markula (2006, 2011) uses Deleuzian concepts of the body without organs and assemblage as a way to deterritorialise the practice of Pilates from dominant health and fitness discourses which define the image of the fit feminine body. Using an ethnographic research design, Markula (2011) becomes a qualified Pilates instructor and teaches a Pilates class once a week for 12 months. Markula investigates, from a Deleuzian perspective, what she can do as a researcher to 'problematize the fitness industry' and at the same time, unsettle individualised notions of identity construction of the participants in her class (Markula 2011: 66). Taking extensive notes from her participant observation of the classes, Markula attempts to analyse the 'folds' typically involved in fitness practices such as Pilates, and to find ways to unhook the practices of Pilates from the normative 'purpose' of the practices (such as 'toning' and controlling the 'feminine' body), to 'continually problematize building a self, a body and a practice' (Markula 2011: 74).

Coleman's (2008, 2009) research focuses on girls' bodies and their relations with images using a Deleuzian framework of 'becoming', in the place of more widespread feminist analyses of girls in which their bodies and subjectivities fall victim to the 'effects' of media images. Through interviews and focus groups with 13 13-year-old and 14-year-old girls from two schools in London and Oxfordshire, England, Coleman explores the ways the girls connect with various images through discussing photographs and creating their own montages of images that are important to them. Rather than studying the effects of images on the girls, Coleman is concerned with 'the ways in which the girls' bodies can be understood as *becoming through* their relations with images' (Coleman 2008: 170, original emphasis).

In Jackson's (2010) feminist ethnographic study of subject formation of senior adolescent girls in rural, southern USA, she presents a Deleuzian analysis focusing on the 'becoming and difference' of Jesse, a cheerleader. Jackson explains that she is motivated to 'work with the girl as an event, to notice how Jesse unfolds herself through micro-particular movements with her others', rather than focusing on the 'surface' to see the uniformity or categorisation of Jesse as a cheerleader (2010: 580). Drawing on Deleuzian theorisations of becoming, including terminology of molar and molecular and

54   Researching the body

'the event' of movement or expression through which becoming occurs, Jackson explores micro-processual ways that Jesse simultaneously occupies the molar territory of cheerleading ('a dominant form that attempted to stabilize her identity') while at the same time 'molecular processes of her becoming deterritorialized this space' (2010: 582).

Studies by Ringrose (2013), Renold and Ringrose (2008, 2011) and Ivinson and Renold (2013; Renold and Ivinson 2014) have also been particularly influential in drawing Deleuzian understandings of subjectivity and the body to disrupt post-feminist descriptions of gender in the midst of moral panics around girls' premature sexualisation. A range of work in the field of education has similarly drawn on and developed Deleuzian concepts in empirical research with young people (Mazzei and McCoy 2011; Youdell 2010; Youdell and Armstrong 2011; Lenz Taguchi and Palmer 2014).

Deleuzian theoretical perspectives have also been developed in the field of health sociology by Potts (2004), Duff (2010, 2014a) and Fox (2002a, 2002b, 2011, 2012) in particular. Potts's (2004) study explores men's and women's experiences of sexuality through Viagra as a treatment for erectile difficulties. This study contrasts the biomedical 'healthy' body, which aims for predictability and stability, with the Deleuzian 'healthy' body, which aims to multiply its capacity for affect. Fox and Ward (2008) outline a theoretical basis for the study of identities based on a Deleuzian framework of embodied subjectivity (2008: 1008). They highlight subjectivity as originating in the 'dialogical confluence between social context and the affirming, creative and embodied experimentation/engagement of the living body' (Fox and Ward 2008: 1008). Elsewhere, Fox (2002a, 2002b, 2011, 2012) has discussed Deleuze's theoretical framework and how it may be applied to understandings of health, illness and health care in the context of thinking through the relationship between bodies and society. Deleuzian theoretical perspectives are also increasingly being drawn upon in sexualities research (Potts 2004; Alldred and Fox 2015; Fox and Alldred 2016) as well as in research in young people's drug use (Duff 2014b; A. Farrugia 2014).

What all of these studies have in common is their approach to the body and the social. The prime theoretical focus which informs these studies understands the body's relationship with society in a particular way. It begins from the premise that the body is a process (rather than primarily a subject/object) that is made and remade through its 'multiplicity of continuous connections with other bodies' (Budgeon 2003). It is the connection and processes between bodies and the world that affect how bodies are experienced, and how they may be lived. My understanding of body work is also informed by this approach. The practices of body work are an outcome of the body's broader connections and relations with other bodies and the world. This involves a shift from a concern for 'being' to 'becoming', and for the different connections that are always in process between bodies and the world. The research project described below takes up these understandings to examine the processes and practices of body work.

The research project

This research draws on Deleuzo-Guattarian concepts to inform a methodology of bodies and practices of body work in relation to gender and health primarily. I define body work practices as a series of affective relations between the body and its environment; and as an embodied process. Body work practices require a conscious investment in the appearance and function of the body; yet the body itself in its affective capacities also motivates the processes of body work. The practices undertaken as 'body work' can include any practices which involve the intent to alter the body's appearance, as well as altering the subjective experience of the body (such as practices aimed at 'feeling healthier').

This study examines the affective relations involved in body work, including the ways that health and gender assemblages are produced and affect participants' bodies. The central research questions are drawn from the ontological and epistemological frameworks I have outlined based on Deleuzian approaches to the body:

- How are knowledges, understandings and experiences of bodies produced through body work practices?
- How do social relations (such as gender and health) intersect with body work practices, and what does this mean for understanding bodies from a Deleuzian perspective?
- How do social relations and body work practices affect the body's possibilities?

These questions were explored drawing on data from face-to-face, in-depth semi-structured interviews with 22 men and women aged 18–33 in Melbourne, Australia. The participants were recruited through the social networking site Facebook, using personal contacts to distribute advertisements electronically to their Facebook 'friends' who were not contacts or acquaintances of my own. Recruiting through social media and electronic advertisements was time and cost-effective, as it allowed me to distribute a large number of advertisements and reach a diverse group of potential participants very quickly. Another advantage of this recruitment method is that it is relatively unobtrusive, since participants did not have to take any direct action or engagement with the advertisement unless they were interested in accessing more information or wanted to participate in the research.

The recruitment flier described the study as exploring 'what the body means to young people currently in society'. It stated 'In contemporary society, the body is often worked on, maintained or changed in many ways. I want to hear from you about these issues, and how this may relate to your own experiences of your body.' Participants self-selected to participate, and contacted me through Facebook messenger or email to ask for more information or to volunteer.

56   *Researching the body*

The flier did not seek participants who undertook particular kinds of body work, such as gym work or dieting, and participants were not asked to specify what forms of body work (if any) they undertook prior to the interview. This allowed participants to speak about any 'body work' practice relevant to them, ranging from the more 'intensive' such as cosmetic surgery, through to the more 'everyday' such as hairstyle or going for walks.

All undertook some kind of 'body work', but the practices, frequency and meanings differed. Some did 'very little' exercise, for example, but described their hair or make-up practices as very important to their presentation of self; others had a very regulated approach to eating and exercise (see Coffey 2013b). All participants connected body work practices related to exercise and eating with health. Body work practices undertaken by the participants in this study ranged from 'healthy' eating and other dietary features; physical exercise (including participation in fitness classes such as Pilates, yoga, 'Boxercise' and 'Zumba'), jogging, swimming and cycling; styling and colouring of hair and applying make-up; removal of body hair; tanning; tattooing and piercing; and cosmetic surgery including Botox, liposuction and breast enlargement. Many of these practices were undertaken by both men and women, with the exception of wearing make-up, tanning and cosmetic surgery, which were exclusive to the women in this study.

Participants were predominantly white[2] and self-identified as middle class,[3] and around half were tertiary educated. Two women described themselves as having Asian heritage (Japanese/Chinese/Vietnamese), and all participants were born in Australia. One male participant identified as homosexual. Images of white, middle-class bodies embody the ideal healthy citizen (Dworkin and Wachs 2009), and this may help to explain their broad endorsement of body work practices aimed at achieving 'health'. Participants' ages ranged fairly evenly from 18–33 years old, with the majority in their twenties. Two men and two women were students at universities with part-time jobs, and others had roles in various professions. The women (who were not full-time students) were currently working in hospitality, retail, the health and beauty industries (as a make-up artist, dental assistant and beauty therapist), marketing, or as a nanny or administrative assistant. It is notable that many of these roles are traditionally 'feminised' forms of work in the 'care', beauty and service sectors. The men who were not full-time students were in less traditional gendered occupations than the women; two were musicians also working in other professions such as sound engineering or graphic design, and two other men worked solely as a graphic designer and as a sound editor for film and television. The occupations of the other five men in the study were an accountant, a barber, a nurse and a firefighter and professional footballer.

Interviews took place between March and October 2010 in cafes, parks and other public spaces in around Melbourne, and lasted up to two hours. A loose topic guide[4] was used to explore participants' experiences of body work and broader understandings of health and gender. Interviews were audio-recorded

Researching the body 57

and transcribed verbatim. Emergent coding was used, in which key themes and issues were identified as they emerged from the words of the participants, and linked to issues around their understandings and experiences of body work, gender and so on. Following Fox and Ward (2008), I used the method of interviewing to enter into a discussion to 'gather the relations and affect, those things that affect an individual' (2008: 1013). Where participants in this study make statements like 'I feel better about myself when I have been exercising', I have interpreted that such a statement can be explored or understood using the concept of affect. I analysed the data thematically and inductively, following analysis techniques described by Minichiello *et al.* (2008) and Willis (2006). The approach to data responds to recent calls to find ways to engage Deleuze methodologically as well as conceptually (Mazzei and McCoy, 2011). This approach shares a parallel concern with post-structural feminist approaches to data analysis which emphasise the multiplicity and variations within and across human identities, rather than a focus on the individual participant's interview data as being compatible with the representation of a coherent 'self' (St Pierre 1997; Mazzei and McCoy 2011).

This study does not aim to be representative, though I attempted to explore a range of perspectives and experiences through recruiting through networks of personal contacts. Although the participants were predominantly white, heterosexual and middle class, there was a high level of variety in participants' body work practices, as well as in their understandings and descriptions of experiences related to bodies. I use the data to illustrate theoretical arguments, approaching the body not as an object or entity but as an event of becoming, in which the affects and relations in encounters are crucial to the formulation of change or action.

The relations and affects of the bodies are the primary concern in this study, and health, consumer culture and gender were particularly important to participants' understandings and experiences of bodies. Affect and becoming can be studied in the context of any connections a body has; with other people, abstract ideas, activities and social constructs (Fox and Ward 2008). Further work in the future could focus specifically on the affects and relations of body work practices and understandings of bodies from a range of cultural and ethnic contexts; or could focus on homosexuality in relation to body work and understandings and experiences of bodies.

The societal context in which bodies are located and in which body work practices take place are also central for understanding the participants' descriptions of their bodies and body work. Gender and consumer culture which include health ideals, individualism and 'image' are key features of the current social, economic and historical context in which body work takes place and meanings of bodies are negotiated. The primary methods used in youth studies research are explored further below, before a discussion as to how approaches towards studying the body and embodiment may be better mobilised methodologically.

58 *Researching the body*

Methods in youth research

As described in the studies above, qualitative methods, primarily in-depth interviewing and ethnography, are the most widely used methods in youth studies. Participatory research is a key strand in youth studies (Kenway *et al.* 2006; Campbell *et al.* 2009; Bagnoli and Clark 2010; Cahill and Coffey 2013). Participatory approaches commonly use methods such as interviewing and focus groups with the aim to 'produce alternative knowledge and more effective ways of understanding complex situations and relationships' (Bagnoli and Clark 2010: 103). In-depth interviewing is a well-established method aligned with feminist approaches, premised on the importance of meaning-making and subjectivity in social research (Rubin and Rubin 2005; Travers 2010). Focus groups and in-depth interviews used in youth research aim to generate rich, narrative-based accounts of young people's experiences and the meanings they draw from these (see Nayak and Kehily 2008b; Ringrose 2013).

Ethnography is another key method used in youth research (Thompson *et al.* 2013). Nayak's extensive study of the embodied negotiations of working-class identities uses the method of multi-site ethnography (Nayak 2003, 2006; Nayak and Kehily 2014). This method comprised a range of other approaches, including participant interaction, observations and encounters in settings such as when young people were with friends or family, in local shops, hanging out on the street, attending urban music events or using public transport. Nayak describes that living in the area in which the ethnography was undertaken enabled a 'lived familiarity and appreciation of the rhythms and routines of everyday neighbourhood life' (Nayak and Kehily 2014: 1332). Kehily also used the method of school-based ethnography to explore issues of sexuality in relation to young people; first in a study of young men (Kehily 2001) and more recently exploring the transition to motherhood among a diverse sample of 62 first-time mothers in the UK (Nayak and Kehily 2014). Ethnography is also a key approach in youth culture and subcultural studies as a way of doing 'insider research', as Hodkinson (2005) discusses. Ethnographic methods are also being extended to study digital communication and young people's use of the internet and social media. Harvey *et al.* (2013) for example used a combined methodology of qualitative interviews and focus group discussions and ethnographic observation of young people's online interactions to explore young people's use of digital media technologies. They use this data to analyse the ways that masculinities and femininities impacted on the gendered forms of value related to the images that circulated through mobile online technologies.

Traditional methods of interviewing are increasingly being supplemented by visual methods such as photovoice and photo elicitation as a way of producing more detailed data on young people's experiences and the meanings they make (Power *et al.* 2014). These methods can be used to go beyond 'words alone' and provide more complex and nuanced understandings than may be available in interviews. In Power *et al.*'s study for example, they argue

Researching the body 59

that the element of photovoice highlighted aspects of young people's sense of space and community that were either 'largely absent or were obfuscated in focus groups and interviews with a researcher-driven agenda' (2014: 1114). In another example, Jackson's study used methods of focus groups and visual methods including drawings, making scrapbooks and cameras to investigate 'how girls make sense of "sexualised" popular culture and how they use it and/or refuse it in their everyday lives' (S. Jackson 2014: 5). The project also asked girls to record media video diaries to enable the participants to narrate and show examples of the media they used every day, as well as enabling them to produce and direct the material they wanted to share. These methods also seek to counteract the 'top-down' relations of power between researchers (adults) and participants (young people) in youth research (see Allen 2008). Allen argues visual methods including photo diaries and photo elicitation enable young people to set the parameters of research and are thereby 'less exploitative' (Allen 2008).

In the primary study of body work described in this book, interviews were used as a way of exploring the participants' descriptions of experiences of their bodies, while not claiming that interviewing offers privileged authentic insights to the 'true selves' of participants (Sandelowski 2002). Rather, as in other qualitative approaches, interviews were used in this study as a method to explore the ways in which participants described their experiences, and especially their practices and negotiations of their bodies through body work. In the next section I will further unpack some methodological tensions associated with attempts to 'embody' youth sociological research.

Embodying research

In feminist work aimed at 'bringing the body back in', 'reflexivity' has been a key ethical priority, through which the researcher reflects on and discusses the ways their own thoughts and feelings may have influenced the collection of the data and its analysis. Only rarely is the researcher's own physicality directly discussed (Throsby and Gimlin 2010). My own bodily appearance and practices matter in the research process, yet they can be awkward to write about in the traditional academic conventions of scholarly writing (Throsby and Gimlin 2010: 109). From a feminist Deleuzian perspective, rather than producing research that only interprets, rhizomatic research sees that both participant and researcher are in processes of becoming, of affecting and being affected (Merceica and Merceica 2010). It is important to visibilise my own embodiment in the research to disrupt the privileged position of disembodied researcher (Ryan-Flood and Gill 2010).

My physicality, in my age, body size and shape, and general appearance, are important in the intersubjective and affective dimensions of encounters with participants in this study. They also have important ethico-political dimensions. At the time of the study I was aged in my late twenties. I am

60 *Researching the body*

white and middle class. I have blonde hair; I am relatively tall and my body shape is slim. My body marks me as benefiting from a range of privileges in racial, classed and physical shape dimensions including 'thin privilege' (Bacon 2009). Because of the themes of the research, I was uncomfortable about the potential of my body to reinforce dominant ideals of slim femininity (Bordo 2003). I was concerned that my own body shape would lead participants to assume that I endorse slimming forms of body work to achieve the 'feminine ideal'. Participants may also have assumed that I would be critical of them if they did not undertake much 'body work', such as when Steph said although she hardly has any spare time, 'that's a pretty shit excuse' not to do exercise. I made a concerted effort to open a space to 'problematise' the slender feminine body, and many participants elaborated on their perspectives of a range of female body shapes being 'beautiful' to them beyond the 'slender ideal'. My age and ethnicity was very similar to most participants, and was likely also important in the interview encounter in providing a basis of 'common ground', through which participants may have assumed I would implicitly understand their perspective as a (relatevely) 'young person' like them. My body may also have made me seem like an 'insider' to those women (and men) in this study who undertook the most intensive forms of body work. As Throsby and Gimlin (2010) argue however, being an 'outsider' to research related to body practices can mean that participants give rich explanations of their practices to someone who is 'unknowing'. There were times such as in Beth's description of anorexia, and Kate's and Isabelle's cosmetic surgery practices, as well as Ben's weight lifting and Adam's AFL training that I was (likely) encountered as a sympathetic 'outsider', and they gave me generous, rich descriptions of their experiences.

A focus on 'the body' is aligned with conceptual approaches which aim to redress the body's marginalisation in theoretical and empirical work at the expense of 'rationality' and a focus on the human mind. Paying attention to the body opens up a range of possibilities for empirical work, through exploring the dimensions of experience that are often invisible or not foregrounded in research that relate to the body, such as affect, embodied sensations. It is about opening analysis beyond people's *ideas* about things, to exploring sensate, physical dimensions of living which are involved in producing action and change. Foregrounding embodiment and the material body can be difficult to achieve (Ryan-Flood and Gill 2010), particularly when combining a non-representational theoretical framework of embodiment with empirical research (Vannini 2015). Developing approaches in which the body and visceral experience is central, rather than marginal, poses both challenges and new opportunities in research with and about young people in the sociology of youth. The methodological implications related to the challenges and opportunities of embodied approaches for the sociology of youth are taken up again in the final chapter of the book.

Conclusion

This chapter has detailed the current existing research focusing on the body, and has called for an increased focus on the body in youth studies theory and research. A focus on embodiment and the body is about opening analysis beyond the cognitive dimensions of experience to also exploring the sensate, physical dimensions of living which are involved in producing action and change. The body has generally not featured as a key focus of study in the dominant strands of 'transitions' and 'cultures' perspectives in youth studies. In the case of youth transitions research, a focus on the body could contribute to richer, more nuanced understandings of the interrelationships between the macro- and micro-processes of social practices such as those relating to education and work patterns. There has similarly been over-emphasis on cerebral aspects of subcultures at the expense of the body and embodiment in youth cultures research. Increased attention to the body could enhance understandings of the dynamics between embodied experience and broader patterns of practice. A focus on the body can add much-needed nuance and richness in studying the diverse and complex dynamics between young people's lives and the social. It can also be useful in disrupting and critiquing dominant knowledge 'about' youth, for example, in concerns around 'risky' practices which often implicitly centre on the body. As I argued using the case example of 'sexting', a focus on the body assists in showing the limitations of media risk discourses for understanding young people's engagements with the practice.

The study of young people's body work practices aims show the potential and promise of the call to 'embody' youth sociological research. Studying body work is a way of placing the body as central empirically through specific practices and activities related to gender and health, whilst also aligning with the broader understanding of the body formed as an active process. New ways of engaging this active process of embodiment through new methods, or through carefully exploring the ontological underpinnings of more traditional methods, will continue to be developed as the body becomes more prominent theoretically and empirically.

Notes

1 www.rollingstone.com/culture/news/sexting-shame-and-suicide-20130917; http://toda y.ninemsn.com.au/article.aspx?id=8265778; http://kidshealth.org/parent/firstaid_sa fe/home/2011_sexting.html.
2 In terms of race and ethnicity, the sample largely identified as 'white', 'Anglo Saxon' or 'Caucasian'. As Dworkin and Wachs (2009) have argued, white bodies dominate bodily ideals. Although I had distributed advertisements to a range of personal contacts who themselves would not identify as 'Anglo/white Australians', and to many friends whom I knew to have friends from a range of ethnic backgrounds, overwhelmingly, it was the 'white' Australians who self-selected to participate in this study.
3 A question on the demographic information sheet completed by participants at the conclusion of the interview asked what 'class' they would identify with. With the

62 *Researching the body*

exception of six participants, all asked me to clarify the question; for example, Jason asked, 'Um, class? What should I put here?' I would respond that the question was 'sort of referring to middle, working class or upper class' and tell participants not to worry about leaving the question blank. Three did leave it blank; others wrote 'middle'. Just under half (10) had attained university degrees, six had completed TAFE or other practical tertiary training, five listed VCE as their highest level of education, and one reported year 10 as being their highest level of education. (TAFE = technical college certificate and VCE = Victorian Certificate of Education, which means graduating from high school; high school in Victoria, Australia runs from grades 7–12.) Of those who did not ask what it meant, three wrote 'middle-upper' (those participants held bachelor's degrees and had attended prestigious private schools), one wrote 'White/middle' (also had a bachelor's degree); two wrote 'lower middle' (one had a bachelor's degree, the other had completed VCE); and one wrote 'all', probably due to the wording of the question, and his interpretation of the word 'identify'. Issues surrounding class were not directly discussed in the interviews, however most were able to engage with the sorts of 'health' and 'fitness' lifestyles that are currently privileged. The bodily ideals prevalent in 'healthism' and consumer culture underscore white, middle-class bodies (Dworkin and Wachs 2009); and many of the participants in this study could be considered part of this privileged, dominant classed and raced group. As McLeod and Yates specify in their study on young people in Australia, 'to use "class" as a focus and interpretative marker is to address issues of social distinction, hierarchy, power in individual identities and in the patterns of social relationships between individuals' (2005: 161). Class categories and terms are difficult to pinpoint in contemporary Australia, though class distinctions undoubtedly exist and are lived out by everyone (McLeod and Yates 2005). Even in England, a much analysed 'classed society', class is not a category young people themselves think with, according to a study by Phoenix and Tizard (1996).

4   Interviews followed a loosely structured topic guide: Life context: work and/or study, living arrangements, general life discussion. 'Ideal' bodies: what sorts of bodies (men's and women's) are presented as 'ideal'? What are their features? What do you think of these bodies? What sorts of work would be involved in the appearances of these bodies? Body work: do you do anything to work on your body? Discuss in detail. What does it mean to you? What are your motivations for doing this? How does your body feel when you do these things? Would you do more/less? Demographic answer sheet completed at the end of the interview.

References

Aapola, S., Marnina, G. and Harris, A. (2005). *Young Femininity: Girlhood, Power and Social Change.* New York: Macmillan.

Addlakha, R. (2008). Disability, Gender and Society. *Indian Journal of Gender Studies, 15*(2), 191–207. doi: 10.1177/097152150801500201

Atkinson, M. and Monaghan, L. F. (2014). *Challenging Myths of Masculinity: Understanding Physical Cultures.* Aldershot: Ashgate.

Albury, K. and Crawford, K. (2012). Sexting, Consent and Young People's Ethics: Beyond Megan's Story. *Continuum,* 26(3), 463–473. doi: 10.1080/10304312.2012. 665840

Alldred, P. and Fox, N. (2015). The sexuality-assemblages of young men: a new materialist analysis. *Sexualities: Studies in Culture and Society.*

Allen, L. (2008). Young People's 'Agency' in Sexuality Research Using Visual Methods. *Journal of Youth Studies,* 11(6), 565–577. doi: 10.1080/13676260802225744

Researching the body 63

Allen-Collinson, J. (2011). Running embodiment, power and vulnerability: notes towards a feminist phenomenology of running. In E. Kennedy and P. Markula (eds), *Women and Exercise: The Body, Health and Consumerism*. New York: Routledge.

Bacon, L. (2009). Reflections on fat acceptance: lessons learned from privilege. Paper presented at the National Association to Advance Fat Acceptance. www.LindaBacon.Org

Bagnoli, A. and Clark, A. (2010). Focus Groups with Young People: A Participatory Approach to Research Planning. *Journal of Youth Studies*, 13(1), 101–119. doi: 10.1080/13676260903173504

Bartky, S. (1990). *Femininity and Domination: Studies in the Phenomenology of Oppression*. New York: Routledge.

Bay-Cheng, L. Y. (2003). The Trouble of Teen Sex: The Construction of Adolescent Sexuality through School-based Sexuality Education. *Sex Education, 3*(1), 61–74. doi: 10.1080/1468181032000052162

Bennett, A. and Robards, B. (2014). *Mediated Youth Cultures: The Internet, Belonging and New Cultural Configurations*. New York: Palgrave Macmillan.

Bird, G. (2008). The White Subject as Liberal Subject. *Australian Critical Race and Whiteness Studies Association e-Journal*, 4(2), 1–14.

Bordo, S. (2003). *Unbearable Weight: Feminism, Western Culture and the Body* (10th anniversary edn). Berkeley: University of California Press.

Bray, A. and Colebrook, C. (1998). The Haunted Flesh: Corporeal Feminism and the Politics of (Dis)embodiment. *Signs: Journal of Women in Culture and Society*, 24(1), 35.

Bridges, T. (2009). Gender Capital and Male Bodybuilders. *Body and Society*, 15(1), 83–107.

Brown, A. R. (2008). Popular Music Cultures, Media and Youth Consumption: Towards an Integration of Structure, Culture and Agency. *Sociology Compass*, 2(2), 388–408.

Budgeon, S. (2003). Identity as an Embodied Event. *Body and Society*, 9(1), 35–55.

Bynner, J. (2005). Rethinking the Youth Phase of the Life-course: The Case for Emerging Adulthood? *Journal of Youth Studies*, 8(4), 367–384. doi: 10.1080/13676260500431628

Cahill, H. and Coffey, J. (2013). Young People and the Learning Partnerships Program. *Youth Studies Australia*, 32(4).

Campbell, C., Gibbs, A., Maimane, S., Nair, Y. and Sibiya, Z. (2009). Youth Participation in the Fight against AIDS in South Africa: From Policy to Practice. *Journal of Youth Studies*, 12(1), 93–109. doi: 10.1080/13676260802345757

Coffey, J. (2013a). Bodies, Body Work and Gender: Exploring a Deleuzian Approach. *Journal of Gender Studies, 22*(1), 3–16. doi: 10.1080/09589236.2012.714076

Coffey, J. (2013b). 'Body Pressure': Negotiating Gender through Body Work Practices. *Youth Studies Australia*, 32(2), 39–48.

Coffey, J. (2014). 'As Long as I'm Fit and a Healthy Weight, I Don't Feel Bad': Exploring Body Work and Health through the Concept of 'Affect'. *Journal of Sociology*. doi: 10.1177/1440783313518249

Coffey, J., Budgeon, S. and Cahill, H. (eds) (2016). *Learning Bodies: The Body in Youth and Childhood Studies*. New York: Springer.

Coffey, J. and Farrugia, D. (2014). Unpacking the Black Box: The Problem of Agency in the Sociology of Youth. *Journal of Youth Studies*, 17(4).

Coffey, J. and Watson, J. (2015). Bodies: Corporeality and Embodiment in Childhood and Youth Studies. In J. Wyn and H. Cahill (eds), *Handbook of Children and Youth Studies*. New York: Springer.

64 *Researching the body*

Coleman, R. (2008). The Becoming of Bodies: Girls, Media Effects and Body Image. *Feminist Media Studies*, 8(2), 163–178.

Coleman, R. (2009). *The Becoming of Bodies: Girls, Images, Experience.* Manchester and New York: Manchester University Press.

Coleman, R. and Ringrose, J. (2013). *Deleuze and Research Methodologies.* Edinburgh: Edinburgh University Press.

Connell, R. W. (1995). *Masculinities.* St Leonards: Allen & Unwin.

Côté, J. and Bynner, J. M. (2008). Changes in the Transition to Adulthood in the UK and Canada: The Role of Structure and Agency in Emerging Adulthood. *Journal of Youth Studies*, 11(3), 251–268. doi: 10.1080/13676260801946464

Côté, J. E. (2002). The Role of Identity Capital in the Transition to Adulthood: The Individualization Thesis Examined. *Journal of Youth Studies*, 5(2), 117–134. doi: 10.1080/13676260220134403

Crawford, R. (2006). Health as a Meaningful Social Practice. *Health, 10*(4), 401–420. doi: 10.1177/1363459306067310

Crossley, N. (2004). The Circuit Trainer's Habitus: Reflexive Body Techniques and the Sociality of the Workout. *Body and Society*, 10(1), 37–70.

Crossley, N. (2005). Mapping Reflexive Body Techniques. *Body and Society, 11*(1), 1–35.

Crossley, N. (2006). In the Gym: Motives, Meaning and Moral Careers. *Body and Society, 12*(3), 23–50.

Crossley, N. (2007). Researching Embodiment by Way of 'Body Techniques'. *Sociological Review, 55*(supplement 1), 80–94.

Davis, K. (1995). *Reshaping the Female Body.* New York: Routledge.

Davis, K. (2003). *Dubious Equalities, Embodied Differences: Cultural Studies on Cosmetic Surgery.* Oxford: Rowman & Littlefield.

Dobson, A. S. (2013). Performative Shamelessness on Young Women's Social Network Sites: Shielding the Self and Resisting Gender Melancholia. *Feminism and Psychology.* doi: 10.1177/0959353513510651

Driscoll, C. (2002). *Girls: Feminine Adolescence in Popular Culture and Cultural Theory.* New York: Columbia University Press.

Driver, C. (2011). Embodying Hardcore: Rethinking 'Subcultural' Authenticities. *Journal of Youth Studies*, 14(8), 975–990. doi: 10.1080/13676261.2011.617733

Driver, C. and Bennett, A. (2014). Music Scenes, Space and the Body. *Cultural Sociology.* doi: 10.1177/1749975514546234

Duff, C. (2010). Towards a Developmental Ethology: Exploring Deleuze's Contribution to the Study of Health and Human Development. *Health, 14*(6), 619–634. doi: 10.1177/1363459309360793

Duff, C. (2014a). *Assemblages of Health.* New York: Springer.

Duff, C. (2014b). The Place and Time of Drugs. *International Journal of Drug Policy*, 25(3), 633–639. doi: http://dx.doi.org/10.1016/j.drugpo.2013.10.014

Duits, L. and van Zoonen, L. (2006). Headscarves and Porno-Chic: Disciplining Girls' Bodies in the European Multicultural Society. *European Journal of Women's Studies*, 13(2), 103–117.

Duncan, M. C. (1994). The Politics of Women's Body Images and Practices: Foucault, the Panopticon, and Shape Magazine. *Journal of Sport and Social Issues*, 18 (1), 40–65.

Dworkin, S. and Wachs, F. (2009). *Body Panic: Gender, Health and the Selling of Fitness.* New York and London: University of New York Press.

Farrugia, A. (2014). Assembling the Dominant Accounts of Youth Drug Use in Australian Harm Reduction Drug Education. *International Journal of Drug Policy*, 25(4), 663–672. doi: http://dx.doi.org/10.1016/j.drugpo.2014.04.019

Farrugia, D., Smyth, J. and Harrison, T. (2015). Affective Topologies of Rural Youth Embodiment. *Sociologia Ruralis*.

Featherstone, M. (2010). Body, Image and Affect in Consumer Culture. *Body and Society*, 16(1), 193–221.

Fox, N. J. (2002a). Refracting 'Health': Deleuze, Guattari and Body-Self. *Health*, 6(3), 347–363. doi: 10.1177/136345930200600306

Fox, N. J. (2002b). What a 'Risky' Body Can Do: Why People's Health Choices Are Not All Based in Evidence. *Health Education Journal*, 61(2), 166–179. doi: 10.1177/001789690206100207

Fox, N. J. (2011). The Ill-Health Assemblage: Beyond the Body-With-Organs. *Health Sociology Review*, 20(4), 359–371. doi: 10.5172/hesr.2011.20.4.359

Fox, N. J. (2012). *The Body*. Cambridge: Polity Press.

Fox, N. J. and Alldred, P. (2016). The Resisting Young Body. In J. Coffey, S. Budgeon and H. Cahill (eds), *Learning Bodies: The Body in Youth and Childhood Studies*. New York: Springer.

Fox, N. J. and Ward, K. J. (2008). What Are Health Identities and How May We Study Them? *Sociology of Health and Illness*, 30(7), 1007–1021.

France, A. and Roberts, S. (2014). The Problem of Social Generations: A Critique of the New Emerging Orthodoxy in Youth Studies. *Journal of Youth Studies*, 18(2), 215–230. doi: 10.1080/13676261.2014.944122

Frosh, S., Phoenix, A. and Pattman, R. (2002). *Young Masculinities: Understanding Boys in Contemporary Society*. New York: Palgrave.

Frost, L. (2001). *Young Women and the Body: A Feminist Sociology*. New York: Palgrave Macmillan.

Frost, L. (2003). Doing Bodies Differently? Gender, Youth, Appearance and Damage. *Journal of Youth Studies*, 6(1), 53.

Frost, L. (2005). Theorizing the Young Woman in the Body. *Body and Society*, 11(1), 63–85.

Gibson, B. E., Mistry, B., Smith, B., Yoshida, K. K., Abbott, D., Lindsay, S. and Hamdani, Y. (2013). Becoming Men: Gender, Disability, and Transitioning to Adulthood. *Health*, 1363459313476967

Gill, R. (2007). Critical Respect: The Difficulties and Dilemmas of Agency and 'Choice' for Feminism: A Reply to Duits and van Zoonen. *European Journal of Women's Studies*, 14(1), 69–80.

Gill, R. (2008). Empowerment/Sexism: Figuring Female Sexual Agency in Contemporary Advertising. *Feminism and Psychology*, 18(35), 35–60.

Gill, R., Henwood, K. and McLean, C. (2000). The Tyranny of the 'Six-Pack'? Understanding Men's Responses to Representations of the Male Body in Popular Culture. In C. Squire (ed.), *Culture in Psychology*. London: Routledge.

Gill, R., Henwood, K. and McLean, C. (2005). Body Projects and the Regulation of Normative Masculinity. *Body and Society*, 11(1), 37–62.

Gill, R. and Scharff, C. (2011). *New Femininities: Postfeminism, Neoliberalism, And Subjectivity*. New York: Palgrave.

Graham, L. and Mphaphuli, M. (2015). 'Let's go 50/50': The Everyday Embodiment of Sexuality amongst African Young People. In J. Wyn and H. Cahill (eds), *Handbook of Youth and Childhood Studies* (pp. 229–242). New York: Springer.

66 Researching the body

Grogan, S. and Wainwright, N. (1996). Growing up in the Culture of Slenderness: Girls' Experiences of Body Dissatisfaction. *Women's Studies International Forum*, 19, 667–673.

Groven, K. S., Solbraekke, K. N. and Engelsrud, G. (2011). Large Women's Experiences of Exercise. In E. Kennedy and P. Markula (eds), *Women and Exercise: The Body, Health and Consumerism*. New York: Routledge.

Hargreaves, J. (2007). Sport, Exercise and the Female Muslim Body: Islam, Politics, and Male Power. In J. Hargreaves and P. Vertinsky (eds), *Physical Culture, Power and The Body*. New York: Routledge.

Hargreaves, J. and Vertinsky, P. (eds) (2007). *Physical Culture, Power and the Body*. New York: Routledge.

Harris, A. (2004). *Future Girl: Young Women in the Twenty-First Century*. New York: Routledge.

Harvey, L., Ringrose, J. and Gill, R. (2013). Swagger, Ratings and Masculinity: Theorising the Circulation of Social and Cultural Value in Teenage Boys' Digital Peer Networks. *Sociological Research Online*, 18(4), 9.

Hauge, M. I. (2009). Bodily Practices and Discourses of Hetero-Femininity: Girls' Constitution of Subjectivities in their Social Transition Between Childhood and Adolescence. *Gender and Education*, 21(3), 293–307.

Hickey-Moody, A. (2007). Intellectual Disability, Sensation and Thinking through Affect. In A. Hickey-Moody and P. Malins (eds), *Deleleuzian Encounters*. New York: Palgrave Macmillan.

Hodkinson, P. (2005). 'Insider Research' in the Study of Youth Cultures. *Journal of Youth Studies*, 8(2), 131–149. doi: 10.1080/13676260500149238

Hodkinson, P. (2012). Beyond Spectacular Specifics in the Study of Youth (Sub)Cultures. *Journal of Youth Studies*, 15(5), 557–572. doi: 10.1080/13676261.2012.663891

Hollands, R. (2002). Divisions in the Dark: Youth Cultures, Transitions and Segmented Consumption Spaces in the Night-Time Economy. *Journal of Youth Studies*, 5(2), 153–171.

Ivinson, G. and Renold, E. (2013). Valleys' Girls: Re-theorising Bodies and Agency in a Semi-Rural Post-Industrial Locale. *Gender and Education*, 25(6), 704–721. doi: 10.1080/09540253.2013.827372

Jackson, A. Y. (2010). Deleuze and the Girl. *International Journal of Qualitative Studies in Education (QSE)*, 23(5), 579–587.

Jackson, S. (2014). Girls and 'Tween' Popular Culture in Everyday Life: A Project Example. *SAGE Research Methods Cases*. London: Sage.

Jackson, S. (2015). Girl's Embodied Experiences of Media Images. In J. Wyn and H. Cahill (eds), *Handbook of Youth and Childhood Studies* (pp. 229–242). New York: Springer.

Karupiah, P. (2012). Modification of the Body: A Comparative Analysis of Views of Youths in Penang, Malaysia and Seoul, South Korea. *Journal of Youth Studies, 16* (1), 1–16. doi: 10.1080/13676261.2012.693588

Kehily, M. J. (2001). Bodies in School: Young Men, Embodiment, and Heterosexual Masculinities. *Men and Masculinities*, 4(2), 173–185. doi: 10.1177/1097184x0100 4002005

Kennedy, E. and Markula, P. (eds) (2011). *Women and Exercise: The Body, Health and Consumerism*. New York: Routledge.

Kenway, J., Kraack, A. and Hickey-Moody, A. (2006). *Masculinity Beyond the Metropolis*. Basingstoke: Palgrave Macmillan.

Kwan, S. and Trautner, M. N. (2009). Beauty Work: Individual and Institutional Rewards, the Reproduction of Gender, and Questions of Agency. *Sociological Compass*, 3(1), 49–71.

Leahy, D. (2014). Assembling a Health [Y] Subject: Risky and Shameful Pedagogies in Health Education. *Critical Public Health*, 24(2), 171–181.

Lee, J., Macdonald, D. and Wright, J. (2009). Young Men's Physical Activity Choices: The Impact of Capital, Masculinities and Location. *Journal of Sport and Social Issues*, 33(1), 59–77.

Lenskyi, H. (1994). Sexuality and Femininity in Sport. *Journal of Sport and Social Issues*, 18(4), 356–376.

Lenz Taguchi, H. and Palmer, A. (2014). Reading a Deleuzio-Guattarian Cartography of Young Girls' 'School-Related' Ill-/Well-Being. *Qualitative Inquiry*, 20(6), 764–771. doi: 10.1177/1077800414530259

Lloyd, M. (1996). Feminism, Aerobics and the Politics of the Body. *Body and Society*, 2(3), 79–98.

Lokman, P. (2011). Becoming Aware of Gendered Embodiment: Female Beginners Learning Aikido. In E. Kennedy and P. Markula (eds), *Women and Exercise: The Body, Health and Consumerism*. New York: Routledge.

Lupton, D. (2012). M-health and Health Promotion: The Digital Cyborg and Surveillance Society. *Soc Theory Health*, 10(3), 229–244.

Lupton, D. (2013b). Quantifying the Body: Monitoring and Measuring Health in the Age of Health Technologies. *Critical Public Health*, 23(4), 393–403. doi: 10.1080/09581596.2013.794931

Mac an Ghaill, M. (1994). *The Making of Men: Masculinities, Sexualities and Schooling*. Buckingham: Open University Press.

McIntyre, M. P. (2011). Keep Your Clothes On! Fit and Sexy through Striptease Aerobics. In E. Kennedy and P. Markula (eds), *Women and Exercise: The Body, Health and Consumerism*. New York: Routledge.

McMahon, J. (2011). Body work – Regulation of a Swimmer Body': An Autoethnography from an Australian Elite Swimmer. *Sport, Education and Society*, 16(1), 35–50.

McRobbie, A. (2001). *Feminism and Youth Culture*. London: Macmillan.

McRobbie, A. (2004). Postfeminism and Popular Culture. *Feminist Media Studies*, 4(3), 255–264.

McRobbie, A. (2007). Top Girls? Young Women and the Post-Feminist Sexual Contract. *Cultural Studies*, 21(4), 718–741.

McRobbie, A. (2015). Notes on the Perfect. *Australian Feminist Studies*, 30(83), 3–20. doi: 10.1080/08164649.2015.1011485

Manago, A. M. (2013). Negotiating a Sexy Masculinity on Social Networking Sites. *Feminism and Psychology*, 0959353513487549

Mansfield, L. (2011). Fit, Fat and Feminine? The Stigmatization of Fat Women in Fitness Gyms. In E. Kennedy and P. Markula (eds), *Women and exercise: the body, health and consumerism*. New York: Routledge.

Markula, P. (1995). Firm But Shapely, Fit But Sexy, Strong But Thin: The Postmodern Aerobicizing Female Bodies. *Sociology of Sport Journal*, 12(4), 424–453.

Markula, P. (2006). Deleuze and the Body without Organs. *Journal of Sport and Social Issues*, 30(1), 29–44. doi: 10.1177/0193723505282469

Markula, P. (2011). 'Folding': A Feminist Intervention in Mindful Fitness. In E. Kennedy and P. Markula (eds), *Women and Exercise: The Body, Health and Consumerism*. New York: Routledge.

68   Researching the body

Mary, A. A. (2013). Re-evaluating the Concept of Adulthood and the Framework of Transition. *Journal of Youth Studies*, 17(3), 415–429. doi: 10.1080/13676261. 2013.853872

Mazzei, L. A. and McCoy, K. (2011). Thinking with Deleuze in Qualitative Research. *International Journal of Qualitative Studies in Education*, 23(5), 503–509. doi: 10.1080/09518398.2010.500634

Mears, A. (2014). Aesthetic Labor for the Sociologies of Work, Gender, and Beauty. *Sociology Compass*, 8(12), 1330–1343.

Merceica, D. and Merceica, D. (2010). Opening Research to Intensities: Rethinking Disability Research with Deleuze and Guattari. *Journal of Philosophy of Education*, 44(1), 80–92.

Minichiello, V., Aroni, R. and Hays, T. (2008). *In-depth Interviewing: Principles, Techniques, Analysis* (3rd edn). South Melbourne: Longman Cheshire.

Monaghan, L. F. (1999). Creating 'The Perfect Body': a Variable Project. *Body and Society*, 5(2–3), 267–290.

Monaghan, L. F. (2001a). *Bodybuilding, Drugs and Risk*. London: Psychology Press.

Monaghan, L. F. (2001b). Looking Good, Feeling Good: the Embodied Pleasures of Vibrant Physicality. *Sociology of Health and Illness*, 23(3), 330–356.

Monaghan, L. F. (2002). Vocabularies of Motive for Illicit Steroid Use among Bodybuilders. *Social Science and Medicine*, 55(5), 695–708. doi: http://dx.doi.org/10.1016/S0277-9536(01)00195-00192

Nayak, A. (2003). *Race, Place and Globalization: Youth Cultures in a Changing World*. Oxford: Berg.

Nayak, A. (2006). Displaced Masculinities: Chavs, Youth and Class in the Post-industrial City. *Sociology*, 40(5), 813–831. doi: 10.1177/0038038506067508

Nayak, A. and Kehily, M. J. (2006). Gender Undone: Subversion, Regulation and Embodiment in the Work of Judith Butler. *British Journal of Sociology of Education*, 27(4), 459–472.

Nayak, A. and Kehily, M. J. (2008a). *Gender, Youth and Culture*. Houndmills: Palgrave Macmillan.

Nayak, A. and Kehily, M. J. (2008b). *Gender, Youth and Culture: Young Masculinities and Femininities*. New York: Palgrave Macmillan.

Nayak, A. and Kehily, M. J. (2014). 'Chavs, Chavettes and Pramface Girls': Teenage Mothers, Marginalised Young Men and the Management of Stigma. *Journal of Youth Studies*, 17(10), 1330–1345.

Nettleton, S. and Watson, J. (eds) (1998). *The Body in Everyday Life*. London: Routledge.

Olivardia, R., Pope, H., Borowiecki, J. and Cohane, G. (2004). Biceps and Body Image: The Relationship between Muscularity and Self-Esteem, Depression, and Eating Disorder Symptoms. *Psychology of Men and Masculinity*, 5(2), 112–120.

Phoenix, A. and Tizard, B. (1996). Thinking through Class: The Place of Social Class in the Lives of Young Londoners. *Feminism and Psychology*, 6(3), 427–442.

Pike, E. (2011). Growing Old (dis)gracefully? The Gender/Aging/Exercise Nexus. In E. Kennedy and P. Markula (eds), *Women and Exercise: The Body, Health and Consumerism*. New York: Routledge.

Potts, A. (2004). Deleuze on Viagra (or, What Can a 'Viagra-Body' Do?). *Body and Society*, 10(1), 17–36. doi: 10.1177/1357034x04041759

Power, N. G., Norman, M. E. and Dupré, K. (2014). Rural Youth and Emotional Geographies: How Photovoice and Words-Alone Methods Tell Different Stories of

Place. *Journal of Youth Studies*, 17(8), 1114–1129. doi: 10.1080/13676261.2014.881983

Priestly, M. (1998). Childhood Disability and Disabled Childhoods: Agendas for Research. *Childhood*, 5, 207–223.

Renold, E. and Ivinson, G. (2014). Horse-Girl Assemblages: Towards a Post-Human Cartography of Girls' Desire in an Ex-Mining Valleys Community. *Discourse: Studies in the Cultural Politics of Education*, 35(3), 361–376. doi: 10.1080/01596306.2014.888841

Renold, E. and Ringrose, J. (2008). Regulation and Rupture: Mapping Tween and Teenage Girls' Resistance to the Heterosexual Matrix. *Feminist Theory*, 9, 314–339.

Renold, E. and Ringrose, J. (2011). Schizoid Subjectivities? Re-theorizing Teen Girls' Sexual Cultures in an Era of 'Sexualization'. *Journal of Sociology*, 47(4), 389–409.

Retallack, H., Ringrose, J. and Lawrence, E. (2016). 'F*** Your Body Image!' Teen Girls, Twitter Feminism and Networked Affect in a London School In J. Coffey, S. Budgeon and H. Cahill (eds), *Learning Bodies: The Body in Youth and Childhood Studies*. New York: Springer.

Rich, E., Evans, J. and De Pian, L. (2011). Obesity, Body Pedagogies and Young Women's Engagement with Exercise. In E. Kennedy and P. Markula (eds), *Women and Exercise: The Body, Health and Consumerism*. New York: Routledge.

Ringrose, J. (2011a). Are You Sexy, Flirty, or a Slut? Exploring 'Sexualization' and How Teen Girls Perform/Negotiate Digital Sexual Identity on Social Networking Sites. In R. Gill and C. Scharff (eds), *New Femininities: Postfeminism, Neoliberalism, And Subjectivity*. New York: Palgrave (pp. 99–116).

Ringrose, J. (2011b). Beyond Discourse? Using Deleuze and Guattari's Schizoanalysis to Explore Affective Assemblages, Heterosexually Striated Space, and Lines of Flight Online and at School. *Educational Philosophy and Theory*, 43(6), 598–618.

Ringrose, J. (2013). *Postfeminist Education?: Girls and the Sexual Politics of Schooling*. New York: Routledge.

Ringrose, J. and Harvey, L. (2015). Boobs, Back-off, and Small Bits: Mediated Body Parts, Sexual Reward and Gendered Shame in Teens' Networked Images. *Continuum: Journal of Media and Cultural Studies*, 29.

Ringrose, J., Harvey, L., Gill, R. and Livingstone, S. (2013). Teen Girls, Sexual Double Standards and 'Sexting': Gendered Value in Digital Image Exchange. *Feminist Theory*, 14(3), 305–323. doi: 10.1177/1464700113499853

Rubin, H. and Rubin, I. (2005). *Qualitative Interviewing: The Art of Hearing Data*. London: Sage.

Ryan-Flood, R. and Gill, R. (2010). *Secrecy and Silence in the Research Process: Feminist Reflections*. New York: Routledge.

St Pierre, E. A. (1997). Methodology in the Fold and the Irruption of Transgressive Data. *International Journal of Qualitative Studies in Education*, 10(2), 175–189.

Sandelowski, M. (2002). Reembodying Qualitative Inquiry. *Qualitative Health Research*, 12(1), 104–115. doi: 10.1177/1049732302012001008

Sanders, J. and Munford, R. (2008). Losing Self to the Future? Young Women's Strategic Responses to Adulthood Transitions. *Journal of Youth Studies*, 11(3), 331–346. doi: 10.1080/13676260801946480

Sharp, M. and Nilan, P. (2014). Queer Punx: Young Women in the Newcastle Hardcore Space. *Journal of Youth Studies*, 1–17. doi: 10.1080/13676261.2014.963540

70 Researching the body

Siibak, A. (2010). Constructing Masculinity on a Social Networking Site the Case-Study of Visual Self-presentations of Young Men on the Profile Images of SNS Rate. *Young*, 18(4), 403–425.

Skeggs, B. (1997). *Formations of Class and Gender: Becoming Respectable*. London: Sage.

Spitzack, C. (1990). *Confessing Excess: Women and the Politics of Body Reduction*. New York: State University of New York Press.

Thompson, R., Russell, L. and Simmons, R. (2013). Space, Place and Social Exclusion: An Ethnographic Study of Young People Outside Education and Employment. *Journal of Youth Studies*, 17(1), 63–78. doi: 10.1080/13676261.2013.793793

Thorpe, H. (2011). *Snowboarding Bodies in Theory and Practice*. New York: Palgrave Macmillan.

Thorpe, H. A. (2009). Bourdieu, Feminism and Female Physical Culture: Gender Reflexivity and the Habitus-Field Complex. *Sociology of Sport Journal*, 26(4), 491–516.

Throsby, K. and Gimlin, D. (2010). Critiquing Thinness and Wanting to Be Thin. In R. Ryan-Flood and R. Gill (eds), *Secrecy and Silence in the Research Process: Feminist Reflections* (pp. 105–116). London; New York: Routledge.

Travers, M. (2010). Qualitative Interviewing Methods. In M. Walter (ed.), *Social Research Methods* (2nd edn). Sydney: Oxford University Press.

Unterhalter, E., Epstein, D., Morrell, R. and Moletsane, R. (2004). Be Yourself: Class, Race, Gender and Sexuality in South African Schoolchildren's Accounts of Social Relations. *Pedagogy, Culture and Society*, 12(1), 53–72. doi: 10.1080/14681360400200189

Vannini, P. (2015). Non Representational Research Methodologies: An Introduction. In P. Vannini (ed.), *Non-Representational Methodologies: Re-Envisioning Research*. London and New York: Routledge.

Wacquant, L. (2005). Carnal Connections: On Embodiment, Apprenticeship, and Membership. *Qualitative Sociology*, 28(4), 445–474. doi: 10.1007/s11133-11005-8367-0

Walkerdine, V., Lucey, H. and Melody, J. (2001). *Growing Up Girl: Psychosocial Explorations of Gender and Class*. Basingstoke: Palgrave.

Waquant, L. (1995). Pugs at Work: Bodily Capital and Bodily Labour among Professional Boxers. *Body and Society*, 1(1).

Watson, J. (2000). *Male Bodies: Health, Culture and Identity*. Philadelphia: Open University Press.

Willis, K. (2006). Analysing Qualitative Data. In M. Walter (ed.), *Social Research Methods*. Oxford: Oxford University Press.

Willis, P. E. (1977). *Learning to Labor: How Working Class Kids Get Working Class Jobs*. New York: Columbia University Press.

Woodman, D. and Wyn, J. (2015). *Youth and Generation: Rethinking Change and Inequality in the Lives of Young People*. London: Sage.

Wray, S. (2011). The Significance of Western Health Promotion Discourse for Older women from Diverse Ethnic Backgrounds. In E. Kennedy and P. Markula (eds), *Women and Exercise: The Body, Health and Consumerism*. New York: Routledge.

Wright, J., O'Flynn, G. and Macdonald, D. (2006). Being Fit and Looking Healthy: Young Women's and Men's Constructions of Health and Fitness. *Sex Roles*, 54(9–10), 707–716. doi: 10.1007/s11199-11006-9036-9039

Wyn, J. and Woodman, D. (2006). Generation, Youth and Social Change in Australia. *Journal of Youth Studies*, 9(5), 495–514. doi: 10.1080/13676260600805713

Wyn, J., Lantz, S. and Harris, A. (2012). Beyond the 'Transitions' Metaphor: Family Relations and Young People in Late Modernity. *Journal of Sociology*, 48(1), 3–22. doi: 10.1177/1440783311408971

Youdell, D. (2010). Queer Outings: Uncomfortable Stories about the Subjects of Post-Structural School Ethnography. *International Journal of Qualitative Studies in Education*, 23(1), 87–100. doi: 10.1080/09518390903447168

Youdell, D. and Armstrong, F. (2011). A Politics beyond Subjects: The Affective Choreographies and Smooth Spaces of Schooling. *Emotion, Space and Society*, 4(3), 144–150. doi: http://dx.doi.org/10.1016/j.emospa.2011.01.002

4 Assembling gender: body work, identities and the body

Introduction

In contemporary sociology, practices geared to shaping the body and physical control (such as through diet, fitness regimes and presentation of the body through consumption) are understood as increasingly central to people's sense of self-identity. The body and 'body image' is a central concern for young people, and a key focus of government policy in Australia. The National Advisory Group on Body Image was set up by the Australian government in 2009 to find strategies of addressing the problems associated with body image. In February 2012, the first international summit on body image was held by the UN. The increase in health, beauty and fitness industries is aligned with an increase in attention to the body, and 'body image' for both women and men. 'Body image' issues are presented in the popular media and psychology as predominantly individual pathologies, but also linked to the negative 'effects' of images (Coleman 2009). The dynamics of embodiment and body work practices are highly complex, and require a different way of thinking about bodies and the relationship between bodies and society. I develop the term 'body work' to theorise the dynamic process by which bodies and societies shape each other.

The presentation of bodies is strongly delineated by gender norms. Though men are now argued to be moving towards the 'dubious equality' as consumers of health, fitness and cosmetic products (Featherstone 1982), participants' descriptions of men and women's 'ideal' bodies broadly linked with dominant conceptualisations of masculinity and femininity as exclusive, dichotomous categories, in line with conventional gender relations (Frost 2003). Body work practices are thus 'gendered' and are shaped by a broader context of unequal gender structures, patterns and norms. Binary gender arrangements can be understood as key elements which 'territorialise' the body. The idealised woman's body in this context is slender, while the idealised man's body is toned and muscular (Bordo 1999, 2003; Dworkin and Wachs 2009). Participants' descriptions of men and women's 'ideal' bodies broadly reflected these gendered characteristics. The gendered physicalities of these 'ideal' bodies connect to a range of underlying assumptions around

Assembling gender 73

men's 'natural' physical strength and prowess, and women's 'natural daintiness', as one participant in this study described. The rise in men's concern for the body can be understood as linked to their increasing participation in consumption practices around the body such as gym culture (Crossley 2006). The body work practices both women and men undertake in this context are strongly geared towards emphasising, or producing, gendered differences through the body (territorialisations). Numerous examples can be understood as producing molar gendered identities through participants' body work practices. Importantly, while these arrangements are taken as important in understanding the current significance of body work, they are not approached as neatly *explaining* body work. Instead, a focus on gender as a process through which bodies are assembled, rather than a force inscribed on a passive body, enables the nuances and ambiguities in the examples to be drawn forth to also show the contingent and non-essential ways in which gender is engaged in producing the body and body work. The Deleuzo-Guattarian theoretical framing of the body and the concept of assemblage introduced in Chapter 2 are discussed first to ground the empirical examples of gender and body work which follow.

Theorising gender as an assemblage

A Deleuzo-Guattarian approach understands the body as produced through encounters, relations, forces and practices. This approach moves beyond 'human nature' as the prime ontological category of analysis to also explore the ways in which matter, affect, biology, technology, politics and other forces are crucial in 'assembling' what we understand as human and natural (Rose 2007). It places attention on the numerous things or forces the body engages with, including discourses, affects, ideals, norms, practices, institutions and other bodies and objects.

An assemblage is 'always collective, [and] brings into play within us and outside us populations, multiplicities, territories, becomings, affects, events' (Deleuze and Parnet 2002: 51). An assemblage 'designates something which happens between two terms which are not subjects, but agents, elements' (Deleuze and Parnet 2002: 51). Another definition of assemblage is a functional collection of connections (see Currier 2003). Assemblages are functional because they create the conditions for orientation towards action. It is for this reason that assemblages are often described as 'active'. Assemblages can therefore be understood as functional, active collections of connections. The key ontological basis for this concept is that assemblages are not 'transcendent structures' which can be traced to an imaginary essence; i.e. do not map back onto social orders, including male/female, mind/body. They are not fixed to an 'immutable order', and are instead 'continually in flux' (Currier 2003: 321).

The concept of assemblage can also be used to describe the ways gender relations operate to territorialise bodies. Territorialisation assists in explaining

74 *Assembling gender*

the process by which forces of the social such as gender, class, ability and ethnicity for example regulate and produce bodies through social categories and hierarchies (Fox 2002: 353). Territorialisation can be understood as a key dimension of a body's process of assembling, denoting an active process and body rather than passive inscription of the body by social norms, such as representations of 'ideal bodies'. Bodies assemble through a 'functional collection of connections' (see Currier 2003), including discourses, norms, ideals, institutions, bodies, affects and practices. Understanding gender as an assemblage sees it as a functional, active arrangement of connections which operates as only a temporary articulation or territorialisation rather than an essential identity category. This is not to say that gender as an assemblage is benign and neutral; gender is certainly cut across by dominant power relations, or what Deleuze and Guattari would term 'binary machines'. Current arrangements of gender can be understood as produced by the binary machine because a binary model of biological sex still frames dominant social understandings and gender arrangements. The perspective of gender as an assemblage, however, assists in disrupting this binary position, and insists that the current dominance of current arrangements has *no essential or originary basis.*

Following Fox, assemblages can be understood as 'elaborated from disparate elements that can be material, psychic, social and abstract/philosophical' (2011: 364). Fox gives an example of this through delineating elements of an 'eating assemblage, [comprising] (in no particular order), at least: Mouth – food – energy – appetite' (2011: 364).

Following this example, a relational gender assemblage might comprise at least (and in no order):

> The (biological, sexed) body – bodily presentation – body work – discourses – norms – ideals – images – performance – expectations – sexuality

These concepts have been drawn on by a number of feminist authors to assist theorisations of bodies and gender. One key reason this perspective is attractive and seen to hold promise relates to Deleuze and Guattari's (1987) insistence on there being no essential or biological basis for current dominant relations of power and resulting inequalities; instead, they focus to recognising positive potential and affirmation of difference. For these reasons, this approach can add important dimensions to analysis of the embodiments and productions of gender in everyday life.

Examples will show the ways gender is performed and produced in relation to gender as a complex relational assemblage. From this perspective, gendered embodiments are not simply the reproductions of dualist gender formations; rather, gender is engaged, negotiated and produced continually through affects and relations. This approach to gender as continually produced through affects, relations and doings enables the ambiguities and complexities

Assembling gender 75

of gender to be explored, including the bodily and sensate dimensions of sociality beyond the discursive.

Gender and body work

Gender was a central theme in participants' discussions of their bodies and body work practices. Understandings of the body which focus on embodied sensations are crucial to analysing participants' explanations of their experiences of body work in this context. Some participants explain that their experiences of body work and the embodied sensations involved relate directly to their experience of self or identity. Exercise and discourses of gender and health also link into the participants' understandings and experiences of their bodies and selves. These factors together go towards comprising the gender assemblages of participants.

The practices of body work undertaken by participants in this study varied greatly, but in many instances were patterned by familiar gender arrangements. Exercise was an aspect of body work for almost all participants and included playing team sports (such as netball, baseball and soccer); jogging; swimming; cycling; yoga and doing fitness classes at the gym (such as 'boxercise' or 'Zumba'). Only men spoke of going to the gym to lift or train with weights, however, and almost all (nine out of 11) of the men practiced this form of body work. Men as well as women spoke about being careful about their diet, such as through avoiding fatty foods and eating 'healthier' fruit and vegetables or avoiding carbohydrates to control their weight. Being 'overweight' or 'fat' was viewed by most participants as unacceptable for men or women in broader society; although being specifically 'skinny' or slender was understood as being more important to women's 'body image' than men's. Three women in this study spoke about eating disorders; two (Beth and Isabelle) had suffered from an eating disorder, and Clare had a close friend who had. Others though noted that the vast majority of those who suffer from eating disorders are women. Cosmetic surgery was also discussed as being primarily undertaken by women, though Isabelle said she had noticed an increase in male patients at the cosmetic surgery day clinic at which she is employed. Isabelle and Kate had undergone cosmetic surgical procedures. Other forms of body work included wearing make-up, which all of the women (and no men) wore. Isabelle, Anna, Gillian, Victoria and Beth said they wore make up most days, and described wearing it as generally important to feeling 'good' or 'comfortable'. Sara, Angela, Kate, Kim, Clare and Steph said they liked to wear make-up sometimes, but also felt comfortable not wearing it, such as when going to the gym or to the shops. Most women, and no men, also discussed 'tanning' (from the sun, solarium or fake tanning creams) as a form of body work they undertake sometimes. Hair styling was discussed by most women, and two men, Simon and Paul. The practices that were most clearly defined and associated with traditionally gendered bodily norms were lifting weights, which was done only by men; and wearing make-up,

76　*Assembling gender*

undergoing cosmetic surgery or suffering eating disorders related only to women in this study.

I will now explore the ways in which 'ideal' physical characteristics were described as gendered by the participants and link with broader cultural and social discourses of gender before going on to discuss some of the paradoxes and complications involved with these seemingly rigid gendered forms of body work.

Negotiating 'ideal' (gendered) bodies

Participants' descriptions of men and women's 'ideal' bodies broadly linked with dominant conceptualisations of masculinity and femininity as exclusive, dichotomous categories, in line with conventional gender relations (Frost 2003). Their descriptions can be read as territorialisations which produce and regulate bodies through social categories and hierarchies (Fox 2002: 353). Women, for example were broadly described as being more 'self-conscious' about their appearance than men, with their body work practices centred mainly on 'slimming' activities such as dieting or exercise (Gimlin 2002; Dworkin and Wachs 2009). By contrast, appearance was construed as something men generally did not care about. This is ironic, given that ideal men's bodies were described as looking muscular, which requires body work practices of lifting weights and necessitates a great deal of attention to the body's aesthetics (Atkinson and Monaghan 2014). These generalisations can be understood as linking into broad cultural conceptions of femininity as body based, and masculinity as associated with strength, power and intelligence (Witz 2000). Although many participants did not endorse these 'ideal' figures, or do the sorts of body work required to 'achieve' these bodies, all identified them as the mainstream ideal. While these narrow understandings of men's and women's bodies were used by participants to make sense of others' bodies, their experiences and understandings of their own bodies and body work practices were much more complex. The concept of affect assists in drawing out these complexities and ambiguities, as will be discussed later in the chapter.

The following examples show how physical characteristics are gendered and frame participants' discussions of 'ideal' men's and women's bodies.[1] The comments below illustrate how some participants described the characteristics of 'ideal' women's bodies:

> Just like a slim toned figure, tanned, and long legs, and that sort of thing.
> (Sara, 24, dental nurse)

> I think girls … they don't want the curves. They want the shiny skinny sexy legs that they see on TV. They want that slender look, the skinny

arms and not muscly but really skinny and thin, they want to look like models who look like that.

> (Adam, 23, footballer and university student)

Tall, good body, skinny, definitely not fat. Good looking, I always picture like, long hair and all that sort of stuff. Good body means toned, not too skinny, average size and fit, that sort of thing.

> (Clare, 18, high school student)

I like, sort of, a thin, well not, thin, but sort of er ... not under-thin but not large sort of a person. I think some degree of toning but not someone who's muscly, or anything like that.

> (Tom, 24, firefighter)

Slenderness and muscle tone is described as ideal. Women's ideal bodies were 'definitely not fat', but not 'under-thin' or 'too skinny' though, either. Being 'toned' is described as important, but being 'muscly' transgresses dichotomised norms of femininity because of the connotations between muscularity and masculinity (Grogan *et al.* 2004; Bridges 2009).

Men's 'ideal' bodies were described as 'rugged', 'athletic', 'tall' and 'strong'. The following are some descriptions of 'ideal' men's bodies:

> Someone who's quite built, a chiselled jaw ... I keep going back to what I think is attractive! Probably someone who's relatively tall, built, not like overly muscular, but probably in between, not scrawny, toned I guess?
>
> (Kim, 24, administrative assistant)

Quite athletic, broad chest, um ... yeah. I'd just probably say strong and athletic-type image.

> (Sam, 26, nurse)

Tall. Sporty. Muscly. [giggles]

> (Clare, 18, high school student)

They've got sort of the 6 pack [defined abdominal muscles] and the 'V' going [muscular torso] and the sculpted sort of body with the muscles and that.

> (Adam, 24, footballer/student)

Um, definitely toned! Not too big though in the arms, not too like buffed out and puffy, sometimes that looks a bit too fake, but definitely, toned stomach and toned arms, and ... tall, not too tall but probably 6 foot.

> (Victoria, 23, marketing officer)

78 *Assembling gender*

Being 'built' or having a 'sculpted' muscular body; along with looking 'strong' but 'not too big' (but also 'not scrawny') were all emphasised as characteristics of 'ideal' male bodies. Others also said ideal men's bodies should be 'definitely not fat' or overweight, and this is a similarity between men's and women's idealised bodies: fat is reviled (Lupton 2013). The sorts of descriptions however between men's and women's ideal bodies above rely on gendered oppositions, and link more broadly to hierarchal categorisations of gender (Connell 2009). This is illustrated in Sam's example. When discussing 'ideal' bodies for men and women, he says:

> I guess men are looking for that more athletic, muscly type of figure. Sort of harking back to the classic 'man' sort of thing, you know strong, make you feel safe, that sort of thing. You don't want a guy who's all prissy-looking. You kind of want a man to be a man. And on the flip side, I guess you want women to be petite, and dainty, and I don't know. You don't really want the butch, hard-looking woman that could beat the crap out of you!

> (Sam, 26, nurse)

Sam describes dichotomous gender ideals as 'natural', supported by bodily or biological differences between men and women. To exemplify his perception as how men and women's bodies should look and how they should behave, he uses examples of the 'prissy' guy and the 'butch, hard-looking woman' as repellent, transgressive figures, in order to emphasise revered 'classic' and 'natural' versions of a man. Examples such as these have typically served to naturalise men's and women's bodily differences as the basis for gendered inequality (Grosz 1994). Traditional, patriarchal and heterosexist versions of femininity are also strongly asserted, when Sam argues 'you want women to be petite and dainty', and that it is his instinct to be 'protective' of women. These sorts of comments demonstrate the binary logic and molar gender categories which can territorialise the body. Deleuze and Guattari (1987) refer to social structures and institutions such as the state, gender, class and other dominating and normalising forces (including discourse) that operate on binary logic as 'binary machines'. The normalising gender and heterosexist discourses which operate in Sam's example are one key aspect by which the gender assemblage is produced. This assemblage is functional; the discourses within it assist in producing the conditions of possibility for further interactions and engagements. Though few participants described gender and bodies in normalised or restrictive ways as Sam, these examples of the ways 'ideal' bodily norms link with dominant, binarised gendered characteristics are important in contextualising some of the current discourses of gender which frame young people's body work practices. Their descriptions of bodily norms and idealised appearances give important detail on the discursive framings of gender norms as they connect with the production of particular bodies. Gender discourses, however, are only one dimension of a gender assemblage;

Assembling gender 79

the way gender operates also includes affective and material dimensions. Seeing gender as a functional assemblage involves exploring the ways all of these elements together produce the body's possibilities in relation to gendered embodiment. The discursive and affective dimensions of gender assemblages are explored in the next sections on 'luminous' gendered bodies.

Femininity, visibility and consumer culture

This section further explores the current emphasis on the body's appearance and how some women in this study described their practices of body work in the context of 'luminous' femininities (McRobbie 2009), linking gender with other social assemblages and contemporary social contexts, including consumer culture and sexuality.

The different sorts of body work undertaken by men and women was broadly described in the study as relating to different social expectations or 'pressures' around men's and women's bodies. Men and women emphasised that women are judged more for their appearance than men, linking in with gender and heterosexual discourses in which women's beauty is central in attracting a male partner. As Kate explains:

> I get caught up in 'this is how I'm supposed to look, this is what I'm supposed to be'. And it's really crappy. It gives you that low self-esteem. And very rarely do you see men, like it's very rare for a man to have an eating disorder ... obviously the pressure for women to look really skinny, they cave under that pressure and they go 'oh I need to go and have plastic surgery, I need to stop eating, I need to go and do all these things'. Men, not so much. You don't really see a man who's had a nose job. It's not as much of a thing. But for women it is. And women I think are scared. Like 'my husband's gonna leave me if I don't look younger, or if I'm not this'. It becomes less about who they are and their personality than about how they look.
>
> (Kate, 24, administrative assistant/nanny)

Kate is critical of the gendered expectations surrounding men's and women's bodies, and the responsibility women bear in relation to the appearance of their bodies and the impact this has for heterosexual relationships. Kate describes that women perceive the need to 'look really skinny', have plastic surgery or a 'nose job', or 'stop eating' or 'look younger' because women are 'scared' they will lose their partners if their 'attractiveness' diminishes. Kate is critical too of the underlying assumption that a woman's appearance is indicative of 'who she is' or her personality; and argues that societally, men's bodies do function as symbolic for their entire being in the way women's bodies do.

As McRobbie (2009: 118) has argued, 'female body anxieties are intricately tied up with the high value which society places on spectacularly coded styles

80   *Assembling gender*

of feminine beauty and sexuality'. The ways that bodies are lived by both women and men may involve such 'anxieties' (as will be discussed), and many of the women, including Kate, highlight the ways they feel constrained through societal pressure to live up to such 'spectacular' feminine forms of beauty. Other participants say they feel 'pressure' to monitor their appearance because of the broader societal expectation that women are viewed as 'on display' (Davis 1995):

> I think the media places a lot of pressure on women to look a certain way, to be a certain way ... and guys don't really get [experience] that.
>
> (Kim, 24, administrative assistant)

Similarly, Paul criticises consumer culture and the fashion and beauty industries for contributing to women feeling 'under pressure' to live up to idealised forms of femininity, creating a situation in which there is 'more in the world for women to worry about':

> For women, of course there's just so much more of an industry towards women and appearance. I mean there's make up, there's diet, there's clothes and whatever. From wherever that came from or whatever that's based on, there's definitely ... more ... um ... more in the world for women to worry about.
>
> (Paul, 32, sound editor)

Gillian also discusses the theme of women being under more 'pressure' linking with popular and consumer culture including the media, advertising, beauty and fashion industries, but also extends her comments to the wider experiences and actions of men and women:

> Women definitely have it harder. Yep. Oh, just the pressure. Well maybe it's the pressure they put on themselves? Coupled with pressure from society, pressure from men. And of course, I think in the media, I think women's beauty and physical attributes are much more, there's much more importance placed on that than there is on men's appearance. So, yeah, I think definitely women have a harder time.
>
> (Gillian, 31, make-up artist)

Gillian's view that there is more importance placed on a woman's appearance than a man's appearance is a key aspect of many of the other comments regarding gender and bodies made by participants in this study, by both men and women. This view links with feminist critiques of the appearances 'required' of women's bodies (Bartky 1990; Wolf 1991; Bordo 2003), which implicate the media, consumer culture and patriarchy as contributing to the gender structures which promote idealised and highly stylised images of women and femininity. Gillian also individualises her experience, blaming

Assembling gender 81

herself for 'putting pressure on myself and putting ideas in my head', despite having just criticised men's and the media's roles in this context. There are many factors at work in Gillian's example which link broadly to the ways gender relations, images and the media are negotiated (Coleman 2009; Featherstone 2010), particularly in an individualised neo-liberal context in which people are encouraged to problematise and monitor their own predicaments rather than looking to broader societal patterns of inequity (McRobbie 2009).

Feminine luminosities and shopping centres

The dynamics of being 'visible' or 'noticed' related to femininities' modes of bodily presentation are particularly apparent in discussions of shopping centres. The material space of the shopping centre is crucial in producing the affects associated with luminous feminine bodies who 'stand out' and look 'special' through specific modes of bodily presentation.

Sara describes the ways that some women are more visible or noticeable than others in a social space such as a shopping centre:

SARA: If there's a girl that's got a lot of make-up on, walking around shopping, and with a lot of make-up on and really dressed up, you can tell they look after themselves? I think you can tell on some people [what sort of person they are]. I think you look at them twice because they're so ... done up so well, but it doesn't mean I want to look like that.

JULIA: Yeah. What about other things ... does it go the other way, if people look the opposite of that?

SARA: Yeah, you don't really look at them. You don't acknowledge them at all really. Cos there's nothing to, there's nothing special to see, they're just casually dressed and hair tied back or whatever. I think it's just the people who do themselves up really nicely they sort of stand out.

(Sara, 26, dental assistant)

Sara describes a particularly visible form of femininity in which 'a girl with a lot of make-up on, really dressed up ... stands out'. This example also links in with theories which argue that social space is organised around opportunities for display and surveillance. In these social spaces, some are more visible than others. The display of consumer goods such as in shopping centres, department stores and supermarkets, encourages voyeuristic consumption in which 'the individual is increasingly on display as he/she moves through the field of commodities on display' (Featherstone 1982: 19). Practices of body work, such as wearing make-up and other techniques associated with what Sara calls 'doing yourself up nicely', are part of 'an expanding market for the sale of commodities' in consumer culture (Featherstone 1982: 19).

A new materialist perspective of affect enables a focus on the specificities and micro-relations of context – in this case, the 'fashion–beauty complex'

82   Assembling gender

(Bartky 1990) associated with femininities in the post-feminist consumer space of the shopping centre (Jackson *et al.* 2012). Another participant, Isabelle, describes feeling 'yuck' and avoiding people's gaze if she goes to a shopping centre after work when she is not wearing make-up:

> I find if I go to a shopping centre after work and I have no make-up on and my hair's yuck, I don't really make eye contact with people, because I feel yuck? ... I get anxious, like if I'm in the shopping centre and I look yuck, even though I don't look bad but I feel like I do, I feel like people are staring at me and then I get panicky, and like I can't breathe and I have to go home.
>
> (Isabelle, 24, beauty therapist)

McRobbie argues that it is increasingly difficult to be visible and 'to function as a female subject without subjecting oneself to those technologies of self that are constitutive of the spectacularly feminine' (2009: 60). Sara's example links with McRobbie's argument, when she contrasts a 'girl' who wears a lot of make-up and who is 'dressed up' and as being worthy of looking at 'twice', with the woman who does not display femininity in this highly cultivated way, who is dressed casually with her 'hair tied back', 'nothing special to see' who 'you don't acknowledge at all really'. McRobbie argues, 'the global fashion beauty complex charges itself with the business of ensuring that appropriate gender relations are guaranteed' (2009: 61). The dynamics of visibility are a core to feminine luminosities in consumer culture spaces exemplified by the shopping mall, and the affective dimensions of this image is particularly intensive (Featherstone 2010). Gendered practices of consumption, such as through being 'really dressed up' in fashionable clothes and wearing a lot of make-up are required to be 'noticed'. Isabelle and Sara's examples show that this process is not only discursive, but is also profoundly affective and registered through embodied sensations including feeling 'yuck' and out of place if the body is not presented in a way that is perceived as expected in that particular space.

The implications of not performing femininity as 'expected' is taken further in another example from Isabelle below, in which she describes the importance of being seen 'as feminine' (and, by implication, heterosexual) through bodily presentation:

> If a woman's a tradie [Aus. slang for 'tradesman' or blue-collar worker] and she looks a bit butch, you don't see her as feminine, so ... people don't really, women don't really want that ... Some people say it'd be easier to be a man, but I don't wanna be a man. I like getting all dressed up, looking nice, looking pretty. It's a lot of work but I *like* it.
>
> (Isabelle, 24, beauty therapist; emphasis added)

Isabelle perceives that spectacular femininity enables one to be recognised as feminine, and to be 'visible' in binary heterosexual gender relations. As

Assembling gender 83

Ringrose and Walkerdine have argued, the requirements of post-feminism and heterosexuality work alongside neo-liberalism, as the goals of heterosexual desirability are key aspects of femininity in contemporary make-over culture (2008). Isabelle explains that women have to 'do more (body) work' than men because it's expected that 'women always try and look good', and that she enjoys doing this. This must be strictly enacted, however, since failure to perform this is to risk looking a 'bit butch', which 'people, women don't really want'. This is an intensification of the gender binary: gender relations are territorialised and closed down. Falling outside of clear categorisations of gender and femininity carries the consequences of being labelled as 'butch', and embodying a figure that 'no one really wants', that may result in (heterosexual) invisibility ('you don't see her as feminine'). This process is mapped on to the body through bodily performances of gender such as body work practices, and is also registered affectively in the body through feeling 'panicky' if this mode of presentation is not performed. The 'cost' of being stigmatised in these ways is evident in Isabelle's 'butch tradie' and Sam's repudiation of the 'butch, hard-looking' woman, and links with the ways that heterosexuality is produced through gender binaries (Renold and Ringrose 2008; Ringrose 2011). Isabelle and Sam's disapproval of 'butch' female figures also clearly point to implied heterosexuality sustained through gender binaries, wherein heterosexuality is presumed and immutable and all other possibilities for sexuality are closed off (Butler 1993). These binaries underpinning Isabelle and Sam's examples are crucial to the maintenance of heterosexuality as seemingly 'natural' and self-evident.

Gender, consumer culture and the 'visible' male body

In the media and popular culture, 'men's bodies are on display as never before' (Gill *et al.* 2005: 38). In the current social and cultural context, men too are 'increasingly drawn into the consumer culture body image game and are becoming more critical and vulnerable about their bodies' (Featherstone 2010: 202). Although the (young) female body and 'spectacular femininity' continues to be particularly visible in the context of consumer culture through an emphasis on slenderness, the young athletic and muscular male body can be seen as embodying a 'spectacular' form of masculinity (Coffey 2015) which is increasingly visible in popular culture and the media (Gill *et al.* 2005; Featherstone 2010).

Appearance and bodily presentation was important to all male participants in the study. All but two men described wanting to be 'bigger' or to maintain a physique that is 'big and strong':

> I want to be muscular, I want to be seen as like, strong, in everything.
>
> (Finn, 32, Graphic designer)

84　*Assembling gender*

> I want to look the best I can, to have that classic male, slim, muscly build.
>
> (Sam, 25, nurse)

Shilling (2003) argues that the male 'muscular mesomorph' ideal can be linked to three social trends: the decrease in stigmatisation of gay men's bodies through the practice of bodybuilding in the 1980s and 1990s; a 'muscular backlash' as a response to greater numbers of women entering the public sphere across recent decades; and the corresponding issue of replacing a male 'breadwinner' identity with activities of consumerism geared towards cultivating the body's appearance.

Though most men wanted to be 'bigger', a number of them distanced themselves from the 'excessive' muscles of bodybuilders, and emphasised 'tone' rather than 'bulky muscles' as their aim.

> You don't wanna go too over the top. It's funny you should say this, like yesterday my mate and I were looking up muscle men on YouTube. That's over the top.
>
> (Tom, 24, firefighter)

> Not the bodybuilder muscle-bound type, but that muscular frame but really athletic at the same time.
>
> (Ben, 32, sales rep)

> I guess muscles and stuff, although not too big.
>
> (Stephen, 18, student)

These dynamics of muscularity but 'not too big' align with participants' discussions of 'excessive muscularity' and steroid use as 'gross' in another study of male body image and identities (Ravn and Coffey 2015). Instead muscles and going to the gym in moderation were described as being ideal for men and as cohering with a general image of 'health'. As Daniel says, 'There's probably guys going to the gym too, but a lot of them would just be for health maybe'.

Along with the invitation to care about the body's appearance and to consume products to aid in the body's aesthetic improvement, a growing emphasis on individual responsibility for health is also central in understanding the rise in a concern for the body's appearance for men, and in general (Crawford 1980; Gill *et al.* 2005). Bell and McNaughton (2007: 112) however argue that men's current concern with their bodies is not particularly new, and that men have not been immune to aesthetic pressures for some time, particularly surrounding 'fatness'. It is in this context of increasing attention and 'visibility' of the (young, athletic, muscular) male body that body work is experienced by some of the men in this project, such as Adam.

Adam is 23 years old and plays Australian Rules football professionally. Adam is also a part-time student at university and works as a voice actor in

Assembling gender 85

radio advertisements. In describing the sort of work involved in attaining a 'football body', he says it took him about three years to 'go from being a skinny guy' to having the 'sculpted body' of a professional footballer. Adam discusses how his body shape as an athlete enables him to be visible or 'noticed by girls':

> I guess before I started playing football, as an 18 or 19 year old, I wanted that body that would get the girls I guess! I'd go to the gym 5–6 days a week to work on that. That was it for me, for me it was just a lot of gym work. The more I did that the better results I would see, so that was my motivation – I want a body that gets me noticed. And that did start to get me noticed, by girls especially. That was my main objective I think at the time.

Specific male body shapes are becoming more 'visible': athletes such as AFL (Australian Football League) footballers and soccer players' physiques were widely described by participants in this study as being most attractive and 'ideal' for men. Although Adam's aim is to have a body that will afford him heterosexual capital to get him 'noticed' by women, the athletic and muscular male figure is also noticed as 'attractive' in homosexual relations, as Simon (who identified as gay) described a body like Adam's as attractive and ideal to him. Many participants, including Simon, explained that muscles are 'ideal' for men's bodies because muscles are seen to denote 'health', vibrancy and the capacity for action. In this context, as a football player, Adam understands that his physique draws the attention of women (and men) because he fits the masculine 'ideal'.

Perhaps unsurprisingly, as Solomon-Godeau has pointed out, 'contemporary representations of masculinity, either in elite or cultural mass forms, reveal significant correspondences to older visual paradigms of ideal masculinity' (1997: 21–2). This means that traditional gender relations are often aimed at closely physically resembling an ideal (and opposing) physical representation of gender. The relations surrounding the increasing visibilities of men's bodies (which are almost always muscular) are important for understanding the ways that young men's bodies may be experienced and lived, particularly given that masculinity and men's bodies have often not been included in analyses of gendered experiences. Analysing the dynamics of these bodily practices is also important given the amount of work, effort and rigour it takes to 'sculpt' a muscular body into a desired size and shape. Adam says, 'naturally [men's] bodies will sculpt eventually when you do lots of push ups or bench presses because of hormones and all that stuff'. Though muscles are described as 'natural' to men (and not women, as was explicitly stated), attaining a muscular physique requires highly regulated practices and regimes involving a space and equipment to facilitate weights training, a controlled diet, regular periods of free time to train, money, and often other people (such as a professional trainer or knowledgeable friends to assist or

86 *Assembling gender*

advise). It is important to disrupt the naturalisation of gendered physiques such as muscularity with masculinity to unpack the specific and deliberate ways in which gender is produced socially, and produced through the body. As Bell and McNaughton argue, we should ensure we locate men's as well as women's experiences in gender relations, given the tendency for men (and particularly white, middle class men) to 'enjoy both the privilege and the curse of invisibility' (2007: 112). Adam's desire to be visible or 'noticed' for his masculinity may be a particularly new element of masculinity, linked with dominant, hierarchized forms of masculinity through sports such as AFL (Drummond 2011).

Although some aspects of visibility and the status of the male body may be changing (Dworkin and Wachs 2009), such as in Adam's desire to have a body that will 'get him noticed', the politics of meaning around men's and women's bodies in this context are different. As Paul explains, visibility is not part of the traditional discourse on masculinity, though it may be part of a man's embodied experience:

> I don't know, but ... I certainly don't think about my appearance any-where near as much as women I know. I don't have to. I can if I want, but it sort of starts to stress me out after a very small amount of time.
>
> (Paul, 32, sound editor)

Paul can choose to think about and work on his appearance, but is not obliged or expected to because this is not an expectation in normative masculinity. Paul's comment that when he does think about it, it 'stresses [him] out' quite quickly indicates that a concern for his appearance nevertheless affects him (and other men, such as Adam). There are palpable gendered inequalities however underpinning these examples of visibility due to the different social meanings and values attached to masculinity and femininity, and the costs associated with (in)visibility in different contexts.

The footballer–body–assemblage

Most of the examples relating to body work and bodies described so far can be understood as hooking into 'molar' descriptions of gender. The 'molar' is 'something that is well-defined, massive and governing – such as large structures or identity categories' (Jackson 2010: 581). The identity categories of masculinity and femininity are mobilised through Adam's pursuit of a 'footballer's body' that would 'get him noticed' by girls and garner respect from his team-mates, opposition team-mates and 'in the street'. This molar masculine gender identity goes towards 'constituting' Adam's body as an assemblage. In Adam's example, gender is a 'performative doing' through comportment and bodily techniques of a footballer, which includes the regime and routine of going to the gym five to six times a week and following a strict diet. Being part of a football club means that other bodies such as team-

Assembling gender 87

mates and training staff; the material spaces of the football field and gym; and the 'respect' he feels his body garners on the street are also important for understanding the dynamics by which his body is produced.

Assemblages are produced through the engagements of 'disparate elements that can be material, psychic, social or abstract/philosophical' (Fox 2011: 364). Fox gives the example of the sexuality assemblage, which comprises at least:

sex organ – arousal – object of desire

The gender assemblage, then, could be understood as comprising at least:

sexed body – norms – body practices – identity

In Adam's case, we can expand his gender assemblage to include at least (and in no particular order):

football (masculine ideals of strength, speed, control, ability) – heterosexual desire – body work (the gym – weights – diet) – muscles – sexed body – motivation

Approaching gender as an assemblage attends to the discursive, performative and regulative aspects of normative gender categories, and also to the affective, embodied, sensate and unpredictable dimensions as it is lived. These 'gendering' dimensions of Adam's identity may be assembled differently at other points in time in the future. Countless other aspects equally contribute to assembling Adam's 'body-regime', including speech, thought, will, passion (Rose 1996: 186) and other formations including race (his particular positioning as a white Anglo-Australian); place (he lives, works and trains in a wealthy urban suburb in Melbourne); class (he has received a private school education and attends one of the top universities in Australia) and sexuality (he is heterosexual). These dimensions assist in placing Adam's body-regime, and the particular dominant or molar dynamics of his gender assemblage, in context as Adam is positioned in the dominant group in each of these categories.

Affects and capacities

The range of possibilities for bodies beyond the molar or binary machines depends on whether affects are multiplied or intensified. Exploring the range of possibilities available to bodies involves assessing whether affects can be multiplied or opened up, or whether affects are closed down and intensified (Fox 2002). For example, Isabelle's and Sam's insistence that women must dress and behave in a 'feminine' way in order to be recognised as women (and humans) intensifies and reasserts the binary machine of gender, limiting other possibilities for living through gender. Their examples demonstrate what a

88 *Assembling gender*

sharp regulation and policing of gender looks like and indicates how repressive and limiting molar gender assemblages can be. However, because assemblages are the outcome of a body's diverse and dynamic relations, the assemblage (including the gender assemblage) is also dynamic. It is because of this dynamism that Deleuze and Guattari (1987: 216) can make statements about the ways in which something 'always escapes' from binary organisations.

Jackson (2010) argues that statements which shift binary logic betray the inherent instability of molar structures such as gender, and can be termed 'becoming'. Any statement, comment or action that destabilises and undermines binary logic, no matter how small, is directed towards experimentation, difference and change, rather than what is already known. Such movement away from the molar and binary machines can be understood as becoming. In this way, the participants' critiques of gender norms related to appearance and heterosexuality can be seen as oriented towards experimentation and change; to the potential of becoming otherwise. However, as seen in Isabelle and Sam's examples, the binary machine also closes down possibilities for becoming otherwise. Where the molar, binary machine of gender is endorsed and reiterated it is intensified, and possibilities for living gender differently are closed down.

It is important to pay attention to the configurations of consumer culture and spectacular forms of femininity and masculinity because they are implicated in the mediating forces (territorialisations) which work to produce the body. The examples above suggest some of the ways gender is assembled through body work practices and a multitude of other aspects: including (hetero)sexuality, media images, others' bodies, materials and spaces. The ways that participants explain their body work and negotiate broader gender structures are explored further in the remainder of this chapter, with a particular emphasis on the micro-processes that 'escape' the molar gender assemblage.

In-between gender: ambiguities, contradictions, ruptures

A focus on the micro-processes of instability and change that are inherent in molar structures such as gender recognises that bodies are not contained and completely reducible to molar understandings of gender and the subject (Armstrong 2002). Bodies assemble through a 'functional collection of connections' (see Currier 2003), including territorialising discourses, norms, ideals, institutions, as well as less predictable engagements with bodies, affects and practices. Exploring the instances when the broader structures of gender frame body work practices are critiqued, or at least not endorsed by participants in this study is a way of engaging with the molecular, the 'tiny things that destabilise the perception of a whole' (Jackson 2010: 582). The following examples illustrate instances of critique, ambiguity or contradiction in participants' descriptions of gender, body work and the body.

Assembling gender   89

'I can't be bothered'

Many women were critical of the physical expectations related to gender and normative femininity. Kate, for example discusses the sorts of requirements of femininity in the 'fashion-beauty-complex' (McRobbie 2009) that she often 'can't be bothered with':

> Women are expected to have their nails done, have their eyebrows waxed, have their hair dyed, have a tan, have this, have white teeth, have, you know what I mean? I get so tired [of it]. Half the time I just go 'uh uh, I can't be bothered waxing my eyebrows, I can't be bothered', you know. It's pretty, sort of ... I dunno, you wish that you could that there were more sort of natural-looking women out there.
>
> (Kate, 24, nanny/administrative assistant)

Similar to Kate, Angela questions why girls would bother wearing a lot of make-up:

> I know a few other girls from school and they have so much make-up on and I think 'why go to all that trouble?' It's like a mask covering their face, but then some girls just don't care [about wearing make-up], like genuinely don't care [laughing] and I like that.
>
> (Angela, 18, graphic arts student)

In another criticism of feminised 'beauty work', Kim says she sometimes feels like shaving off all of the hair on her head to escape from the pressures surrounding femininity and beauty:

> Sometimes like, I wish I could shave all my hair off, because that has a lot to do with being a woman, women have the long hair, and guys have short hair. There's just so much emphasis placed on women and their hair ... In an ideal world, I wouldn't have to make an effort. I'd still look good, but wouldn't have to make an effort. I'd love that! Yeah. I guess since leaving high school I've sort of understood that you only look a certain way, but that's not who you really are ... looks are nothing without brains.
>
> (Kim, 24, administrative assistant)

Kim explains that her occasional impulse to shave off all of her hair is associated with a desire to escape from the 'effort' and maintenance involved in feminine body work. Although she says she wishes she did not have to make the efforts required by the cultural norms of feminine beauty and body work, she says she still wants to 'look good', but also emphasises non-physical attributes such as intelligence as really important to 'who you are'.

90 *Assembling gender*

Although none of these examples from Kate, Angela or Kim wholly reject or deconstruct feminine beauty practices and the broader gender relations which underpin them, they do complicate and critique, in small ways, the sorts of body work practices they undertake and relate them to broader expectations of femininity. Through their forms of body work, Kate, Angela and Kim engage with but also critique broader gender discourses. Their bodies and discursive practices associated with gender can be understood as enfolded, and produced through, one another (Barad 2007). The negotiations and intra-actions between bodies and gender structures produce both. Bodies, because they connect in this way, are inherently productive, rather than passive. Bodies are produced through, but not determined by, their relations (Coleman 2009: 214).

The ways that Kate, Angela and Kim connect with binary gender structures through their criticisms of some feminine requirements of beauty can be understood as molecular, comprising a slight shift away from the acceptance and practices of molar gender structures. According to Deleuze, such comments entail the opening of new possibilities for action and productivity. Kate, Angela and Kim's comments do not enable them to literally 'escape' gendered subjectification, but rather point to the micro-events that have the potential to destabilise dominant gender narratives, small as these 'escapes' may be. Through these examples I have aimed to show that critiques of the dominant are important in Deleuzian analysis. This perspective of the body as in processes of becoming does not endorse the apolitical perspective that 'anything goes'; that all becomings are positive. The point is not to show that gender is endlessly fluid or loose, but rather that it is actively produced in ways that are both restrictive and creative, often simultaneously. A focus on the micro-politics of different situations, examples and assemblages is a way of both critiquing and exploring in fine detail how the current contexts come to assemble, while also recognising that there is inherent capacity for change in these arrangements.

'The gym is a f***ed place'

A number of men in the study were critical of the 'macho' environment of the gym and the hierarchy of masculinities in this space. Simon describes that he avoids going to the gym altogether specifically because of the 'macho' environment:

> I'm all skinny and little and stuff and I'd be a bit put off, feel a bit inadequate, it would make me feel insecure … Everyone would have better bodies and stuff and I think that would be intimidating … I'm happy with my body, but if I was around people [like at the gym] then maybe I'd feel a bit inadequate and a bit inferior to them.
>
> (Simon, 18, university student)

Assembling gender 91

Similarly, Peter has only recently started going to the gym, and says he has 'finally worked up the courage to go into a place like that'. The gym, for Peter is also an intimidating environment because of the particularly 'dominating' form of masculinity associated with lifting weights and muscularity. Peter is caught between the desire he has had for a long time 'to get bigger' and 'to be more muscular' and the disdain he has for the 'macho' masculinity of his trainer at the gym:

> The gym is a fucked place. I don't understand those people. I just sort of feel that I'm doing my best to assimilate every time that I walk in there. And I know that they know I'm not meant to be there. I have a trainer so I see him once a week, I saw him today. I kind of, I like him but he's a real weirdo ... he said to me what are my goals and I felt like, on the spot, I didn't know what to say. So I said 'I want to get bigger', for some reason, that isn't really what I want. And he's taken that on board for how he's trying to get me fired up and I just find that really patronising. So like when I walk in, he'll be there scoffing a can of tuna going 'Yeah, great, there are 27 grams of protein in this!' And he says to me, there will be him in a big group of trainer people hanging out, and he'll see me and will call out 'Hey Peter how are you? Ready to get massive?' [in loud booming voice] and I'm just like, 'yeah dude! I'll just go upstairs and get massive with you, won't I' [sarcastic] and I just feel real patronised.
>
> (Peter, 27, barber)

Peter distances himself from 'those people' at the gym, and disavows his desire to 'get bigger', saying 'that isn't what I really want', although elsewhere in the interview he says he has always wanted to be more muscular. Peter says he feels patronised by his trainer whose aim is to make him 'massive', and also feels uncomfortable because of his body: 'I know that they know I'm not meant to be there'. Like Simon, Peter feels insecure about his physical size compared to dominant and dominating physiques of the muscular men at the gym, his trainer in particular.

> I think you stick out if you're like me, and you don't have much, like the skinny man at the gym. Like in the free weights area, I feel like I stick out like a sore thumb. I wanted to, like, you know how women have like Fernwood [a women's-only gym franchise]? I thought it would be sweet if there was a gym just for, like, skinny guys. Called Wormwood or something!

For Peter and Stephen, being 'the skinny man at the gym' makes them feel uncomfortable, unwelcome and out of place. Both describe wanting to achieve physical distance from these spaces to avoid the 'massive' male bodies who embody forms of masculinity they find 'intimidating' or 'patronising'.

92 *Assembling gender*

Peter's and Simon's examples show the variations in men's understandings of their bodies related to discourses and affects associated with dominant masculinity. In these examples, normative, muscular masculinity is complicated and opened up. Rather than reinforcing hegemonic masculinity, such as in previous comments made by Sam like 'a man should be a man', which close down possibilities for masculinities other than the dominant 'ideal', Simon and Peter denaturalise hegemonic masculinity by showing how carefully constructed and difficult to embody it can be. Their examples open up difference in the molar category of masculinity; they can be understood as molecular, 'individual responses to becoming' (Jackson 2010: 582). Merceica and Merceica (2010) in their research on disability argue for example that propositions made by participants such as 'this school is not inclusive', from a Deleuzian perspective, need to be acknowledged as bringing about an alteration in the intensities not only of the person but of the whole world, and 'it is this shift in intensities that Deleuze's thought invites us to engage and experiment with, and explore' (Merceica and Merceica 2010: 86). The intensities and openings towards difference have been explored in this chapter through participants' critiques and (micro) problematisations of gender structures and related practices of body work.

Images, affect and 'body pressures'

Though women are discussed by men and women in the study as being subject to more body 'pressure' relating to broader gender discourses, men also described feeling 'pressure' to emulate physical gender ideals. The main difference between men and women in the study is that men did not connect their experiences of body pressure as being common to other men's experiences. As the above examples show, narrow categories of masculinity and femininity can be profoundly limiting and difficult to live up to, and require a great deal of work to sustain (Butler 1993). Further, there is less space for men to discuss their bodies and gender as being problematic in relation to dominant discourses of masculinity, and, as such, men often have the 'privilege and curse' of invisibility in relation to 'body issues' (Bell and McNaughton 2007: 112).

In the following examples, both Kate and Jason used almost exactly the same language to describe the process of looking at others' 'ideal' gendered body characteristics and wanting to look like them:

> There are such a lot of expectations on women nowadays, in all the magazines that come out or fashion television … I get caught up in 'this is how I'm supposed to look, this is what I'm supposed to be'.
>
> (Kate, 25, administrative assistant/nanny)

Assembling gender 93

When we see those [football] players running around it puts, kind of, an image in your mind, like 'oh that's what I need to look like, that's how I need to be', and so you go to the gym.

(Jason, 22, accountant and amateur footballer)

Images of gendered ideal bodies – whether in the 'real' physical bodies of football players or magazine images of 'perfect women' – affect Kate's and Jason's bodies and body work practices.

Featherstone (2010) argues that the intensified focus on men in advertising and consumer culture is altering the dynamics of masculinity to be more focused on appearance and presentation. There are significant parallels in Kate's and Jason's experiences of their bodies in relation to masculine and feminine 'ideals'. McCaughey (1999: 121) argues that 'we are so used to positioning women as passive dupes of sexist culture, and men as wilful agents who gain meaning and material rewards from their activities, that we have missed the parallels between the two body projects'. Though the images are demarcated by gendered norms, placing focus on the process by which they are 'affected' by images helps to tell a more complex story relating to gendered body work practices and the gender assemblages they comprise.

Kate and Jason used almost exactly the same phrasing to describe how others' bodies *affect* them. This is a good example of what the concept of affect entails and how it is useful for understanding body norms and body image for both women and men. Featherstone insists that images are not merely visual, and are felt as a sense of energy, force or intensity: they are affective (2010: 199). Affects relate to embodied sensations which mediate what happens next: the capacity of a body for action. 'Becoming' can be understood as the outcomes of those affective relations between bodies and things; or 'what a body can do' (Deleuze 1992). Hence, gender ideals affect Kate's and Jason's bodies and body work practices; they have particularly intensive affects in their relations with the 'gendered ideal' bodies they see, which has implications for how they feel and think about their bodies, and what they do in terms of body work practices.

Conclusion: opening gender and the body

This chapter has discussed that body work practices are a central way that gender is performed and negotiated materially. Through exploring the current context in which the body's appearance is a crucial issue of concern for young people, I have aimed to show the potential of an approach which understands the body as an active, productive force. This relational approach to understanding the body and the social is useful for understanding why the body is so significant for contemporary youth. This perspective assists in understandings of embodied, gendered identities and sees them as formed through the dynamics between bodies, affects, discourses, norms, practices and socio-material forces.

94 *Assembling gender*

This approach enables an understanding of the multiple and complex ways bodies are negotiated through affective relations with forces such as gender and within the context of numerous other assemblages. Bodies can be seen as 'events' of becoming, rather than subjects or objects, as in numerous other feminist studies of the body (Budgeon 2003). Gender is a key mediating force which works to form the event of the body, part of a series of negotiations which comes to bear on the corporeality of the body. Because the focus is on the connections bodies make and their reconfigurations that result, seeing the body as an event is to acknowledge the multiple negotiations it undertakes (Budgeon 2003). Body work practices are a key aspect of this process.

Gendered embodiments are not simply the reproductions of dualist gender formations; rather, gender is engaged, negotiated and produced continually through affects and relations. The study of these micro-relations and how they link with the broader socio-historical context has been termed 'micro-politics' (Fox 2014). The point is not to show that gender is endlessly fluid or loose, but rather that it is actively produced in ways that are both restrictive and creative, often simultaneously. A focus on the micro-politics of different situations, examples and assemblages is a way of both critiquing and exploring in fine detail how the current contexts come to assemble, while also recognising that there is inherent capacity for change in these arrangements. As Houle describes, the micro-political ontology of Deleuze and Guattari has capacity inherent within it: the insistence that things could be otherwise (2011: 110). It is important to pay attention to these complexities and nuances and the processes by which bodies and the social assemble to understand the conditions of possibility for more open gender arrangements and social change more broadly.

This perspective has been drawn on by numerous feminist scholars in an effort to develop a critique of gendered embodiment which wants to move beyond the dynamics of domination/subordination or dualistic analytic frameworks (Budgeon 2015). It is important to look at the dynamics of gender as actively engaged in and negotiated to understand the full range and contradictions associated with gendered embodiments. To say that gender is actively negotiated is not to say that it is straightforwardly 'challenged' or 'resisted' by participants towards some form of emancipation or empowerment. As these examples have shown, gender is actively produced through encounters in a range of ways, including those can be read as more or less positive or restrictive. We are all enmeshed in this dynamic process. Some positions provide us with more room to move than others, such as those which are more accommodating of a broader range of identities and perspectives than those presented in Isabelle's or Sam's examples, who insisted on normative, restrictive and repressive models of femininity in opposition to traditional, dominant masculinity. This perspective can also assist in casting light on areas obscured by traditional models of gender; for example, relating to the similarities in how the body is experienced and negotiated by both men and women.

Assembling gender 95

While most men in the study assumed that body image and body pressure is not as relevant as an issue for men as it is for women, the body's appearance was a clear concern for almost all of them. One of the only differences between men and women in the study was that unlike women, men were not broadly understood to have body concerns, though they did. Many other researchers have unintentionally (and often understandably) not included men in approaches to the body when critiquing the different gendered contexts framing body presentation and broader dimensions of gender inequality. Deleuze and Guattari's concepts offer tools for placing at the centre of focus 'the practices between gender ... the contradictions, plays, experimentations, swappings, ambiguities and passings' within gender (Skeggs 2004: 27). This approach to the body enables a consideration of the similarities in the processes by which the body is shaped, including social binary territorialisations of gender, while retaining a focus on context and unequal dimensions of gender relations. As a result, this perspective has the potential to contribute to creating a rich and detailed picture of the dynamics of young, gendered embodiments.

Note

1 Early in interviews, I asked participants to describe what they perceived to be the 'mainstream' ideal body for men and women seen in the media, for example. I asked this question to get in to the 'zone' of asking about bodies and body work to break the ice. This is because in the first few interviews participants often didn't know what I meant by 'body work'. Asking about ideal bodies gave a point of reference for the perceived 'mainstream ideal', and a way of linking in to the perceived dominant framings of gender and health in relation to bodies and appearances. This also enabled a 'way in' to asking about body work, as I asked subsequently 'what sorts of things do you think people have to do to look like that?' I was also careful to introduce a space where I was not simply asking them to 'endorse' these images. Many asked the, 'do I describe what I think is ideal or what other people think?' This opened a space to discuss the diversity rather than conformity of body image ideals beyond the narrow and limiting images usually presented in the media.

References

Armstrong, A. (2002). Agency Reconfigured: Narrative Continuities and Connective Transformations. *Contretemps: An Online Journal of Philosophy*, 3, 42–53.

Atkinson, M. and Monaghan, L. F. (2014). *Challenging Myths of Masculinity: Understanding Physical Cultures*. Aldershot: Ashgate.

Barad, K. (2007). *Meeting the Universe Halfway: Quantum Physics and the Entanglement of Matter and Meaning*. Durham and London: Duke University Press.

Bartky, S. (1990). *Femininity and Domination: Studies in the Phenomenology of Oppression*. New York: Routledge.

Bell, K. and McNaughton, D. (2007). Feminism and the Invisible Fat Man. *Body and Society*, 13(1), 107–131.

Bordo, S. (1999). *The Male Body: A New Look at Men in Public and Private*. New York: Farrar & Giroux.

96 *Assembling gender*

Bordo, S. (2003). *Unbearable Weight: Feminism, Western Culture and the Body* (10th anniversary edn). Berkeley: University of California Press.

Bridges, T. (2009). Gender Capital and Male Bodybuilders. *Body and Society, 15(1)*, 83–107.

Budgeon, S. (2003). Identity as an Embodied Event. *Body and Society*, 9(1), 35–55.

Budgeon, S. (2015). Theorizing Subjectivity and Feminine Embodiment: Feminist Approaches and Debates. In J. Wyn and H. Cahill (eds), *Handbook of Youth and Childhood Studies* (pp. 243–256). New York: Springer.

Butler, J. (1993). *Bodies that Matter: on the Discursive Limits of 'Sex'*. London: Routledge.

Coffey, J. (2015). 'I put pressure on myself to keep that body': 'health'-related body work, masculinities and embodied identity. *Social Theory and Health*. Available online 4 September 2015. doi: 10.1057/sth.2015.27

Coleman, R. (2009). *The Becoming of Bodies: Girls, Images, Experience.* Manchester and New York: Manchester University Press.

Connell, R. W. (2009). *Gender* (2nd edn). Cambridge: Polity Press.

Crawford, R. (1980). Healthism and the Medicalisation of Everyday Life. *International Journal of Health Services*, 10(3), 365–388.

Crossley, N. (2006). In the Gym: Motives, Meaning and Moral Careers. *Body and Society*, 12(3), 23–50.

Currier, D. (2003). Feminist Technological Futures. *Feminist Theory*, 4(3), 321–338. doi: 10.1177/14647001030043005

Davis, K. (1995). *Reshaping the Female Body.* New York: Routledge.

Deleuze, G. (1992). Ethology: Spinoza and Us. In J. Crary and S. Kwinter (eds), *Incorporations*. New York: Zone.

Deleuze, G. and Guattari, F. (1987). *A Thousand Plateaus: Capitalism and Schizophrenia* (B. Massumi, trans.). Edinburgh: Edinburgh University Press.

Deleuze, G. and Parnet, C. (2002). *Dialogues II* (H. Tomlinson and B. Habberjam, trans. 2nd edn). New York: Columbia University Press.

Drummond, M. (2011). Reflections on the Archetypal Heterosexual Male Body. *Australian Feminist Studies*, 26, 103–115.

Dworkin, S. and Wachs, F. (2009). *Body Panic: Gender, Health and the Selling of Fitness.* New York and London: University of New York Press.

Featherstone, M. (1982). The Body in Consumer Culture. *Theory, Culture and Society*, 1, 18–33.

Featherstone, M. (2010). Body, Image and Affect in Consumer Culture. *Body and Society*, 16(1), 193–221.

Fox, N. J. (2002). Refracting 'Health': Deleuze, Guattari and Body-Self. *Health, 6(3)*, 347–63. doi: 10.1177/136345930200600306

Fox, N. J. (2011). The Ill-Health Assemblage: Beyond the Body-With-Organs. *Health Sociology Review*, 20(4), 359–71. doi: 10.5172/hesr.2011.20.4.359

Fox, N. J. (2014). The micropolitics of obesity: materialism, neoliberalism and food sovereignty. Paper presented at the British Sociological Association Medical Sociology Annual Conference, Birmingham.

Frost, L. (2003). Doing Bodies Differently? Gender, Youth, Appearance and Damage. *Journal of Youth Studies*, 6(1), 53.

Gill, R., Henwood, K. and McLean, C. (2005). Body Projects and the Regulation of Normative Masculinity. *Body and Society*, 11(1), 37–62.

Gimlin, D. (2002). *Body Work: Beauty and Self Image in American Culture.* Los Angeles: University of California Press.

Grogan, S., Evans, R., Wright, S. and Hunter, G. (2004). Femininity and Muscularity: Accounts of Seven Women Body Builders. *Journal of Gender Studies*, 13(1), 49–61.

Grosz, E. (1994). *Volatile Bodies: Towards a Corporeal Feminism*. St Leonards: Allen & Unwin.

Houle, K. (2011). Micropolitics. In C. J. Stivale (ed.), *Key Concepts: Gilles Deleuze: Key Concepts (2nd Edition)*. Durham, GBR: Acumen.

Jackson, A. Y. (2010). Deleuze and the Girl. *International Journal of Qualitative Studies in Education (QSE)*, 23(5), 579–87.

Jackson, S., Vares, T. and Gill, R. (2012). 'The Whole Playboy Mansion Image': Girls' Fashioning and Fashioned Selves within a Postfeminist Culture. *Feminism and Psychology*, 0959353511433790

Lupton, D. (2013). *Fat*. London: Routledge.

McCaughey, M. (1999). Fleshing Out the Discomforts of Femininity: The Parallel Case of Female Anorexia and Male Compulsive Body Building. In J. Sobal and D. Maurer (eds), *Weighty Issues: Fatness and Thinness as Social Problems*. New York: Aldine De Gruyter.

McRobbie, A. (2009). *The Aftermath of Feminism: Gender, Culture and Social Change*. London: Sage.

Merceica, D. and Merceica, D. (2010). Opening research to Intensities: Rethinking Disability Research with Deleuze and Guattari. *Journal of Philosophy of Education*, 44(1), 80–92.

Ravn, S. and Coffey, J. (2015). 'Steroids, it's so much an Identity Thing!' Perceptions of Steroid Use, Risk and Masculine Body Image. *Journal of Youth Studies*. doi: 10.1080/13676261.2015.1052051

Renold, E. and Ringrose, J. (2008). Regulation and Rupture: Mapping Tween and Teenage Girls' Resistance to the Heterosexual Matrix. *Feminist Theory*, 9, 314–339.

Ringrose, J. (2011). Beyond Discourse? Using Deleuze and Guattari's Schizoanalysis to Explore Affective Assemblages, Heterosexually Striated Space, and Lines of Flight Online and at School. *Educational Philosophy and Theory*, 43(6), 598–618.

Ringrose, J. and Walkerdine, V. (2008). Regulating the Abject: The TV Make-over as Site of Neo-liberal Reinvention toward Bourgeois Femininity. *Feminist Media Studies*, 8(3), 227–246.

Rose, N. (1996). *Inventing Our Selves: Psychology, Power and Personhood*. Cambridge: Cambridge University Press.

Rose, N. (2007). *The Politics of Life Itself: Biomedicine, Power, and Subjectivity in the Twenty-First Century*. Princeton, NJ: Princeton University Press.

Shilling, C. (2003). *The Body and Social Theory* (2nd edn). London: Sage.

Skeggs, B. (2004). Context and Background: Pierre Bourdieu's Analysis of Class, Gender and Sexuality. In L. Adkins and B. Skeggs (eds), *Feminism after Bourdieu*. Oxford: Blackwell.

Solomon-Godeau, A. (1997). *Male Trouble: A Crisis in Representation*. London and New York: Thames & Hudson.

Witz, A. (2000). Whose Body Matters? Feminist Sociology and the Corporeal Turn in Sociology and Feminism. *Body and Society*, 6(2), 1–24.

Wolf, N. (1991). *The Beauty Myth: How Images of Beauty Are Used against Women*. New York: William Morrow.

5 Health, affect and embodiment

Introduction

The body's 'health' is a central focus in contemporary society. Body work practices such as those undertaken with the aim of 'fitness', 'slimming' or growing muscle also intersect with gender norms and bodily ideals. These practices are key to understanding the dynamics of young people's concern for the body's appearance and contemporary embodiments. The current emphasis on the body's appearance, or the aesthetic body, can be linked to a range of social, cultural and economic factors including the expansion of health, leisure, cosmetic, beauty and fitness industries since the 1980s (Lupton 1995; Shilling 2003). Sociological work has traced these shifts to cultural changes in advanced capitalist societies which occurred during the second half of the twentieth century in which conspicuous consumption became central in the ethos accompanying hard work in the realm of production (Featherstone 1982; Shilling 2007). As a result of this shift, embodiment and the physical body came to be treated as both a 'project' and a 'form of physical capital' (Bourdieu 1977; Shilling 2003, 2007; Mears 2014). The increasing focus on 'health' in all spheres of life is particularly important for understanding the significance of the aesthetic body (Atkinson and Monaghan 2014). The media is a crucial dimension of the growing industry of health through health and fitness magazines (Dworkin and Wachs 2009), the popularity of reality television shows promoting weight loss and fitness (Moore 2010) and social media sites such as Instagram, Twitter, Tumblr and Facebook which are fast becoming the prime means of marketing and advertising (Holmes 2014). These sites are key mediators of bodily representations and gender norms (Perloff 2014; Reade 2014; Tiidenberg and Gómez Cruz 2015).

Social media is a key instantiation of contemporary consumer culture. Consumer culture is obsessed with the body, and that through consuming products and pursuing health 'strategies', the positive benefits of bodily transformative work form the dominant narrative related to the 'image' of health (Featherstone 2010). 'Transformations' of the body achieved through cosmetic surgery and the 'look good, feel good' logic of consumer culture 'is presented as within the reach of all' (Featherstone 2010: 202). In this

Health, affect, embodiment 99

environment, 'looking healthy' is equated with looking 'young' and 'sexy' (Atkinson and Monaghan 2014). Numerous authors have theorised the link between cultural developments with an emphasis on consumption and the effect this has had on the way the body is approached as an 'object' to be worked on and improved (Bartky 1990; Bordo 2003; Crossley 2006; Dworkin and Wachs 2009). In this, the focus on 'body work' seeks to address these dimensions in relation to the body's significance in contemporary society. Body work practices are key aspects of what can be termed 'health assemblages' (Duff 2014). In this chapter I argue that understanding health and embodiment as assemblages (Duff 2014) produced through a range of networks and relations can assist us to understand the complex and contradictory ways health is engaged with and produced in young people's lives.

Health assemblages

A Deleuzo-Guattarian (Deleuze and Guattari 1987) perspective understands the body as an 'assemblage' rather than a discrete entity (see Chaper 2). It is a relational perspective which places focus on things the body engages with, including discourses, affects, ideals, norms, practices, institutions and other bodies and objects. Health assemblages are one such aspect which bodies engage with, and which compose bodies. Health assemblages are 'a function of encounters between bodies, between forces and between practices' (Duff 2014: 186). This approach can assist in unsettling simplistic links between health and 'healthy' practices, and health and appearance, giving new insights into the complexity and messiness of health embodiments. This focus can also assist in developing further theoretically grounded understandings of the body and the social.

According to Deleuze (1988), what we are capable of is directly related to embodied sensation (affect), and it is the relations of affect that produce a body's capacities (Coleman 2009). The process informs what a body can do; the range of possibilities that are available stemming from engagement with the many dimensions of numerous assemblages, including health in these examples. 'Becoming' can be understood as the outcomes of those affective relations between bodies and things. Rather than asking 'what are bodies', or questioning the being of bodies, Deleuze (1992) asks 'what can a body do?'. To study becoming is to study the micro-processes of change through the body's affective relations through engagements with other assemblages (Hickey-Moody and Malins 2007).

In this chapter I focus on 'health affects' in particular. I draw on it both as a conceptual model which frames the ontological approach of the research, and as an analytic tool exploring the embodied sensations that participants describe in relation to their bodies and body work practices. Where participants in this study make statements like 'I feel better about myself when I have been exercising', I have interpreted that such a statement can be explored

100 *Health, affect, embodiment*

or understood using the concept of affect following Fox and Wards's (2008) example. According to Deleuze, what we are capable of is directly related to embodied sensation (affect), and it is the relations of affect that produce a body's capacities (Coleman 2009). To affect and be affected is, for Deleuze, becoming. I use the concept of affect as a way of focusing on the connections or encounters between bodies (and assemblages) and what these encounters produce: what can a body do? Or, in relation to health which is the focus of the examples in this chapter: what are the health affects which compose health assemblages, and how do these affect what a body can do?

Numerous authors have noted that 'in relation to the body and health, neo-liberalism calls upon individuals to self-govern through endless examination and self-care' (Leve *et al.* 2012: 124). Health in this context is related to moralised, individualised ideologies associated with neo-liberalism (Crawford 2006), as well as gender, as was introduced in Chapter 4. These relations affect the body and what it can do. The range of possibilities that are open or available are a result of the body's affects and relations (Fox 2002).

All participants highlighted health as an important aspect of their body work practices. Health was discussed in varying ways: as a set of ideas linked to morals and individual responsibility (Kate says 'I don't feel as healthy as I should') and applied to others' bodies (Adam respects 'people who respect their body and respect their health'); as a feeling (Gillian, Clare and Peter discuss the embodied sensations linked to exercise such as increased heart rate and endorphins); as related to identity and the experience of the self ('I just want to feel healthy so that I feel happy', as Paul says; Sam, Jason and Finn say they feel 'better' about themselves when they are 'fit and strong'); and as linked to image and appearance (Angela, Kim and Victoria say that exercise helps them to maintain a 'healthy shape'). These themes can be understood through approaching health as an assemblage – comprising discourses, images, affects and relation to the self – enabling an exploration of the ways these elements interconnect and operate in contemporary embodiments.

First in this chapter, I explore how health is discussed, defined and experienced by participants, and how health links with their understandings of bodies and body work practices. Their definitions and descriptions of health – what it is, what it feels like, and how it can be 'achieved' or worked towards – are complex. Participants' conceptualisations and experiences of health can be understood in the context of discourses and moral rhetoric surrounding health. Here, neo-liberal economic policies connect with consumer culture to encourage individualised, moralised forms of bodily control, linked to health and well-being (Crawford 2006). While being linked to dominant discourses of health, however, participants' experiences and understandings of health are often ambiguous and paradoxical; they are certainly not straightforward. Opening up the concept of health to focus on the intensities and affects involved, the 'always more', widens our perspective (Merceica and Merceica 2010: 86). In this spirit, it is important that understandings of health explore the affective or sensate dimensions of body work practices, such as exercise.

Health, affect, embodiment 101

The affects and relations involved here are integral for exploring what a body can do; what are its capacities and its limits?

Health: ideals, discourses, affects and practice

Health can be understood both as a discourse, relating to individualised self-responsibility and a 'culturally sanctioned way of being' in contemporary, neo-liberal Western states such as Australia (Featherstone 1982, 2010; Crawford 1987), as well as a set of practices undertaken in an effort to become healthier. Health is also a profoundly affective and embodied process, and may be better conceptualised in this way rather than a state of being that can be attained (Coffey 2014). It also has paradoxical links with particular gendered images of health in the landscape of consumer culture (Coffey forthcoming). In participants' discussions, however, 'health' as it was 'felt' was much messier than simply mapping on to dominant ideals. The discursive framings of health which inform health assemblages are described first, before a discussion of the more complex and contradictory dimensions of health as affective and sensate in participants' discussions.

'Health' was described by participants as produced through undertaking 'healthy' behaviours, such as eating a diet low in fat and sugar, and undertaking regular exercise. These practices are central in the 'new paradigm of health' (Moore 2010), in which 'health promotion has prematurely exhorted the public to undertake a large number of different behaviors' (Becker 1993: 1). The terms health, shape, image, appearance were often conflated or used interchangeably by participants in the interviews. 'Looking good' or attractive was often synonymous with health. To look healthy, as many described, is to 'look good'. Health is thus deeply linked to image and appearance, and related to consumer culture in which work on the self through work on one's appearance is an imperative (Featherstone 2010).

The moral and individualistic dimensions of 'health' were apparent in many instances in the interviews. Many spoke of how they felt 'lazy' or 'slack' if they have not been exercising. Health, or practices that were considered to lead to 'health' such as exercise, were discussed as though they were a common requirement, which, if not being met, warranted explanation and justification. In this way, body work practices are linked to the pursuit of 'health'. The ethos of individual autonomy, choice, personal responsibility and control over one's fate are core characteristics of attitudes towards the body in advanced liberal societies (Rose 2000: 329), in which the idealised status of 'health' is an individual, moral responsibility. For example, Steph discusses how her work hours have increased, and she is no longer at college where she used to play organised team sports:

JULIA: Before you were saying that you would want to exercise more if you weren't working so much?
STEPH: Yeah, it's probably a pretty shit excuse to be honest! [laughs]

102 *Health, affect, embodiment*

JULIA: What do you mean?
STEPH: Oh, like everybody works and heaps of people find time to work out.

(Steph, 21, server)

Steph says that working long hours is a poor 'excuse' for not exercising, illustrating the moralised dynamics of individual responsibility for health (Crawford 1980; Lupton 1995). Kate also refers to health as an idealised state and as an objective standard of 'being' that would allow the feeling of health to be met or 'achieved':

> I wouldn't do it [exercise] to improve my body to get a six-pack or to get toned. I'd do it more just to feel good ... I think I focus more on looking healthy, but as far as feeling it, I don't think I feel it as much as I should. I definitely should get out and do more exercise. I feel so much better when I do.

The appearance of health is not enough; Kate explains that she wants to focus more on *feeling* healthy: 'I don't think I feel it as much as I should'. Here, health is assumed to be not only a practice or appearance, but is also valued as an embodied sensation.

'Health' was also frequently described as in opposition to 'fat'. In describing why athletic bodies are ideal for men and women, Simon reasons 'it all comes down to health':

> If you're free to move and stuff, if you're fit you can run and stuff and you have stamina and all those kind of skills, and stuff. Um yeah, I guess that's healthy. And just not lazy I guess, I don't know, I associate fat with laziness.

(Simon, 18, university student)

People who were 'fat' or 'overweight' were defined as 'definitely not healthy' by all participants, and as seriously contravening health as an idealised 'state'. Participants described those who are 'fat', 'overweight' or 'obese' as lazy, lacking self-esteem and self-restraint, and deserving of the increased surveillance and criticism they receive. As Dworkin and Wachs describe, 'while the fat body remains stigmatised as lazy, undisciplined, or as a poor member of the social body, the fit body becomes a metaphor for success, morality and good citizenship' (Dworkin and Wachs 2009: 38). Even though Clare asserts that 'people should just be happy the way they are', this sentiment does not extend to those who are 'incredibly overweight', and the discursive constructions of health and individualism help Clare to justify this:

> I think that if you're incredibly overweight and obese you need to do something about it. There was a girl at my school as an example, she has dropped out now, but she was huge and she was always saying 'I'm so fat, I need to lose weight, I need to do exercise', and we said 'we'll support

Health, affect, embodiment 103

you, we'll help you' and then the next second she'd be buying cheese jaffles, a Big M and a massive Freddo Frog for breakfast every morning at school. And it's kind of the point where, it's ridiculous, you're not being healthy, you're not doing anything to help yourself.

(Clare, 18, VCE student)

Clare is most critical of the girl's individual failure of responsibility to 'do anything to help herself'. Tom makes similar generalisations about his housemate's lack of self-discipline, and assumes that she would like to lose weight, even though in a later section of the interview Tom says he has never heard her express this.

My housemate, she's overweight; she knows that she's overweight, but she's lazy. Despite the effort, you know, or she wants to do something about it but at the same time, does nothing. So, she'd be quite happy to eat what she eats in the quantity that she does, but there's no effort or commitment to a plan. And no drive I suppose. Whereas, I think if you look at confident people, most of them are probably pretty fit kind of people, fairly driven sorts of people. And this is just generalisations as well, I'm sure there are exceptions to the rule, but overweight people are generally, I find, more shy. Or withheld. I think it would be true to say, to generalise again, that a lot of people that are overweight have some self-esteem issues.

(Tom, 25, firefighter)

The moral implications of health are most evident in statements such as these, which attach a negative moral judgement of 'lazy', or positive judgements of 'healthy' to specific body shapes. As many others have argued (Lupton 1996, 2013; Grimshaw 1999; Gimlin 2002; Crossley 2006), being 'fat' is culturally stigmatised, and comes to symbolise a range of other negatively inscribed aspects of self, such as laziness, poor 'self-esteem' and a 'lack of effort or commitment'; the opposite of successful and 'driven' and other characteristics most valued in neo-liberal consumer culture. Those deemed 'fat' are also subjected to greater surveillance, such as when Clare lists the different sorts of food eaten by the girl at her school, or when Tom emphasises the quantity of food his housemate consumes.

Where looking or being 'fat' was considered 'unhealthy' and condemned by participants as a result, individualised self-discipline through body work regimes was exalted. Adam and Victoria both equated body work, through physical exercise and maintenance of body weight with 'respect'. Adam explains that he respects people who:

Respect their bodies and respect their health and take it seriously. I think everyone should be able to make time to be healthy.

(Adam, 23, footballer/university student)

104 *Health, affect, embodiment*

These examples illustrate some of the more regulatory discursive framings associated with 'healthism' (Crawford 1980). The moral and symbolic order underpinning Adam's respect for others who 'respect their own bodies' through undertaking 'healthy' activities is gendered, classed and racialised (Dworkin and Wachs 2009). This marginalises corporeal forms which are not white, middle class or slim in particular. Adam's view that health is something that can be achieved by 'everyone' negates the significant costs of time and money required in the pursuit of health. The expectation that 'everyone should make time to be healthy' obscures the classed and structural aspects of health and body work, such as socio-economic, living and working conditions. 'Health' and forms of body work required to 'achieve' health are available to the more privileged middle or upper classes with more available disposable income and free time. Dworkin and Wachs argue that the primary consumers of health and fitness products such as magazines are 'white and middle class', and that the constitution of emphasised masculinity and femininity (Connell 1987) through body work practices of this dominant group intersect with class and race privilege (Dworkin and Wachs 2009: 162–3). These factors are important in understanding and contextualising participants' descriptions of health and body work practices. As the examples in the next section discuss, however, 'health' is not always the straightforward result of undertaking 'healthy' practices, and these practices require negotiation so as not to slip over and become 'dangerous' such as through under-eating or over-exercising.

Shifting boundaries: health as 'becoming dangerous'?

The actual practices associated with 'health' undertaken by participants were highly varied, although eating a 'healthy' diet and physical exercise activities were mentioned by all participants as being 'healthy', regardless of participants' own practices. This process was also described in much more complex ways.

Angela describes what she thinks is involved in achieving a 'healthy body':

> I guess eat regularly, like six small meals, just even go for a walk like three times a week. I don't think it would take that much effort to keep like a pretty healthy body. Just as long as you don't over-indulge in everything all the time. I don't think it should be that hard to maintain a healthy body weight.
>
> (Angela, 18, visual art student)

Angela's idea of health is less rigid than that of other participants, many of whom emphasise the importance of intensive fitness regimes or strict control over eating different sorts of foods and in specific quantities. Clare for example is much more specific in her description of health and healthy practices

Health, affect, embodiment 105

than Angela, particularly in relation to food and what constitutes 'healthy eating':

> I do eat quite healthily ... but I eat a LOT. I love my food and stuff like that, so, you know, I'd have a couple of packets of chips and some popcorn, like air popped, and then for lunch I'd always have veggies, my capsicum, cucumber and carrot and an apple, I had, like, a veggie patch in my lunchbox! I'll usually indulge on a Friday because I'll have four and a half hours of dancing coming up that night, where I know, whatever I eat now I'm going to work off, just as long as I keep it in small doses and I exercise in healthy doses, not unhealthy doses.
>
> (Clare, 18, high school student)

Clare lists the food in her lunch box in a way similar to a 'confession' (Rose 1996), 'admitting' to the 'unhealthy' foods such as packets of chips and popcorn as well as listing the many vegetables and fruits she eats. The particular authority in how diet connects with health shows how 'personal life' is linked with broader health discourses, which comprise a 'particular form of power' (Rose 1996: 96). In Clare's example, exercise and eating particular foods are the 'healthy' practices.

In describing eating and exercising practices being undertaken in 'healthy' doses, Clare shows that the boundaries of 'health' are fluid and must therefore be carefully managed. Practices such as 'healthy' eating habits and exercise do not straightforwardly guarantee the experience of health (as nebulous as it this may be), and has limits or boundaries. The 'dose' of these practices is crucial. Clare suggests that health is not contained in one set of practices, but rather has the potential to exceed or extend beyond these practices, to become something else. In another example, Clare discusses the 'full on' physical exercise of her after school dancing class:

> We do very intense warm-ups and everything to get everyone going. The other night everyone was just sweating and disgusting! It's very full on and they make sure we stay healthy at the same time.

The intense physical exercises accomplished in Clare's dancing class do not constitute 'health' alone, although similarly intensive physical exercise is widely considered a 'healthy' practice by other participants. Clare's assertion that health is ensured by her instructors 'at the same time' as the intense exercise strongly implies that such exercise is in danger of exceeding its status as a 'healthy' practice. Health, then, is not contained in 'healthy' practices.

Sara and Daniel, among others, referred to body work practices such as going to the gym and exercising as being potentially 'addictive', saying 'people can get obsessed with it'. Sara describes intensity and frequency regarding exercise routines delineate between the activities being 'healthy' or 'obsessive'.

106 *Health, affect, embodiment*

SARA: Men and women can both become, like almost obsessed with it [working on their bodies], and do their routines every day and exercise and eat well and all that sort of thing, sure.

JULIA: So ... you're saying that people can get obsessed with going to the gym and things like that? Do you know people like that or ...?

SARA: I know people like that, and I know people who, you know, how guys can use steroids or drugs to make themselves look better, and I've heard stories that once they start doing it, it becomes addictive and they have to do it every day ... Like, you can look good but you don't have to, it doesn't have to be an obsession, you can work out twice a week and be healthy. You don't have to go every day.

JULIA: So you think that's the better way to be?

SARA: Yeah definitely, do it, like, healthily.

(Sara, 26, dental nurse)

Sara describes there is 'nothing wrong' with wanting to 'look good'; however, she understands the practices of those who exercise at the gym every day or use steroids as 'obsessive' rather than 'healthy'. Sara's exhortation that there's nothing wrong with looking good and exercising can be linked to ideological norms governing the individualised, self-reliant and responsible neo-liberal subject which reward and encourage people to be healthy through 'lifestyle choices' (Atkinson and Monaghan 2014: 19). She is also, however, critical of men in particular for 'going too far' and putting more effort into the aesthetic appearance of muscles through intensive training and use of steroids. There is tension here between the cultural idealisation of 'fit-looking bodies' and the significant work required towards this aesthetic ideal which may involve the use of synthetic hormonal drugs such as 'steroids'. However, as Atkinson and Monaghan (2014: 23) have discussed in relation to bodybuilders and postmodern images of health and fitness, 'the fit-looking (lean, muscular) body functions as a social symbol of health' and healthy existence. As Sara suggests, in this context, there is often a gap between health 'per se' and intensive activities aimed at the symbolic representation of health. Another participant, Ben, who had been lifting heavy weights almost daily for almost 10 years to maintain a 'big, muscly' appearance says: 'I could say it was for the health benefits and everything, but ... I can't really say that's the main reason for it.' Health is available as a discourse he 'could' draw upon to justify or explain his body work. The appearance of muscularity is typically linked with the image of 'healthy' masculinity, which can help to explain the continuing appeal of bodybuilding and the increasing popularity of muscle-building more generally (Atkinson and Monaghan 2014).

Clare, like Sara, also problematises and complicates 'health' and practices that are generally understood by others as 'healthy' such as eating vegetables and exercising. A key reason for this is that Clare's former best friend suffered from anorexia. Clare describes this as the central example of what can

Health, affect, embodiment 107

happen when seemingly 'healthy' practices of eating 'healthily' and exercising can be taken too far and 'become dangerous':

> One of my, um, she used to be my best friend, we're not close any more – she got anorexia this year through stress and just, very bad treatment – like, she's very fit and healthy but all she ever did was exercise. And she, she ate, all I'd ever see her eat was lettuce. And she got to the point where she was becoming too healthy and it was just becoming dangerous.
>
> (Clare, 18, school student)

Clare describes that the practices of eating 'healthy' foods such as lettuce and exercising in themselves are not essentially 'good' (healthy) and may become problematic or even 'dangerous' if they are done 'too much'. Here, 'health' as practices can be just as dangerous as 'unhealthy' practices. 'Unhealthy' practices were particularly typified in Clare and others' examples of people they knew who were 'very overweight', who 'eat a lot of junk food and don't exercise'. Echoing arguments made by Webb and Quennerstedt (2010: 791), these bodies can be understood as 'risky'. 'Risky' bodies are read as unhealthy, overweight, 'not obedient and useful', and transgressive in what Webb and Quennerstedt (2010: 791) term a 'neoliberal, performative culture of health surveillance'.

The examples in the next section explore some further complexities associated with health embodiments and exercise. Through the concept of affect I explore participants' descriptions of experiences of how body work practices such as exercise *feel*, and what this means for how their bodies are lived.

Exercise, health and the self: 'inhabiting my flesh'

Exercise was described as a particularly important aspect of body work for most participants. Almost all (20 out of 22) of the participants made specific reference to physical activities as having an impact on how their body feels, which I analyse as the embodied sensations, or affects, related to their exercise. Many echoed very similar descriptions of how exercise contributes to feeling 'good', or 'better'. In most cases, I did not ask participants about specific practices of exercise, but let participants define exercise related to their own experiences and understandings.

Most participants broadly agreed that their 'exercise' practices linked to the way their body feels. For example, Anna discusses how she used to play in team sports at college but no longer does because her circumstances have changed: she has finished her undergraduate university degree and is working full-time hours as a waitress to save money to travel overseas. She says:

> I normally feel, like, a lot better if I have been exercising, but just, like, little things if I do them now I'm like, 'phew! That was a bit of a struggle! That's a bit embarrassing!' But, um, yeah, I generally do like it when I

108　*Health, affect, embodiment*

am exercising a little bit more. Although a lot of the times I can't really be bothered but I know, you do, you do feel a little bit better if you know that you're doing something, but I have been very slack the last couple of months.

(Anna, 21, server)

Comments such as Anna's were common throughout the interviews, and many participants agreed that doing exercise equated with 'feeling good' or 'feeling better' in some way. As Anna explains, 'I think you just generally feel better for it [exercise] because you don't feel like you're lazing around and being a bit of a couch potato'. Exercise here has a moral dimension in ways similar to those described in the previous section, and enables her to feel moral satisfaction related to physical activity; though there are numerous times she 'can't really be bothered'. 'Knowing you're doing something', related to exercise specifically is also an important aspect of body work.

Similarly, Victoria explains that she really enjoys her routine of going to the gym three or so times a week. She says, 'I like going. I feel good.' In explaining this further, Victoria says her main motivations for going to the gym regularly are:

VICTORIA: To keep fit. Probably to maintain a good shape really. Yeah. And be yeah, healthy, and maintain a healthy shape.
JULIA: So it's sort of about how you outwardly look?
VICTORIA: Um … yeah mainly how I look. Yeah. And how I feel inside.

(Victoria, 23, marketing officer)

Appearance is a key motivator for Victoria's body work, and physical exercise affects how Victoria feels on the 'inside' as well. Examples from other participants suggest that this 'inside' feeling is linked with their outward appearance. In Victoria's example, she explains that she enjoys physical exercise because it enables her to 'maintain a healthy shape' and that achieving this, or at least 'doing something' about it, is what feels good on the 'inside'. As Victoria explains it, the process of exercise for appearance 'feels good', yet although this may seem straightforward and simple, this is complicated in numerous other participants' descriptions of their experiences.

As in examples from Anna, Steph and Victoria, the embodied sensations of 'exercise' practices of body work were related to 'feeling better' about themselves, or in how they look. Paul also explains what it is that makes him 'feel good' after doing yoga:

PAUL: After a yoga class I walk out feeling more limber, and yeah, you know, just healthier, generally happier, because blood and oxygen has gone to all parts of my body, my muscles are all warmed up, I'm walking straighter, I have less sore joints and whatever it is … I sleep better. It's a general psychological and physical improvement, all over.

Health, affect, embodiment 109

JULIA: Ok. So it's like feeling better on the inside ... and the outside as well?
PAUL: Er, yeah, there's a degree of that? Knowing that I'm taking care of myself, and I dunno. I guess that might partly have something, [some] insight into why healthy people look better. Definitely there's – I feel better about the way I look when I'm not putting on weight, when I'm losing weight, my body's a bit better and ... yeah. Also I've got really bad posture so when I'm healthy I stand straighter and present better and feel more confident I guess.

(Paul, 31, sound and film editor)

Paul explains the connections and associations between the kinaesthetic elements related to his body resulting from yoga, such as feeling 'limber' with 'warm muscles', and his sense of feeling 'generally happier and healthier'. Paul's body 'feels better' after yoga because the embodied sensations associated with blood oxygenating his organs and warming his muscles make him feel 'healthier' and thus 'happier'. The bodily sensations he associates with 'health' make him feel 'happy', and he also relates the feeling of health with appearance: 'healthy people look better'. Looking 'better' involves not putting on weight, or losing weight, and he feels better when he is achieving this – through doing things like yoga. Feeling 'better' is very much related to how the body looks in Paul's example, but also extends beyond this to the bodily sensations associated with the specific practices of stretching and breathing involved in yoga.

In a similar way, Kate explains what health 'feels' like. As has been discussed, for Kate, exercising and 'health' is not only related to her appearance, and is more about how she 'feels':

KATE: I don't think I feel it [health] as much as I should. I definitely should get out and do more exercise. I feel so much better when I do.
JULIA: Do you mean you feel more confident or have more energy, or something?
KATE: Both. A bit of both. Like, if I run around The Tan [the Botanical gardens in Melbourne] and come home and have a shower I'm like 'ooh I feel really good'. You've stretched out your legs and got some fresh air and got your heart rate up and everything like that. And when I eat healthy too, I guess when you're feeling inside 'I feel really healthy today' I think it shows on the outside, do you know what I mean? You've got more of a glow about you, same as if you've got a lot of rest, I make sure I get about eight hours' sleep.

(Kate, 24, administrative assistant/nanny)

When Kate describes what 'feels really good' about exercise, the feeling she describes after running is kinaesthetic, embodied. Like Paul, she mentions her organs (heart rate), legs (which have been 'stretched out') and oxygen (fresh air) in explaining what 'health' feels like. It also includes aspects such as

110 *Health, affect, embodiment*

posture and rest The numerous kinaesthetic, physical and mental connections involved in this 'feeling' mean that the way health is experienced is complex and multiple. Using a Deleuzian understanding of bodies, Fox (2002: 360) argues that the affects associated with health are 'dynamic and continually multiplying' depending on the connections and relations between bodies and the world. This perspective enables a way of understanding the contradictions and complexities of participants' descriptions and experiences of 'health'.

Health is not only confined to its embodied sensations on the 'inside', but as something that can also be visibly present. 'Looking healthy' is not enough, as Kate describes; she does not 'feel' it as much as she 'should'. Further, 'healthy' practices (such as dietary controls, jogging, yoga) which purportedly lead to the sensations of 'health' (such as increased heart rate, warm muscles, inhaling 'fresh air') 'show on the outside'. The practices of health are explained by Kate as leading to the feeling of health, which in turn lead to the appearance of health: 'you've got more of a glow about you'. While the practices, feelings and appearances of health are very closely connected, they do not always function in the straightforward way that Kate explains. For many participants, health and appearance are more complicated. For many others, the affective experiences of the body involve the connections between the 'appearance' and image, and are associated with the experience of the 'self' and identity.

Some participants explained that their experiences of body work and the embodied sensations involved relate directly to their experience of self or identity. Rose (1989: 214) has argued that the body has become central to 'transformation of the alienation, repression and fragmentation of the self in modern times'. In more recent work, Rose conceptualises the relations and connections between 'the capacities of the human subject and the practices in which he or she participates' (2000: 325) as a series of continuing modulation; part of the rhizomatic flows characteristic of liberal control societies (Deleuze 1995). In this way, practices of the body and self, such as forms of body work related to health, can be understood in the context of the particular set of circumstances in which individuals are 'obliged to be prudent and responsible for their own destinies'; to take control of their 'selves' (Rose 2000: 324).

Work on the self through body work practices was described by many participants as related to 'feeling comfortable' with their body and 'self'. To a large extent, the practices of exercise, and 'health' were explained as the means towards this:

> I want to maintain a good shape, a good body, just to feel comfortable in my self.
>
> (Clare, 18, school student)

Similarly, Kim explains 'I feel more comfortable in my skin' when she has lost weight as a result of jogging and doing yoga. Paul also terms exercise as contributing to the way he 'inhabits [his] flesh':

Health, affect, embodiment 111

PAUL: I've always gone to the gym a little bit. Mostly just to, you know, stay active and feel better ... about ... I mean partly physically, but ... partly the way I look, but also partly the way I feel about inhabiting my flesh. These days I'm doing less weights and I'll swim a couple of times a week and I've started running with my girlfriend, just started a programme with that, and riding my bike. I think just staying ... maintaining the exercise these days is as much about keeping my mindset positive as it is about ... I mean I don't like it when I'm not exercising when I'm overweight ... I do have a tendency for my weight to blow out ... quite easily ... um, and I don't, really don't like the way I look, my clothes look when I'm like that; the way I feel, etc. And I prefer it when I'm doing something about it. But I'm not after, I'm not, I don't have an image of myself in mind, I'm not going for rock-hard abs or, you know.
JULIA: It's just more of an overall sort of, um, self-care or something?
PAUL: Yeah. I just wanna feel healthy, in some sort of, within some sort of level of a solid, good fitness so that I feel happy and ... yeah.

(Paul, 32, sound editor)

Paul does not like the way he *feels* when he has put on weight. This feeling relates not only to his appearance, but the way he inhabits his 'flesh'. Involved in this process are numerous elements: physical, mental, affective, kinaesthetic sensations all contribute to his experience of the 'flesh', and what it is like to 'inhabit' his body. As Paul explains, his 'self' is constructed and experienced in the context of all of these factors, and is an ongoing process. Paul's relations to his 'self' through forms of body work take place in a context in which individuals are encouraged to take a critical investment and approach to the 'self' in its entirety, through work on the body and attention to thoughts and 'state of mind' (Rose 1996). The particular relations Paul is involved with when describing what it feels like to 'inhabit his flesh' occur in a context in which self-analysis is encouraged. This in turn is related to numerous social influences including psychology and confessional 'self-help' trends. As Dworkin and Wachs (2009: 13) note, 'the practices of seeing, telling, listening, marking, defining, judging and changing behaviours is well integrated into the fabric' of Western, neo-liberal consumer societies such as the USA and Australia. Further, as in some of the other previous examples, Paul equates feeling healthy with feeling happy. According to Paul (as well as Kate and others), 'happiness' can be achieved through body work practices in a linear, straightforward way: as Paul says, 'I just want to feel healthy, so that I feel happy'.

Exercise, health and 'happiness'

The entanglement of ideas about health, happiness and appearance as they relate to the way the body is experienced is shown in numerous other examples:

112 *Health, affect, embodiment*

> You don't have to be thin to look good, but I don't feel very healthy at the moment. When I am exercising regularly, even if my weight hasn't shifted at all, I just feel that little bit better about myself. I'm not an overly showy person, I don't think if I was skinnier, I'd get my legs out more, it's just … I don't know. You'd just have a little bit more confidence about yourself. It's not … I wouldn't get fit so that I could show off my body, I'd get fit so that I could be happy. I don't know, just if anyone did see it I wouldn't be worried about it. I don't know, I'm not a big fan of, I don't even think I've been to the beach these holidays, I get really nervous when I have to get down to a bikini and stuff. Um … yeah, just, it'd be just one less thing to worry about I guess. If you're just a little bit skinnier or a little bit whatever it's just one less thing to worry about. I don't know.
>
> (Steph, 21, waitress)

Exercising regularly with the goal of being 'a little bit skinnier' as Steph explains would mean she has 'one less thing to worry about' and enable her to 'feel that little bit better' about herself. Again, exercise, appearance (in looking 'skinnier') and the experience of the body relates to the self and connect to gendered patterns of embodiment related to slenderness, as the previous chapter discussed. Further, the connection between body work and 'happiness' is demonstrated: 'I wouldn't get fit so that I could show off my body, I'd get fit so that I could be happy'. There are affects and connections involved in Steph's idea of 'happiness' centring around the body as it is felt, and as it is seen by others, such as at the beach – which is a space of particularly intensive bodily display in Australian 'beach cultures' (Booth 2012). It is interesting that Steph makes a specific point that she would not display her body more if she lost weight (through wearing revealing clothing) or 'show it off'. For Steph, her priority is that 'if anyone did see' her body, she would not have to 'worry about it'. Although the body's public visibility in the context of consumer culture has been explained by some theorists as paramount (Featherstone 2010), in Steph's example, visibility is not the most important aspect of her body work. More complexly, Steph imagines that exercise has the potential to form a new and improved experience of the self in which would be 'happier', through being 'skinnier'.

Anna echoes Steph's words, and explains that exercise is the solution to feeling 'self-conscious' about her body, and a way of having 'one less thing to worry about':

> I think, you know, you have a tighter, toner, slightly slenderer body you can feel more confident, because sometimes you can feel a bit, self-conscious, like 'oh', the old cliché, 'does my butt look big in this', or 'is my stomach, does my stomach look huge in this' … I guess if you're in tip-top shape then I guess it's just one less thing that you have to worry about.
>
> (Anna, 21, waitress)

Health, affect, embodiment 113

Steph and Anna describe that monitoring of the body ('does my stomach look huge in this') and feeling 'self-conscious' only happens when they are not exercising. They both envisage 'very fit people' as 'happy' who do not suffer from insecurity about their bodies, and who do not need to monitor or 'worry about' their bodies any more. However, as other participants who exercise more intensely explain, their exercise practices do not cause them to worry less about their bodies, and may even form an ongoing series of relations between body work and the self that may limit possibilities for living the body in other ways.

As the previous section suggested, this link between healthy practices and the experience of health and its psychologised associations with happiness are not assured. The following section expands on this using a case study example of one participant, Gillian, drawing together analysis of the body's affects related to health assemblages as shaping 'what it can do'.

What can a body do? Body work as 'liberation' and constraint

Gillian, 31, works as a make-up artist and server at a busy café in Melbourne. Gillian's physical body work practices involve running, doing yoga and carefully controlling her diet. She runs 10 km two or three times a week, does one yoga class a week, and her job as a server at a restaurant is also 'very active'. She explains that these practices enable her to 'feel better' about her 'self'. Gillian explains that not eating at the end of a long shift at work 'makes a massive difference' to not gaining weight, despite often being 'exceptionally hungry':

> I'll often do a six-, seven-, eight-hour shift with no breaks and it's very active, high-stress work, and I'll get to eat beforehand a little bit and often there'll be food left over at the end of the night that I can eat. So, um … when I'm trying to eat healthier I don't eat the food at the end of the night, because I find that makes a massive difference to me. When I eat that food I put on weight, when I don't I actually take off weight … I don't – in theory I don't believe in denying myself, but … it's just, I dunno.
> (Gillian, 31, make-up artist)

Although 'in theory' Gillian does not believe in 'denying' herself food (even if she is 'exceptionally hungry'), maintaining her desired weight is the most important factor: 'it makes a massive difference to me'.

In ways paradoxically similar to those which Anna and Steph imagine, Gillian explains that exercise, through jogging and yoga provide a way of 'liberating' her self and body from 'feeling bad' – feeling physically unattractive, and inadequate:

> I've gotta make the best out of what I've got, and so I think when I'm doing yoga or jogging, it's my way of liberating myself, instead of feeling

114   *Health, affect, embodiment*

> sad about myself because ... I feel attractive if I'm in a fit state, or if I'm taking good care of my body, healthy, um ... in shape, I feel like, then I don't think 'oh why can't I be like this, why can't I be like that?' I guess that's my way of liberating myself from that constant battle in my head, where you feel bad about yourself. Because as long as I'm fit and at a healthy weight, a decent weight ... I don't feel that.

Although these practices make Gillian feel 'better' and more accepting of her body, her feeling 'better' is contingent on these practices. She must uphold her 'fitness' (or must avoid eating at the end of a shift) in order to be 'liberated' from feeling 'bad'. Gillian's body work, which requires so much effort, thought and time, operates as a great constraint, yet she describes these practices as enabling her to feel 'liberated'. Her example also speaks to the 'schizoid' conditions of post-feminism in which repressive gender norms are recoded through a language of empowerment (Renold and Ringrose 2011).Through this paradox, Gillian's body work practices are clearly central to her positive experience of self. Being in a 'fit state' enables her to negate this feeling of inadequacy and 'unattractiveness', to 'make the most' of her body as it is, she explains, rather than resorting to cosmetic surgical procedures, as she says. The relations and affects between Gillian's body, body work practice and the world define what she can do, and the possibilities that are available to her. While these practices make her 'feel better', the affects related to these body work practices are limited. Where body work practices such as these are framed as her only way of freeing herself from 'feeling bad', other possibilities for experiencing and living her body are not immediately available. The concept of affect works such that 'what bodies can feel is an element of what they can do' (Fox 2015). Gillian, like many other participants, is affected by the 'call upon the individual to enter into the process of their own self-governance through processes of endless self-examination, self-care, and self-improvement' (Peterson 1996: 49). 'Healthy' body work practices are a key means by which the burden of care of the self is embodied and is guided by health affects. Paul, Steph and Anna imagine that doing body work to be 'fitter' will make them 'happier'. Gillian, however, shows that this process is fraught. The embodied experiences related to the discourses, ideals and sensations of 'health' can be understood as a complex process involving the affects and relations between bodies and other assemblages as having an impact on how they feel and what they can do. The significant work involved in Gillian's maintenance of a narrowly defined 'ideal' appearance (linked strongly to femininity and health) that enables her to 'feel good' about her body at the same time perpetuates her body work and closes down possibilities for living her body in other less regulated ways.

Physically hegemonic gender ideals clearly frame body work and bodies, and contribute to the affects which influence the body's possibilities (Coffey 2013). Because, for example, gendered ideals of women's and men's bodies are

Health, affect, embodiment 115

narrow, their possibilities for their bodies and body work are restricted (Coffey 2012).

Health affects and health as becoming

The concept of affect, understood practically as 'something which affects something else' and as 'the experience of intensities' (Featherstone 2010: 195) can be used as a way to think through Gillian's comments here. In this context, Gillian's body work practices, including a strict regulation of what she eats after work, doing yoga and jogging affect her body and what she can (or cannot) do. While these practices make her 'feel better', the affects related to these body work practices are limited. Where body work practices such as these are framed as her only way of freeing herself from 'feeling bad', other possibilities for experiencing and living her body are removed. Affects can be understood as producing 'styles of life', or ways of living. Hickey-Moody and Malins (2007: 3) explain that:

> Styles of life and modes of evaluation that are shaped by resentment, judgment and negation tend to reduce and close off bodily possibilities and potentials for change. By contrast, those which affirm life and its positive capacity for difference, enhance our range of powers and potentials.

Gillian's body work practices are described as integral to her being able to feel good in her body and self, and Gillian explains that feeling good about herself without these practices is unimaginable. The affects associated with Gillian's body work mean that her 'style of life' is shaped by negation, and reduces her potential to live her body in other ways. That Gillian may feel comfortable or content with her body and in herself without undertaking those practices of body work is a potentiality that is not currently available to Gillian. In this way, the embodied sensations surrounding body work which affect her body constrain her and limit the range of possibilities available for living her body. Fox (2002, Fox and Ward 2008) uses Deleuze and Guattari's concept of the body without organs to further describe this process and can help to explain how affect may be useful in approaching Gillian's experience of her body and body work practices. Deleuze and Guattari (1987) understand humans and other bodies as actively connecting and engaging with the world through ongoing 'experimentation', and the body without organs is the concept which describes the locus of these encounters. Social and cultural assemblages (such as gender, in Chapter 4, and health ideologies in this chapter) affect the body. The affects and relations of a body include the psychological, emotional and physical attachments produced in encounters between the body without organs and other assemblages. This process conditions what the body can do. Assemblages, through relations and affects, 'define a person's capacities and his/her limits' (Fox and Ward 2008: 1009).

116   *Health, affect, embodiment*

Becoming involves the 'opening up to difference, to the many rather than the few' (Fox 2002: 359); the opening of possibility. This occurs through the 'multiplication of affects, not the intensification of a single affect or relation' (Fox 2002: 359). A body without organs which is involved in this intensification, rather than a multiplication of affects suffers a 'territorialisation that cannot easily be escaped' (Fox 2002: 359). Where Gillian's ways of 'liberating' herself from 'feeling bad' require the ongoing practices of body work, we can begin to see how Gillian's body (as a body without organs) is involved in particular affective relations with health and gender assemblages (of the slim, feminine body), which close down other possibilities for living her body. This does not mean, however, that Gillian's body is incapable of 'becoming-other'; through multiplying the affects and relations between her body, body work and connecting assemblages, Gillian may find numerous other ways living beyond the imperative of body work practices.

The relations and affects surrounding body work practices and health and gender discourses are multiple and complex. Seeing these practices and examples through the lens of affect allows an analysis which foregrounds the embodied, sensual aspects of the body while linking body work practices to broader socio-cultural contexts. The concept of affect also provides a way of understanding the ways these contexts condition but do not determine possibilities for living. The affective experience of the body, involving the connections between the 'appearance' and feelings of 'health', impacts how bodies and selves 'feel' and what they can do.

What this perspective offers is an understanding of body work practices as not intrinsically good or bad; rather it depends on whether life is restricted or maximised through the relations between the body and its myriad encounters. Because 'what a body can do' is continually being negotiated through relations with new things, affects continually have the potential to be 'redrawn' (Fox 2002). The potential to 'become otherwise' as relations and affects modulate is always possible. Even when becoming-other is inhibited by the intensification, rather than the multiplication of affects, this inhibition is never foreclosed from the outset but may develop through the particular processes of new and unforseen relations and affects.

The concept of affect can contribute to developing sociological study of the body. To pursue methods which encourage an increase in the possibilities available for living has political implications related to inclusivity and equality (Fox 2002). Advocating positive 'styles of life', 'those which affirm life and its positive capacity for difference' (Hickey-Moody and Malins, 2007), may enhance not only our own range of powers and potentials, but may also affect others in our relations with them, for example, through affirming difference between bodies (Coffey 2012). For Gillian, for example, an opening to difference could mean expanding her focus from the aesthetic to the emotional or kinaesthetic dimensions through forms of body work which are not geared towards the body's appearance, such as some forms of yoga, tai chi or meditation. Opening to difference could also be facilitated by a focus on the body's

Health, affect, embodiment   117

non-deliberate changes, such as ageing, or pregnancy or menopause; changes which are not effected by deliberate or intentional 'body work'. The strength with which health discourses and body work practices are currently promoted, and associated affective intensifies related to the health imperative however, could make this a difficult task.

Previous sociological work has explored the aesthetic, cultural and bodily dimensions of judgement related to health practices (Lupton 1995, 1999). Lupton, for example, specifies that non-conformance to health imperatives may be both consciously and unconsciously chosen, with alternative practices of the self being generated at the non-discursive level (1995: 135). While such approaches to not draw specifically on the concept of affect, the need to go beyond rationalist understandings of subjectivity and reflexivity to understand bodily aspects of action has been well established (Lupton 1999). Approaches to 'the body' which draw on Deleuzian ontologies or concepts to analyse empirical data are relatively recent within sociology (see for example, Fox and Ward 2008). This analysis contributes to emerging efforts to draw on Deleuzian methodologies and concepts such as affect. The challenge of pairing Deleuzian epistemology and ontology with post-structural methodologies is being engaged with in the work of St Pierre (1997), Lather (2007), Hultman and Taguchi (2010), Mazzei and McCoy (2010) and others in qualitative education and sociological research. Further work will advance these concepts and questions in sociological and feminist work so that new ways of responding to contemporary challenges of exploring the body and embodied experience can be found, particularly as the body continues to increase as a target for economic forces through the marketing of health.

Conclusion

This chapter has described the complex ways 'health' is conceptualised and embodied in relation to social life. Health was described in interviews as a set of practices, activities or performances that involve the body and that has social dimensions. The health assemblage comprises regulatory discourses of health, such as those relating to moralised individual responsibility for having a healthy-looking body and discriminatory attitudes towards people who are not able to live up to this classed, raced 'slim' bodily form. It also comprises images of healthy bodies and happy people which proliferate in consumer culture, and the juggernaut industries which sell these images and discourses through products and services. Health is also profoundly embodied, and affective, which means that the ways that health assembles in relation to these other dimensions for each person may be different. The examples in this chapter have aimed to show both the strength of those discourses of health, but also to go beyond these in analysis to also include analysis of the more complex and paradoxical elements in young people's health embodiments. These examples showed that experience of 'health' is not the straightforward result of undertaking 'healthy' practices, and these practices require further

118 *Health, affect, embodiment*

management. They also illustrate that though the ideal of health as an image and a way of obtaining happiness was a key dimension informing participants' body work, these links in actuality were shown to be profoundly tenuous or problematic, as Gillian's example illustrated. The chapter mobilised concepts of affect and becoming to explore the complex and contradictory ways health is understood and lived. This perspective shows that the ways in which health and gender assemble in the context of body work practices condition the body's possibilities. As I have shown in this chapter, the possibilities for living that are available can be understood as organised through the processes engagement between bodies and other assemblages. I used the concept of affect as a way of focusing on a body's encounters and what these encounters produce to explore the health affects which compose health assemblages, and how these affect what a body can do.

References

Atkinson, M. and Monaghan, L. F. (2014). *Challenging Myths of Masculinity: Understanding Physical Cultures.* Aldershot: Ashgate.

Bartky, S. (1990). Femininity and Domination: Studies in the Phenomenology of Oppression. New York: Routledge.

Becker, M. H. (1993). A Medical Sociology Looks at Health Promotion. *Journal of Health and Social Behaviour,* 34(1), 1–6.

Booth, D. (2012). *Australian Beach Cultures: The History of Sun, Sand and Surf.* New York: Routledge.

Bordo, S. (2003). *Unbearable Weight: Feminism, Western Culture and the Body* (10th anniversary edn). California: University of California Press.

Bourdieu, P. (1977). *Outline of a Theory of Practice* (R. Nice, trans.). Cambridge: Cambridge: Cambridge University Press.

Coffey, J. (2012). Bodies, health and gender: exploring body work practices with Deleuze*Research Report 34.* University of Melbourne: Youth Research Centre.

Coffey, J. (2013). 'Body Pressure': Negotiating Gender through Body Work Practices. *Youth Studies Australia,* 32(2), 39–48.

Coffey, J. (2014). 'As Long as I'm Fit and a Healthy Weight, I Don't Feel Bad': Exploring Body Work and Health through the Concept of 'Affect'. *Journal of Sociology.* doi: 10.1177/1440783313518249

Coffey, J. (forthcoming). 'She Was Becoming Too Healthy and It Was Just Becoming Dangerous': Body Work and Assemblages of Health. In J. Coffey, S. Budgeon and H. Cahill (eds), *Learning Bodies: The Body in Youth and Childhood Studies.* New York: Springer.

Coleman, R. (2009). *The Becoming of Bodies: Girls, Images, Experience.* Manchester and New York: Manchester University Press.

Connell, R. (1987). *Gender and Power: Society, the Person and Personal Politics.* Cambridge: Polity.

Crawford, R. (1980). Healthism and the Medicalisation of Everyday Life. *International Journal of Health Services,* 10(3), 365–388.

Crawford, R. (1987). Cultural Influences on Prevention and the Emergence of a New Health Consciousness. In N. Weinstein (ed.), *Taking Care: Understanding and*

Encouraging Self-protective Behavior (pp. 95–114). Cambridge and New York: Cambridge University Press.

Crawford, R. (2006). Health as a Meaningful Social Practice. *Health*, 10(4), 401–420. doi: 10.1177/1363459306067310

Crossley, N. (2006). *Reflexive Embodiment in Contemporary Society.* Berkshire: Open University Press.

Deleuze, G. (1988). *Spinoza: Practical Philosophy* (R. Hurley, trans.). San Francisco, CA: City Lights Books.

Deleuze, G. (1992). Ethology: Spinoza and Us. In J. Crary and S. Kwinter (eds), *Incorporations.* New York: Zone.

Deleuze, G. (1995). *Negotiations, 1972–1990* (M. Joughin, trans.). New York: Colombia University Press.

Deleuze, G. and Guattari, F. (1987). *A Thousand Plateaus: Capitalism and Schizophrenia* (B. Massumi, trans.). Edinburgh: Edinburgh University Press.

Duff, C. (2014). *Assemblages of Health.* New York: Springer.

Dworkin, S. and Wachs, F. (2009). *Body Panic: Gender, Health and the Selling of Fitness.* New York and London: University of New York Press.

Featherstone, M. (1982). The Body in Consumer Culture. *Theory, Culture and Society, 1*, 18–33.

Featherstone, M. (2010). Body, Image and Affect in Consumer Culture. *Body and Society*, 16(1), 193–221.

Fox, N. J. (2002b). What a 'Risky' Body Can Do: Why People's Health Choices Are Not All Based in Evidence. *Health Education Journal*, 61(2), 166–79. doi: 10.1177/001789690206100207

Fox, N. J. (2015). Emotions, Affects and the Production of Social Life. *British Journal of Sociology.*

Fox, N. J. and Ward, K. J. (2008). What Are Health Identities and How May We Study Them? *Sociology of Health and Illness*, 30(7), 1007–21.

Gimlin, D. (2002). *Body Work: Beauty and Self Image in American Culture.* Los Angeles: University of California Press.

Goodchild, P. (1997). Deleuzean Ethics. *Theory, Culture and Society*, 14(2), 39–50. doi: 10.1177/026327697014002005

Grimshaw, J. (1999). Working out with Merleau-Ponty. In J. Arthurs and J. Grimshaw (eds), *Women's Bodies: Discipline and Transgression.* London and New York: Cassell.

Hickey-Moody, A. and Malins, P. (eds) (2007). *Deleuzian Encounters: Studies in Contemporary Social Issues.* New York: Palgrave Macmillan.

Holmes, C. (2014). Health messaging through social media. Paper presented at the *142nd APHA Annual Meeting and Exposition* (November 15–19 November 2014).

Hultman, K. and Lenz Taguchi, H. (2010). Challenging Anthropocentric Analysis of Visual Data: A Relational Materialist Methodological Approach to Educational Research. *International Journal of Qualitative Studies in Education*, 23(5), 525–542. doi: 10.1080/09518398.2010.500628

Lather, P. (2007). *Getting Lost: Feminist Efforts toward a Double(D) Science.* Albany, NY: State University of New York Press.

Leve, M., Rubin, L. and Pusic, A. (2012). Cosmetic Surgery and Neoliberalisms: Managing Risk and Responsibility . *Feminism and Psychology*, 22(1), 122–141. doi: 10.1177/0959353511424361

Lupton, D. (1995). *The Imperative of Health: Public Health and the Regulated Body.* London: Sage.

120 Health, affect, embodiment

Lupton, D. (1996). *Food, the Body and the Self.* Thousand Oaks, CA: Sage.

Lupton, D. (1999). *Risk.* London: Routledge.

Lupton, D. (2013). *Fat.* London: Routledge.

Mazzei, L. A. and McCoy, K. (2011). Thinking with Deleuze in Qualitative Research. *International Journal of Qualitative Studies in Education, 23(5)*, 503–9. doi: 10.1080/09518398.2010.500634

Mears, A. (2014). Aesthetic Labor for the Sociologies of Work, Gender, and Beauty. *Sociology Compass*, 8(12), 1330–1343.

Merceica, D. and Merceica, D. (2010). Opening research to Intensities: Rethinking Disability Research with Deleuze and Guattari. *Journal of Philosophy of Education, 44(1)*, 80–92.

Moore, S. (2010). Is the Healthy Body Gendered? Toward a Feminist Critique of the New Paradigm of Health. *Body and Society*, 16(2), 95–118.

Perloff, R. M. (2014). Social Media Effects on Young Women's Body Image Concerns: Theoretical Perspectives and an Agenda for Research. *Sex Roles*, 71(11–12), 363–377.

Peterson, A. (1996). Risk and the Regulated Self: The Discourse of Health Promotion as Politics of Uncertainty. *Journal of Sociology*, 32(1), 44–57.

Reade, J. (2014). The female body on Instagram: is fit the new it? (BA, thesis), University of Melbourne, Melbourne.

Renold, E. and Ringrose, J. (2011). Schizoid subjectivities? Re-theorizing teen girls' sexual cultures in an era of 'sexualization'. *Journal of Sociology*, 47(4), 389–409.

Rose, N. (1989). *Governing the Soul: the Shaping of the Private Self.* London and New York: Routledge.

Rose, N. (1996). *Inventing Our Selves: Psychology, Power and Personhood.* Cambridge: Cambridge University Press.

Rose, N. (2000). Government and Control. *British Journal of Criminology*, 40(2), 321–339. doi: 10.1093/bjc/40.2.321

St Pierre, E. A. (1997). Methodology in the Fold and the Irruption of Transgressive Data. *International Journal of Qualitative Studies in Education, 10(2)*, 175–89.

Shilling, C. (2003). *The Body and Social Theory* (2nd edn). London: Sage.

Shilling, C. (2007). Sociology and the Body: Classical Traditions and New Agendas. *Sociological Review Monograph*, 55(1), 1–18.

Tiidenberg, K. and Gómez Cruz, E. (2015). Selfies, Image and the Re-making of the Body. *Body and Society.* doi: 10.1177/1357034x15592465

Webb, L. and Quennerstedt, M. (2010). Risky Bodies: Health Surveillance and Teachers' Embodiment of Health. *International Journal of Qualitative Studies in Education*, 23(7), 785–802. doi: 10.1080/09518398.2010.529471

6 'Buff culture', cosmetic surgery and bodily limits

Introduction

This chapter further explores the ways that two key assemblages, health and gender, through body work practices, produce a body's possibilities. I extend the previous chapter's focus on health and exercise to include other body work practices that are described by participants as related to 'obsession' or 'addiction'; practices such as intensive weights training and cosmetic surgical procedures. I continue to draw upon Deleuzian concepts such as affect in analysis to explore the ways bodily possibilities are assembled in relation to practices, discourses, experiences and embodied sensations.

One of my central aims here is to explore how affect is implicated in the ways body work practices are lived, and connect with broader social assemblages and discourses. Such a focus involves examining the processes and relations between bodies and assemblages. As I have shown in previous chapters, discourses of gender and health, along with an emphasis on individual responsibility and other neo-liberal ideas are strongly implicated in participants' understandings and explanations of their experiences related to their bodies. Traditional gender arrangements and the contemporary emphasis on individual body practices aligned with 'health' were engaged with by participants to frame their experiences of their bodies. Bodies are understood as the unstable outcomes of the assemblages within which they are caught up (Rose 1996: 184). Following this, I understand gender and health as assemblages that shape and create the 'conditions of possibility for identity, establishing the psychic substrate that both defines a person's capacities and his/her limits' (Fox and Ward 2008: 1009).

Body work and the limits of 'health'

As I explored in the previous chapter, the ways participants define and describe their experiences of 'health' show that health as a concept is profoundly contingent and complex. For some, specific practices of body work become essential to the (positive) experience of the self, wherein the body cannot be experienced positively without these practices. In Gillian's example

122 'Buff culture', cosmetic surgery, bodily limits

in the previous chapter, her practices of body work were organised around her body looking healthy and being a 'healthy shape' and weight, enabling her to 'feel attractive'. For Gillian, ceasing body work (due to injury or life changes) may have profound repercussions for the way her body is experienced and lived. Other participants describe the ways they undertake some forms of body work as being like an 'obsession' or 'addiction'.

Others discussed the potential for body work practices to become an 'obsession' or 'addiction', as Sara and Daniel described in the previous chapter. Sara described how the intensity and frequency regarding exercise routines delineate between the activities being 'healthy' or 'obsessive'.

Others, such as Daniel, Clare and Anna link health and appearance, arguing that 'people should just be healthy', yet since 'health' is highly contingent and complex, such statements are ambiguous. The multiple understandings and definitions of health mean that 'health' is not confined to any set of practices, nor simply a state of 'being' to be worked towards or attained. While most participants pinpoint particular 'limits' of what is or is not considered a 'healthy' practice or activity, as we have seen, the boundaries of health are shifting and understood differently by different participants in the contexts of the relations between theirs and others' bodies. Many used others' bodies to define these limits, such as overweight acquaintances (a girl Clare knew at school, or Tom's housemate), steroid users (men Sara knows through her partner, or men Ben sees at the gym), women who do not eat enough (Clare's friend at school who suffered from anorexia, or Paul's criticism of idealised women's bodies in the media) or people who over-exercise (in Adam's description of the women he sees running endlessly on the treadmill at the gym). 'Caring too much' about appearance or body work may also be defined as unhealthy.

Tom explains how exercise for him is similar to an 'addiction', because the consequences of not 'keeping it up' regularly translate into 'feeling shit':

TOM: I don't know exactly what it is about it, and I suppose you could talk about hormones that get excreted with exercise, but it is addictive. You get addicted to exercise. People do. If I'm really thinking about, if I'll say 'I'll do some exercise today', that's because I'll feel really shit if I didn't. Not feel shit, as in, I'll be happily sitting on the couch and doing nothing, but just mentally, I'd be disappointed with myself. So that's where the motivation starts to come from.

JULIA: Did you feel that today?

TOM: Yeah! That's why I need to go and do some [exercise] later [today] I think! I'll do something. You do, you get a bit addicted to it. And I've gone through phases where you get really into it and you get through that barrier, and your body starts to crave to do something.

Although the word 'addiction' typically has negative connotations and would not commonly be associated with health, Tom (and others) describe

'Buff culture', cosmetic surgery, bodily limits   123

how they feel addicted to exercising, a practice which is defined as 'healthy'. As a result Tom's 'bad feeling' about not doing exercise is complex. He says he will be 'happily' relaxing on the couch, but 'mentally' his compulsion to exercise motivates him to avoid feeling 'disappointed' with himself. The affects associated with exercise compel Tom to continue the particular practices of body work. Here, we can understand that Tom is engaged in a particular set of affective relations with his body work practices and sense of self. If he does not exercise for one day he will 'feel really disappointed' with himself. Through the concept of affect, I will further explore similar embodied sensations of other participants' practices of body work relating to 'addiction', including some of the most complex and confounding forms such as cosmetic surgery and eating disorders.

'Buff culture': muscularity, body work and addiction

As discussed in Chapter 4, many young men are increasingly picking up the invitation to care about the body's appearance and to consume products to aid in the body's aesthetic improvement. This situation is framed by the growing emphasis on individual responsibility for health which is understood in sociology as a central feature driving the rise in concern for the body's appearance in general (Crawford 1980; Gill *et al.* 2005). The configurations of consumer culture and spectacular forms of femininity and masculinity are important because they are implicated in the mediating forces which work to form the body as an event (Budgeon 2003). It is in this context of increasing attention and 'visibility' of the (young, athletic, muscular) male body that body work is experienced by some of the men in this project. The specific aesthetic ideal of muscles related to masculinity in what has been termed in popular media 'buff culture' are discussed first in the example of 'Zyzz', a 22-year-old Australian bodybuilder and internet celebrity famous for his lean, 'cut', muscular physique and party lifestyle who died in 2011.

> Zyzz was the leader of what he called 'The Aesthetic Crew'. He had a body that had been sculpted in the gym; his online self-promotion compared him with Zeus, king of the Greek gods; although it was his personal story that struck a chord with young followers. At the time of his death, Zyzz was 22 years old and a far cry from the skinny teenager of a few years earlier, unable to attract girls and stand up for himself. His rapid transformation was the stuff of fantasy for thousands of skinny teenagers, and it made him a pin-up boy.[1]

Zyzz was the exemplar of 'buff culture' masculinity. He epitomised a youthful, hedonistic lifestyle which revolved around the gym, attending 'every rave and festival' and 'pulling chicks'. Bodily display and an extremely lean, muscular aesthetic was a crucial aspect of Zyzz's popularity; he attended most

124 'Buff culture', cosmetic surgery, bodily limits

music events shirtless and also worked as a stripper. Heterosexual dynamics of attractiveness were also key, as a legion of young men idolised him for the ability to attract women afforded by his body. Though he always insisted his 'aesthetic' was the result of hard work in the gym and a strict diet, speculation of steroid use surrounded his death in a Thai bathhouse, which the coroner found was the result of an undiagnosed heart condition.

Muscles are 'the distinctive symbol of masculinity', and offer a way of affirming or ensuring recognition of possessing a normative masculine identity (Wacquant 1995: 171). Wiegers describes how the current idealisation of muscles is drawn from 'muscular Christian ideology', which originated in the nineteenth-century 'strong-man era' in which bodybuilding began (1998: 149). Bodybuilding was less fashionable in the 1950s and 1960s, and Wiegers (1998) suggests that this is due to the general sense of optimism in the American medical system at this time related to medical advances such as the control of disease through vaccinations. Although it was still considered 'common sense' to be responsible for protecting one's health during this time, the current intensity of concern with health and longevity is vastly different (Wiegers 1998). Bodybuilding and the idealisation of muscularity related to masculine ideals of strength, physical capacity and reappeared in the 1970s when the health and fitness industry was emerging. The masculine aesthetic ideal gained huge popularity in the 1990s as 'the media was focusing on the phenomenon of muscle more than ever before' (Wiegers 1998: 150). The focus on muscularity as aesthetic ideal in contemporary Western societies has intensified as a result of parallel shifts in consumer culture which offers an increasing range of regimes and technologies to 'invest' in creating a 'beautiful body' (Featherstone 2010). The moral logic implied in consumer culture dovetails with health and gender ideals such that the drive towards beautification (for men as well as women) is more an imperative than merely an available option.

> Indeed the consumer culture publicity presents [body work] as an imperative, a duty, and casts those who become fat, or let their appearance go, or look old before their time, as not only slothful but as having a flawed self. On the other hand, it is assumed that people with an enhanced appearance will be able to enjoy a body and face which are more congruent with their 'true' selves. Body work will also transform the self, upgrading it to a newer level replete with positive possibilities, in line with the new body.
>
> (Featherstone 2010: 195–6)

Muscles feature as a key bodily ideal for participants in this study. All male participants named muscles are 'ideal' features for men's bodies, mostly related to sexual attractiveness (heterosexual and homosexual) and because muscles were seen to denote 'health' for men. The following quotes from male participants relate to the 'pressure' to be 'big' or muscular, as some men in the study described.

'Buff culture', cosmetic surgery, bodily limits 125

Ben, a former professional baseball player, describes how he 'can't get out of the habit' of doing the training he did when he was a professional; that he 'can't bring' himself to not go to the gym for more than two days:

> It's funny, I can't really get out of the habit of still doing a lot of training. I don't get to do as much specific baseball stuff. But I can't bring myself to go for more than two days without going to the gym. I've sort of built up a reputation for being, like a big strong guy, and even if I get on the scales and weigh myself and I'll still be the same weight, I feel like if I don't go for a few days I feel not as strong, not as confident. I have to keep going and doing it. [I feel] a lot of pressure on that. I'm 32 and I wonder how long I can keep that up for.
>
> (Ben, 32, sales representative)

Ben's lifting weights is something he 'has to keep going and doing'; he 'has to keep it up'. This description is very similar to Tom's previous description of 'addiction' related to exercise and to the dictionary definition of addiction, as the 'state [of] being enslaved to something … that is habit forming … to such an extent that its cessation causes severe trauma'.[2] Ben's body work practices contribute directly to his identity and sense of self, and how others see him ('as a big strong guy'). He worries he may not be able to continue in this identity for much longer. Body work, for Ben, has significant repercussions that extend beyond discourses of health and masculinity, though both of these discourses are implicated in the meanings of his body work. Body work practices to do with exercise and lifting weights go towards shaping both the physical body and (hegemonically masculine) sense of self. As a result, body work practices are powerful in how the body is experienced and felt. This also means that if the practices of body work are not 'kept up' for whatever reason – through circumstances associated with injury, age, or other life changes such as increased work or family commitments – the embodied consequences and impact on sense of self may be profound.

In a similar way, Adam discusses the tension involved in deciding to not continue training during the off-season of football. Although he 'really enjoyed' being free from his demanding training regime, discontinuing his body work had unforseen consequences for his sense of self and identity:

> Actually last year between seasons and before training started I was like, 'Oh, I'm really enjoying not training', and I let myself go for awhile, and letting myself go was actually putting on about 4 kilos and it wasn't anything to do with muscle weight, it was just me enjoying life and not having to do that vigorous routine, of all those sessions, and actually it made me feel pretty crap. People were still saying to me 'oh you look fit' but I felt actually very unfit and felt like I was putting on weight and none of it's muscle and I'm not actually keeping myself fit, and so after about a month and a half of not doing much at all – I enjoyed it, not

126 *'Buff culture', cosmetic surgery, bodily limits*

doing much – but I also felt pretty terrible at the same time, I could feel myself slipping, down into the, 'Oh I'm unfit, I don't feel good about myself, I'm losing that body image that I worked so hard for', and even after a month and a half, nothing too much had happened, but I felt like I was losing control ... of who I was, almost.

(Adam, 23, footballer and university student)

Despite others telling him he looks 'fit', and as well as 'really enjoying' not training, the visceral experience of his body changed dramatically. Adam describes how soon after he stopped training he began to feel very unfit, and felt anxious about gaining weight that is not muscle weight. For Adam, feeling unfit very quickly equated to feeling 'pretty terrible'. Adam's sense of self is so entwined with his body being fit and muscular that stopping training for only a few weeks made him feel as though his identity and positive sense of himself was slipping, and that he was losing who he was. Adam's and Ben's relations with body work practices are intensely affective. A focus on their affective experiences enables the visceral, embodied complexities of their bodies to be foregrounded. These examples, from the perspective of affect enable us to see the infinitely more complex ways bodies (body without organs) are defined by their relations and affects, opening up or closing down possibilities for the embodied self (Fox 2002: 351).

Other men in the study also experience their bodies and body work having a significant impact for how the self and body are lived. Jason explains the way he goes about his football training as an 'addiction' that compels him to 'keep it up', and that there are numerous affective consequences involved if he cannot train. Recent injuries (including extensive leg injuries from a severe boating accident, and a shoulder reconstruction due to a subsequent mishap) have meant he has spent lengthy periods of time in rehabilitation, unable to train with weights or to run. The consequences of this extend beyond the pain of the injuries themselves, and have an impact on how he feels about his body and his sense of self on a deeper level. It is only in weeks directly prior to the interview that Jason has been able to resume training. He describes his exercise regime as relating to how he feels about and within his body:

I probably do some sort of exercise, five or six times a week. Sometimes even twice a day. It's a bit over the top, I know, I dunno. But ... you get an addiction I think? Um, and as soon as you start to fall behind, or you start to stop going you start to look at yourself differently like you go 'Oh, what's going on here' [examining body, stomach], like a little bit [laughs]. So, yeah. You get a bit addicted to it. I don't know if that's a good thing, but ... oh well ... there are addictions in life I s'pose ... it's probably one of the better ones to have! [laughs] ... Yeah, you kind of look at yourself a little bit different, like, you go, 'oh hang on, I've stopped, I haven't done this for a little while' and you start maybe noticing a little bit, but it's not actually changing, you're just, you trick, you're

'Buff culture', cosmetic surgery, bodily limits 127

playing tricks on your mind to say 'yep, it's changed'. You look in the mirror and go 'Oh, look at that', but really nothing has [changed]. You can't change from [missing] two sessions, or two weeks even. Um, that's probably the addiction part of it [laughs]. And I dunno, you feel like ... you just feel a little bit different.

(Jason, 22, accounts officer)

The relations between Jason's body and the practices of body work (football training, weights and cardio-vascular sessions) involve 'addiction' because, as he describes, 'as soon as you stop going and doing it, you start to look at yourself differently'. Although Jason jokes that compared to other 'addictions' his training is 'probably one of the better ones to have', the affects associated with his body if he has to stop training are significant and intensive. Through his affective relations between his body and training, Jason perceives his body as being 'a little bit different', despite that nothing in his appearance has 'really changed'. Jason, like Adam, perceives himself differently, and sees his body in a way that is not realistic: 'you look in the mirror and go "Oh look at that" [gesturing to his biceps, implying they are smaller in size] but really nothing has changed'. Adam too said he saw himself differently in the mirror and feels differently about himself, and like Jason had the similar experience of his image 'playing tricks' on him.

Featherstone (2010: 197) argues that in consumer culture, which is obsessed with bodies, 'images do complex work', and extend beyond the 'look good, feel good' advertising tagline which invites individuals to care for their appearances and corresponding experience of self. Featherstone insists that images are not merely visual, and are felt as a sense of energy, force or intensity: they are affective (2010: 199). The affective body (such as Jason's or Adam's) in contrast to body image, 'is a body without a clearly defined image'. This means that the affective body is more processual, and 'can convey and receive a range of affective responses, intensities which are palpable, but difficult to decipher and articulate in language' (Featherstone 2010: 201).

Jason's description of his image in the mirror 'playing tricks' on him points to the complex connections between his mirror image and his affective, embodied sensations. From a Deleuzian perspective, the affective body is understood as 'open and incomplete', and as a result can be 'open to misreading' (Featherstone 2010: 200). A Deleuzian approach does not attempt to foreclose or define the body as subjected to the 'purposive rational instrumental' perspective, as driven by the mind (Featherstone 2010: 200). This way of understanding bodies enables a broader analysis than popularised psychological accounts of negative body image caused by images in the media, for example. From a traditional psychological analysis, Jason and Adam's descriptions of appearing different in the mirror would be typically associated with body dysmorphic disorder (BDD). This is a medicalised and pathologised condition related to a 'dysfunction of the brain' and classified as a

128 'Buff culture', cosmetic surgery, bodily limits

somatoform disorder in the DSMIV (Didie *et al.* 2010). Some participants in fact make reference to body dysmorphic disorder in relation to theirs and others' bodies, which suggests the dominance and popularity of psychologised explanations of the body and body image. For example, using strikingly similar language to Adam and Jason, Isabelle describes the mismatch between her image in the mirror and 'reality' as body dysmorphic disorder:

> I can notice [when I have lost weight], with my clothes and stuff. But I think I can ... it's like a bit of body dysmorphia, I might think I look the same but then I weigh myself and look at myself again in the mirror I'm like, 'Oh no, I look really big', if I'm heavier. It's like your mind is playing tricks on you a little bit.

Both Isabelle and Jason refer to their mind 'playing tricks' on them with their image in the mirror, and their perception of their bodies is contingent on numerous factors concerning how the body looks and feels in relation to body work. Analyses which locate body concerns as psychological 'disorders' divert attention from the emphatically social dimensions of bodily concern. These examples show that the body and body image are much more than individual concerns, and instead link with a range of social, historical, interpersonal and cultural factors related to images, ideals, friends, places, activities and the feelings (affects) associated with all of these things. In this context the body can be reconceptualised as a continual 'becoming' rather than static and foreclosed.

As has been examined in the previous chapters, the specificities of body work practices and the correlations with experience are quite diverse and difficult to predict in advance. For example, where Steph and Anna anticipate that 'very fit people would have one less thing to worry about', numerous examples show this may be far from the case. Appearance and body image do not always follow the 'look good, feel good' logic; and many varying relations between the body and self (through body work practices) ensue. We need tools to understand these ambivalent, less coherent experiences of the embodied self (Coleman 2009). Using affect as a concept engages with an ontology and epistemology capable of understanding the body in continuous movement and negotiation and involved in a complex set of relations, 'rather than a thing with a fixed or determined image' (Featherstone 2010: 208), as in pathologised accounts of BDD.

These examples show the ways in which practices associated with health, exercise and going to the gym have the potential to 'slip over' into relations which profoundly affect the experience of the self. Cosmetic surgery and relations with food are other body work practices which involve affects similar to those discussed in the examples above, and involve particularly intensive affects which are meaningful for the ways the body is lived – its capacities and becomings. I explore these themes in the remainder of this chapter.

Cosmetic surgery, affect and the (feminine) body

Cosmetic surgery, along with other interventions such as weight-loss and exercise regimes that were framed by participants in the context of 'health' are marketed in consumer culture with an 'over-simplistic' logic that such practices have transformative potential that 'will result in a more positive and acceptable body image' (Featherstone 2010: 213). The way the body is lived in relation to these practices, however, can have many other more ambiguous and problematic outcomes, such as those I explored above in the context of exercise and lifting weights becoming 'addictive' and shaping a static body and image that is extraordinarily difficult to 'live up to'.

Data on cosmetic surgery in Australia is scarce and partial, based on the self-reporting of only some surgeons. Market research company IBISworld reports that Australians spent more than $850 million on cosmetic procedures in 2012. According to this source, 92 per cent of patients are women, and breast 'enhancement' is one of the most common procedures.[3] Although men as well as women are invited to enjoy the 'dubious equality' (Featherstone 1982: 22) as consumers in the marketplace concerned with the appearance of their bodies, body work practices such as cosmetic surgery clearly continue to be strongly feminised.

Feminism has contributed significantly to the critique of cosmetic surgery and the broader 'cult' of the body in its societal, cultural, historical and gendered context, particularly through linking these practices with gendered inequalities (Davis 1995; Goering 2003; Tait 2007; Leve *et al.* 2012). The connections between feminised practices of health and beauty for women (the 'fashion–beauty complex') and broader gendered inequality have been widely critiqued (Bordo 2003; Bartky 1995). Banet-Weiser and Portwood-Stacer, in their discussion of reality television programmes argue that the way cosmetic surgery is presented in these programmes 'naturalises a faith in the positive effects of cosmetic surgery, (and) also confirms a contemporary post-feminist ideology about individual transformation and the pleasure that eventually comes from constructing the perfect feminine body' (2006: 262). Davis argues against feminist accounts which see women as 'passively complicit' in reproducing a normalised femininity, or as 'cultural dupes'. Cosmetic surgery is a thorny issue for feminism, relating to how the practice can be critiqued as part of dominant gender relations which privilege men and heterosexual dynamics of desirability without 'blaming the women who take part' (Davis 1995: 71). In the examples below, I show how feminist developments of Deleuze and Guattari's concepts can be useful for understanding the nuances of these practices while retaining a critical sociological lens.

130 *'Buff culture', cosmetic surgery, bodily limits*

Kate's cosmetic surgery: 'now I can just really live my life'

Kate was 24, and lived south of Melbourne with her boyfriend. She had a diploma in Arts, and worked part-time as a nanny and administrative assistant. Three years ago, Kate had cosmetic surgery to enlarge her breasts.

> When I was 21 I decided I felt like all I wanted was boobs. And I told my parents, who are really like, hippies, I'm getting a boob job. And they were like, mum was like, 'oh no darling we just love you the way you are', and I was like 'mum, seriously, I haven't grown boobs, I'm 21 years of age, it's not going to happen for me!'

She said that although it was difficult to 'go against' the advice of her family and friends who told her not to have surgery the decision was integral to her overall happiness and sense of comfort in her body:

> All my girlfriends were like, 'Don't do it'. So you're making a decision and you're going against everyone else. And it's a massive, it's a massive thing. But over time, you can't put a price on being happy with your body. I've never once looked back and regretted my decision. And over time, I've had so many moments where I just feel … like I don't have this feeling in my stomach where I'm worried about wearing bathers … Not stressing about summer, and enjoying your life, and just really living it.

Kate described breast implants as a solution to alleviating her suffering; enabling her to live more fully. She described how she used to be teased and 'humiliated' at high school and would feel anxiety and stress related to any activities which involved a swimming pool or the beach. This may have particular significance in Australia where beach culture is a normative part of youth for those living on the coastline (Evers 2006). She said before the surgery she could never wear the clothes she wanted to wear, and felt self-conscious with boyfriends. She contrasted the 'feeling' she had following the surgery with the feeling she had prior to it 'in her stomach' of anxiety, worry and 'stress' that 'eats away at you'. After her surgery Kate felt able to 'just really live her life'. I asked Kate if there was anything else she would get 'done'; she replied 'Nup. I'm me forever now':

> I wouldn't get Botox or anything as I get older. I just want to grow old gracefully. For me [breast implants] was just about being able to try on a dress. And my friends say 'If you'd had small boobs Kate you wouldn't have done it'. If I'd had any boobs I wouldn't have done it! Just any boobs, an A [cup], I would've been happy with that! I don't think, for me – I don't think there would be anything else I'd change. If I was to change anything on my face I'd look in the mirror and go 'Oh I don't look like me anymore!' It'd be weird!

'Buff culture', cosmetic surgery, bodily limits 131

She said she would not change anything else about her appearance as this would cause incongruence with her sense of self: 'I wouldn't look like me anymore!' Kate's explanation of her 'need' for breast implants is similar to many in Davis's study who did not want to have surgery to 'enhance' themselves, but to 'be like everybody else' (1995: 16). Now that she no longer 'looks different', Kate felt that her 'self' is complete, and thus cosmetic surgery practices become irrelevant.

As in Leve et al.'s (2012) study, in Kate's example, ideologies of neo-liberalism shape her decisions about cosmetic surgery as a lifestyle choice:

> I think if it makes you feel more confident ... It's one of those things, I would never judge someone for a decision they make on their body. Um, I'm all for plastic surgery or make-up or anything, if it makes you feel better, and you're on the earth for such a short time, you know?

This example also reflects the normalisation of beauty practices such as cosmetic surgery as 'work on the self' that has the potential to lead to better self-esteem and a healthier 'body image' (Banet-Weiser and Portwood-Stacer 2006; Featherstone 2010). Crucially, cosmetic surgery is also a particularly drastic intervention that relates to *female* bodies in particular, and is critiqued by numerous feminist scholars as the ultimate capitulation of women to patriarchal interests (see Tait 2007 for an overview). Others have suggested that in a post-feminist context, the body is emphasised as a key site of individual empowerment through transformational body practices and this functions as 'a justification for a renewed objectification of female bodies' (Banet-Weiser and Portwood-Stacer 2006: 257). This perspective of cosmetic surgery is particularly individualised. A consequence of this is that the brunt of body (image) failure is borne by the individual alone if cosmetic interventions do not achieve the desired or expected result (McRobbie 2009). Like Kate, Isabelle had breast enlargement surgery to negate 'feeling bad' about an aspect of her body; to 'feel more comfortable' in her appearance. For Isabelle though, no amount of body work was 'ever enough'.

Isabelle's cosmetic surgery: 'when will it stop?'

Isabelle was 24 years old and lived with her mother and sister in a bay-side suburb in outer Melbourne. She was employed as a beauty therapist at a cosmetic surgery day clinic. Administering a diverse range of body modification, improvement and 'maintenance' practices were part of her daily working life. Like Kate, Isabelle has had breast implants. She said she was 'obsessed' with changing aspects of her body she felt 'self-conscious' about, such as her upper arms, hips and thighs, and her face as it 'ages'. Isabelle's affects, body work and related sense of self follow a different course than Kate's. When describing what women would have to do to get the 'ideal' woman's body (in

132   'Buff culture', cosmetic surgery, bodily limits

the context of her work as a beauty therapist at a cosmetic surgery centre), she said 'it's too hard!'

> I think it's, it's too hard to be honest! Like, you'd never get there. You want an ideal body but even if you're at your goal weight, you still don't, it's still not enough.

Isabelle had breast implants to make her breasts 'look normal' as, she explained, one breast was two cup sizes larger than the other. Other aspects of Isabelle's body work such as wearing make-up or dieting to lose weight, were also undertaken with the same goal – to 'feel more comfortable' with her appearance. The technologies of cosmetic surgery so far have not achieved this for Isabelle. Although Isabelle said she was 'a lot happier' after having surgery, she also explained that afterwards she began thinking of other procedures she could have: 'The more I keep doing ... like I had my boobs done and I was like "Right, what else can I do, what can I do next?"'.

She had had Botox injections ('because the nurses need someone to practice on') and was planning to have Liposuction on her arms and thighs:

> I do wanna have Lipo at work, because we get it for free. One of the nurses had it and she looks good. [voice softer] But you think, 'When will it stop?'. I don't know.

Isabelle sensed that there was something inexorable about her relationship with cosmetic surgery. I asked Isabelle if there was a limit to the amount or kind of surgery she would undertake in the future, and she responded 'I'll do everything'. She said her boyfriend wished she would 'grow old gracefully like his mum', but said that her mother had had a number of cosmetic procedures and that it was 'kind of expected in my family'.

Isabelle's experiences of body work have more in common with others in the study – men and women – who said they were 'addicted' to exercise or going to the gym (Coffey 2014) than Kate who had undergone one of the same cosmetic surgery procedures (breast implants). The different trajectories of Kate's and Isabelle's cosmetic surgery can be usefully explored through the concept of affect. Using the concept of affect in analysis means exploring its dynamics: is affect being multiplied and opened up, or is it intensified and closed down (Fox 2002)? Rather than providing a way to attain a better 'body image', Isabelle's relations with cosmetic surgery produced affects which intensified, meaning that she could only imagine one possibility for her body as it aged: 'I'll have everything done'. Isabelle's breast surgery intensified her affects, 'what can I do next? When will it stop?', whereas Kate's surgery enabled a multiplication of affects, 'there are so many moments now where I just feel ... now I can enjoy my life, just really live it'. Kate and Isabelle have different affective experiences of cosmetic surgery, which means that they have

'Buff culture', cosmetic surgery, bodily limits 133

different conceptions of what their bodies can do, and a different range of possibilities for living.

Affects related to femininity, appearance, image and consumer culture logics of transformation and self-improvement constitute Isabelle's and Kate's bodies as assemblages, and open and close certain pathways as being potential options. According to Deleuze (1988), what we are capable of is directly related to embodied sensation (affect), and it is the relations of affect that produce a body's capacities (Coleman 2009). The intensification of affect can prevent new relations from being formed; while the multiplication of affects opens new possibilities that were not previously thought of or available (Buchanan 1997; Hickey-Moody and Malins 2007). Where affects between a person and a practice of body work (such as cosmetic surgery in Isabelle's case) are intensified, it can be difficult to 'escape' or alter this. 'Escaping' requires new affects between Isabelle and her body (and cosmetic surgery) to be formed; however, it is not easy to 'multiply' affect when it has been closed down (Fox 2002).

'Feminine socialisation' (Marsden 2004) and the social ideas that surround women's bodies and their tendency towards cosmetic surgery are significant for influencing the range of body possibilities that are felt to be available for those women who embody the ideas of femininity and bodily perfection. Because cultural scripts associated with feminine appearance are the learned 'ways of being' for Kate and Isabelle from which their cultural evaluations were made, they had particular, diverse relations with practices of cosmetic surgery. These ways of being are already embodied, so new 'ideas need to be embodied' (Marsden 2004: 317), their bodily material realities need to be contested. As Marsden argues, 'it is the body as such that must imagine, not an agent that aspires to control the materiality of which it is itself a part' (2004: 317).

The concept of affect enables a perspective in which Isabelle's cosmetic surgery is *more than* the effect of poor body image or pathologised body dysmorphic disorder, caused by narrow standards of female beauty as portrayed in the media. Affects influence the experience of body work and the self in complex – and non-deterministic – ways. A focus on the affective relations between Kate's body and the surgery enable the complex, highly contingent and ambiguous experiences of body work to be explored beyond the binary of 'cultural dope' or 'subject possessing agency'. The affects related to Kate's cosmetic surgery extend new ways of living her body, even if she is repeating or emulating ideal physical femininity.

Becoming involves the 'opening up to difference, to the many rather than the few' (Fox 2002: 359); the opening of possibility. Kate's body work practices and broader relations with femininity were more open to difference and multiplicity than Isabelle's. One reason for this is perhaps due to Kate's general critique of body work practices; she criticised the culture of femininity and reflected on her position within it. Feminist critique, I argue, can facilitate this 'opening to difference' through a focus on highlighting micro-politics

134 *'Buff culture', cosmetic surgery, bodily limits*

through critique. Where feminism provides a critical lens on dominant ideals of femininity, and can facilitate less restrictive ideals of women's bodies, it might create the potential for new ideas to be engaged with and a broader range of affects to embody. Feminist critiques of cosmetic surgery highlight the broad social forces which reduce women to their bodies and appearance within the social context of a cultural obsession with the body and perfection. It is important to continue to critique the social norms, discourses and idealisations that surround female bodies in particular to denaturalise the body and illuminate the non-essential aspects of current ideals and their associated inequalities.

This perspective of bodies is radically different from analyses which would focus on the capacities of individuals for agency in their practices of body work, or analyses of the degrees to which bodies are structured, limited or repressed by the cultural environment in which their body work practices are located (as in Kwan and Trautner 2009). I have argued elsewhere, explanation and sociological analysis should not 'appeal to agency' as a force that creates unexpected patterns, but must go further to identify the way that identities and practices are negotiated in process with the structures which conventional accounts position as 'boundaries' (Coffey and Farrugia 2014: 12).

The intensities and affects involved in exercise and cosmetic surgery practices may be similar in terms of how they feel. Practices of exercise, where they are undertaken primarily to alter the shape of one's body or 'image' are similar to cosmetic surgical interventions of the body in so far as both are understood as having the potential to change the way a body is lived. As these examples show, however, the range of outcomes are possible which can be unpredictable and difficult to know in advance.

The intensity of the affects associated with the practices of body work connect the experiences of Isabelle, Ben, Jason and Adam particularly, who explain their experiences of body work in the most intensive and complex ways. Their examples complicate the simplistic discourses of health, gender and how images are supposed to 'feel' (such as in the 'look good, feel good' adage) most comprehensively. This perspective also enables an understanding of body work practices as not intrinsically good or bad; rather, it depends on the affective relations surrounding these practices and whether life is restricted or maximised through the affects associated with those practices.

As Fox (2002: 358) argues, 'the intensification of affect can lead to a becoming which reterritorialises and inhibits further lines of flight ... a body without organs which has become (rather than being in the process of becoming) has suffered a reterritorialisation that cannot easily be escaped'. As I argued in the previous chapter in the context of Gillian's slimming body work practices, the affects related to Gillian's body work practices were limited, and limited the range of possibilities for living her body as a result. Where body work practices are positioned as the only way of freeing herself from 'feeling bad', other possibilities for Gillian living her body (in terms of other ways it may feel or be experienced) are not immediately available.

'Buff culture', cosmetic surgery, bodily limits   135

Becoming is understood as the multiplication and proliferation of affects and involves 'opening up to the many rather than the few' (Fox 2002: 359). In the examples of body work practices from Isabelle and others (Ben, Adam and Jason), however, their affective relations between their bodies and body work practices are intensified, rather than multiplied. Isabelle can only imagine one possibility for her body as it ages: 'I'll have everything done'. Where Kate's cosmetic surgery enabled a multiplication of affects, 'there are so many moments now where I just feel ... now I can enjoy my life, just really live it', Isabelle's breast surgery intensified her affects, 'what can I do next? When will it stop?' Cosmetic surgery, like other body work practices, may also reterritorialise the body and a person's 'styles of life' it in a way that cannot easily be escaped.

Isabelle's relations with molar femininity and her body work practices can be understood as more 'rigid folds' (Hickey-Moody and Malins 2007: 12). As Isabelle's affects surrounding her body and cosmetic surgery continue to intensify, the limits as to what Isabelle's body can do are continually and emphatically shaped by molar femininity, as well as through her family and occupation as a beauty therapist. Although 'there is always the possibility for deterritorialisation' or escape (Fox 2002), territories shaped by molar gender categories establish limits that can be particularly difficult to negotiate. However, the body is not simply determined, and from Deleuze's perspective, 'life is not just the progression of ordered sequences from some already given set of possibilities' (Colebrook 2002: 57). Because the self is 'processual, continually unfolding and becoming other', the body's boundaries and possibilities 'can be redrawn, especially if one has a little help' (Fox 2002: 360).

As I have discussed in other chapters, 'ethological' (rather than etiological) understandings of the body refer to a concern for the affects and relations implicated between bodies and other assemblages, rather than positioning bodies in deterministic or reductive 'cause and effect' models. This means, for example, understanding Isabelle's cosmetic surgery as more than the effect of poor body image or pathologised body dysmorphic disorder, caused by narrow standards of female beauty as portrayed in the media. Affects, or 'the experience of intensities' (Featherstone 2010: 195) are a key aspect of bodies and body work practices, and influence the experience of body work and the self in complex ways.

The positivity, capacity and affirmation of bodies through Deleuze's concept of becoming is implicit because of the openness and indeterminacy of becomings. When affects and relations 'do not ensure an open future', when becoming is foreclosed through the 'stopping' of the process of affects and relations, the body without organs can be fatal (Buchanan 1997; Deleuze 1997). Anorexia and other eating disorders have been described by theorists drawing on Deleuze to understand these practices, and have been termed 'deadly practices of the self' (Buchanan 1997). One way of more thoroughly analysing the ways that bodies, body work, affects and relations work together and form various 'becomings' is to examine these processes in the

136 *'Buff culture', cosmetic surgery, bodily limits*

context of anorexia, through Beth's experience of suffering from anorexia some years earlier. Buchanan explains anorexia as a process in which eating is disconnected from hunger, and the relation between food and the body is refigured (1997: 78). Through examining this potentially deadly re-figuration, I intend to show the theoretical depth in the way affect works and can be used to understand other, less harrowing body work practices.

Beth, the anorexic body and recovering

Beth was 19 years old at the time of being interviewed. Beth alluded to having previously suffered from 'body issues' around the middle of the interview, and when I asked her what this meant, she described suffering from anorexia six years ago, and discussed her recovery and experiences.[4]

Beth described anorexia as a 'disease', saying 'it's such a strange disease; it goes against everything that people are supposed to do. Like, our primal instinct is to eat always, to stay alive. But um, you know, when somebody chooses to starve ...' Here, the differing relation with food involved in anorexia is explained as 'going against our primal instinct ... to stay alive'. From a Spinozist perspective, hunger is not a 'drive' or an instinct but a relation between food and the body (Buchanan 1997). For the anorexic, food takes on a different relation. Spinoza and Deleuze have criticised psychoanalytic perspectives which define hunger as a 'drive', specifying that the theory of hunger as a drive neglects the relations in which hunger is situated. An anorexic's relation with food does not prompt the action of eating. Rather than experiencing the hunger-affect which induces eating, another affect is at work, prompting an alternative relation with food (Buchanan 1997). In Beth's case, shame and guilt are the affects concerning food, which produce the relations between food and her body which compel her to avoid food. For Beth, negative, painful affects are associated with food.

In the following example, Beth describes the process of becoming anorexic in relation to her attitudes and actions towards food and eating:

BETH: It's just like, the minute I started to feel self-conscious, like it just took over. It started with going on a diet, and then it just got out of control.

JULIA: Like, once you started one thing, it just snowballed?

BETH: Yeah. Pretty much. Like, I had a really healthy diet, but it was still a conscious diet. And I just started to be really unsatisfied with myself, and then, food started tasting like, just like guilt. Like, having a bowl of food would just be like eating guilt. And it was horrible. Like, it caused me pain, like, emotionally, to eat. And ... like ... I just didn't want that, that feeling, the shame and everything. And then I stopped eating, and I got really skinny. And, I seemed to think that if I ate anything, I'd put all of the weight back on. So I didn't eat at all. I didn't eat at all for 6 weeks. Um, and then I got hospitalised shortly after that.

'Buff culture', cosmetic surgery, bodily limits 137

Beth is clear in her description of food producing a particular affect far removed from the hunger as a 'drive'. Beth's relations with food are not restricted to 'hunger'; rather, Beth's affects related to food are guilt and shame. For Beth, eating is not associated with nourishment, but with 'physical pain'. To avoid the affects of shame, guilt and pain, the relations between the body and food have to be altered: eating is problematic, but this can be resolved through ceasing to eat. The affects related to food (guilt, shame, pain) thus required an alteration to the relation between the body and food.

Buchanan argues that because anorexics cannot change what food does to them, they must change themselves, which demands that new ways of being be found, 'which effectively means a new way of becoming' (1997: 79). Because Beth could not change what food does to her (affects of guilt, shame, physical emotional pain) food was required to be confronted differently; and demanded an attempt towards a new way of being (or becoming). If affect is the capacity of the body to form specific relations (Buchanan 1997: 80), the affects described by Beth pertaining to food and eating can be understood to produce the relations between her body and food which required her to avoid food and eating.

Buchanan argues that 'the problem for the anorexic, and this is the danger of all self-motivated becoming, is that far from accelerating becoming, what he or she actually does is deform it' (1997: 87). Buchanan summarises Deleuze and Guattari's ethics of the body, and delineates the 'healthy' body from the unhealthy body: 'those relations which ensure an open future, which is to say, those which promote the formation of new compounds, are considered healthy; while those relations which lead to the decomposition of old compounds and are not accompanied by the elaboration of new ones are considered unhealthy' (Buchanan 1997: 82). In other words, Beth's affects of shame and guilt produced particular relations between her body and food that prevented her from being able to eat without feeling physical pain. This relation prevented the formulation of new affects surrounding her body and food. If the body is understood as a multiplicity of forces defined by the affects it is are capable of, then Beth's relations with food signal a reduction in her body's force. The anorexic, like the masochist or the alcoholic, reduces his or her capacity of affection through their activities, and in doing so, reduces the force of the body (Deleuze and Guattari 1987; Buchanan 1997: 88). When new connections are not able to be made or to enter into new compositions, these relations become deadly (Buchanan 1997: 88).

Where I described Gillian's body work in the previous chapter as being involved in the intensification of affects relating to slimming practices, Fox suggests that anorexia may be an extension of the affects of the slimming body 'gone critical' (Fox 2002: 358). The affects involved in Beth's suffering of anorexia are even more restricted and intensified than Gillian's and Isabelle's in their affective relations with other body work. The most important aspect guiding these examples is not the practices of body work themselves, but the

138 *'Buff culture', cosmetic surgery, bodily limits*

relations of affect involved. These define the body and its possibilities; what it can and cannot do.

When Beth was hospitalised she was fed through a nasal tube, and she describes her recovery as predominantly focused on gaining weight, rather than psychological support. Beth's recovery can be likened to a 'line of flight', an intensive deterritorialisation or escape (Fox 2002) which refigured the relations of affect between her body and anorexia, when she says 'one day I just decided ...':

BETH: It's like I made myself, and then I was born again. Like, one day I just decided, I'm going to be the person I've always wanted to be. And I had to ... like almost kill the old me and just start over again. And it's like, there's no place for those memories in my new life. So, I try not to think about it, but if I didn't try to consciously avoid those memories, maybe I would think about it.

JULIA: So how is it then, talking about it now? Is that ... does it feel like a tension between the old and the new?

BETH: It sort of feels like I'm talking about somebody else. Like, a memory that happened in a past life sort of. Like, I'm so removed from it. It's just like talking about a dream I had. Well, it's like a nightmare, that happened while I was sleeping. Yeah.

Beth explains that she had to 'kill' the self that she had 'made'; the anorexic self. Buchanan argues that because anorexics cannot change what food does to them, they must change themselves; but Beth did not just change herself in this process, rather, she 'made herself' entirely. Changing herself and her relation with food amounted to remaking herself; such were the intensities of the affective relations between her body and food.

Buchanan (1997) also argues that this perspective makes it possible to thoroughly reconceptualise problematic explanations of anorexia such as psychologistic 'body image' accounts, to instead see the thoroughly active elements of anorexia, and to see the ways these elements operate more fully. As in Dyke's analysis, anorexia can be approached as 'a pre-individual, moving and unfixed event' (2013: 145). Theories of affect, relations and becoming may be even more relevant in the contemporary neo-liberal context wherein the individual is required to seek new ways of becoming, to be 'self-made' and self-responsible. These concepts may provide particularly strong analytic tools in this context. Beth describes deciding to 'become the person I'd always wanted to be', which required 'killing off' her old, anorexic self, and to a certain extent, repressing the memories of that self and dissociating from that way of being. Beth's examples highlight the force and violence that can be implicit in becomings, and exemplify how central effective relations they may be to understanding the way a body, and a life, may be lived. Deleuze and Guattari's (1987) theories do not only assist in building a more detailed understanding of anorexia and other 'deadly practices of the self'

'Buff culture', cosmetic surgery, bodily limits   139

such as drug addiction, alcoholism and masochism. Their work on anorexia also serves to show the ways that these concepts may be comprehended and used as tools in analysing how 'what a body can do' is negotiated through the ongoing relations and affects of bodies. Other recent work has argued for the need for the body to be made central in eating disorder theories (Rinaldi *et al.* 2016) and in theorising the non-linear processes of 'recovery' (Duff 2016).

Conclusion

This chapter further explores the ways that two key assemblages, health and gender, through body work practices, produce the body's possibilities. The previous chapter's focus on health and exercise was extended to explore more intensive or 'extreme' practices such as intensive weights training and cosmetic surgical procedures. I have aimed to show that drawing on Deleuzian concepts such as affect can assist in analysing the ways bodily possibilities are assembled in relation to practices, discourses, experiences and embodied sensations. The affective dimensions of body work are crucial for understanding how the body is lived, and what possibilities for living are available based on the relations and affects between bodies and other forces. The varying intensities of affect, resulting from different relational processes, mean forms of body work culminate in different becomings for different assemblages (bodies).

Where many participants in this research viewed body work practices as having the potential to contribute to life being lived in more positive ways and making them 'happier' (such as exercise and fitness practices for Anna, Steph, Gillian and Paul, and Kate's experience of breast enlargement surgery), body work practices, for many others, involved the body and self being bound in a set of relations associated with body work practices in ways that were termed 'obsessive' or related to 'addiction'. Kate and Isabelle's very different relations with cosmetic surgery illustrated these complexities, as did the descriptions of Ben, Adam and Jason of exercise and lifting weights. Working with Deleuze's concepts of becomings and intensities of affect can help to explain and further understand the complexity of their experiences.

Rather than reducing the body to its functions, Deleuze and Guattari make the question of what a body can do constitutive, refiguring the body as 'the sum of its capacities' (Buchanan 1997: 75). The more a body is opened to difference and multiple possibilities for affect, the more force it has; the more it can do. This point is particularly relevant to analyses of forms of body work such as cosmetic surgery, since many critiques of these practices have previously centred on the pathologies of the individuals (usually women) who undergo cosmetic surgery, or is theorised in terms of its function in binaristic relations of oppression and liberation (Davis 1995). Instead, what a body can do is understood as constituted through the affective events which go on to form the body as an 'event'. The affective relations involved in anorexia affect what the body can do; just as the affective relations involved in exercise practices or cosmetic surgery affect what the body can do. The 'constitutive

140 *'Buff culture', cosmetic surgery, bodily limits*

relationality' through which bodies affect and are affected by their relations mean that because bodies are produced through relations, they cannot be known prior to their relationality: the outcomes of their affective relations cannot be known in advance (Deleuze 1992).

This perspective assists in showing the limits of concepts of 'body image' and simple cause-and-effect narratives explaining the interplay of bodies and the social. Unhealthy body image and body dysmorphic disorder are said to underpin many women's decisions to undergo cosmetic surgery (Gorbis 2004). Poor body image is also linked with body dysmorphic disorder which can lead to eating disorders. The aetiology of these 'pathologies' are widely said to be media images, or more accurately, the narrow standards of female beauty represented in these images. In much popular feminist work, both mainstream and academic, media representations of thin femininity are understood to be the primary cause of eating disorders and cosmetic surgery. As this analysis shows, however, the ways the body is assembled in relation to these practices is profoundly complex and requires a more complex analysis. Rather than an 'entity' which is primarily conceptualised as the 'effect' of culture or social forces, the body can be more productively understood as a process that is continually being formed and re-formed through its relations and connections to other bodies and forces. Understanding the body as being continually produced through shifting affects, relations and engagements can enable the profoundly complex and often unpredictable dynamics of the body's relationships with the social to be more fully explored.

Notes

1 www.abc.net.au/radionational/programs/backgroundbriefing/boys-and-the-buff-culture/3582746#transcript
2 'Addiction'. (n.d.). Dictionary.com Unabridged. Retrieved 21 February 2012, from Dictionary.com website: http://dictionary.reference.com/browse/addiction
3 www.ibisworld.com.au/industry/plastic-surgeons.html.
4 When Beth mentioned anorexia and began discussing it, I asked her if she was sure she felt ok to talk about it. She assured me she was 'fine', and for the next 20 minutes or so I barely said a word while she described her experiences. At the time, and for days afterwards, I felt humbled and appalled by what Beth had gone through. After she had finished I asked if I could help her in any way, through arranging someone for her to talk to such as a counsellor, and she shook her head, smiled and said, 'No, it's ok. I'm fine now'. I felt as though Beth thought I was fussing over her, and I while I wanted to ensure as far as possible that I was ful-filling my ethical duty of care to Beth, I also did not want to annoy or pester her. I emailed Beth a few weeks after the interview to see if she had asked a friend she had mentioned who might be interested in being interviewed, and was able to use this opportunity to make sure she was feeling ok about her interview; she said she was.

References

Atkinson, M. and Monaghan, L. F. (2014). *Challenging Myths of Masculinity: Understanding Physical Cultures.* Aldershot: Ashgate.

'Buff culture', cosmetic surgery, bodily limits 141

Banet-Weiser, S. and Portwood-Stacer, L. (2006). 'I Just Want to Be Me Again!': Beauty Pageants, Reality Television, and Post-feminism. *Feminist Theory*, 7(2), 255–272.

Bartky, S. (1990). *Femininity and Domination: Studies in the Phenomenology of Oppression*. New York: Routledge.

Bordo, S. (2003). *Unbearable Weight: Feminism, Western Culture and the Body* (10th anniversary edn). Berkeley: University of California Press.

Buchanan, I. (1997). The Problem of the Body in Deleuze and Guattari, or, What Can a Body Do? *Body and Society*, 3(3), 73–91.

Budgeon, S. (2003). Identity as an Embodied Event. *Body and Society*, 9(1), 35–55.

Coffey, J. (2014). 'As Long as I'm Fit and a Healthy Weight, I Don't Feel Bad': Exploring Body Work and Health through the Concept of 'Affect'. *Journal of Sociology*. doi: 10.1177/1440783313518249

Coffey, J. and Farrugia, D. (2014). Unpacking the Black Box: The Problem of Agency in the Sociology of Youth. *Journal of Youth Studies*, 17(4).

Colebrook, C. (2002). *Gilles Deleuze*. London: Routledge.

Coleman, R. (2009). *The Becoming of Bodies: Girls, Images, Experience*. Manchester and New York: Manchester University Press.

Crawford, R. (1980). Healthism and the Medicalisation of Everyday Life. *International Journal of Health Services*, 10(3), 365–388.

Davis, K. (1995). *Reshaping the Female Body*. New York: Routledge.

Deleuze, G. (1988). *Spinoza: Practical Philosophy* (R. Hurley, trans.). San Francisco, CA: City Lights Books.

Deleuze, G. (1992). Ethology: Spinoza and Us. In J. Crary and S. Kwinter (eds), *Incorporations*. New York: Zone.

Deleuze, G. (1997). Immanence. *Theory, Culture and Society*, 14(2), 3–7. doi: 10.1177/026327697014002002

Deleuze, G. and Guattari, F. (1987). *A Thousand Plateaus: Capitalism and Schizophrenia* (B. Massumi, trans.). Edinburgh: Edinburgh University Press.

Didie, E. R., Kuniega-Pietrzak, T. and Phillips, K. A. (2010). Body image in patients with body dysmorphic disorder: Evaluations of and investment in appearance, health/illness, and fitness. *Body Image*, 7(1), 66–69. doi: http://dx.doi.org/10.1016/j.bodyim.2009.09.007

Duff, C. (2016). G major to D major to A minor 7 (A Progression to Recovery). In J. Coffey, S. Budgeon and H. Cahill (eds.), *Learning Bodies: The Body in Youth and Childhood Studies*. New York: Springer.

Dyke, S. (2013). Disrupting 'Anorexia Nervosa': An Ethnography of the Deleuzian Event. In R. Coleman and J. Ringrose (eds), *Deleuze and Research Methodologies*. Edinburgh: Edinburgh University Press.

Evers, C. (2006). How to Surf. *Journal of Sport and Social Issues*, 30(3), 229–243. doi: 10.1177/0193723506290394

Featherstone, M. (1982). The Body in Consumer Culture. *Theory, Culture and Society*, 1, 18–33.

Featherstone, M. (2010). Body, Image and Affect in Consumer Culture. *Body and Society*, 16(1), 193–221.

Fox, N. J. (2002). Refracting 'Health': Deleuze, Guattari and Body-Self. *Health*, 6(3), 347–363. doi: 10.1177/136345930200600306

Fox, N. J. and Ward, K. J. (2008). What Are Health Identities and How May We Study Them? *Sociology of Health and Illness*, 30(7), 1007–1021.

142 *'Buff culture', cosmetic surgery, bodily limits*

Gill, R., Henwood, K. and McLean, C. (2005). Body Projects and the Regulation of Normative Masculinity. *Body and Society*, 11(1), 37–62.

Goering, S. (2003). Confirmity through Cosmetic Surgery: The Medical Erasure of Race and Disability. In R. Figueroa and S. Harding (eds), *Science and Other Cultures*. New York: Routledge.

Gorbis, E. (2004). Addiction to plastic surgery www.hope4ocd.com/downloads/gor bis_plastic0703.pdf

Hickey-Moody, A., and Malins, P. (eds) (2007). *Deleuzian Encounters: Studies in Contemporary Social Issues*. New York: Palgrave Macmillan.

Kwan, S., and Trautner, M. N. (2009). Beauty Work: Individual and Institutional Rewards, the Reproduction of Gender, and Questions of Agency. *Sociological Compass*, 3(1), 49–71.

Leve, M., Rubin, L. and Pusic, A. (2012). Cosmetic Surgery and Neoliberalisms: Managing Risk and Responsibility. *Feminism and Psychology*, 22(1), 122–141. doi: 10.1177/0959353511424361

McRobbie, A. (2009). *The Aftermath of Feminism: Gender, Culture and Social Change*. London: Sage.

Marsden, J. (2004). Deleuzian Bodies, Feminist Tactics. *Women: A Cultural Review*, 15(3), 308–319. doi: 10.1080/0957404042000291436

Rinaldi, J., Lamarre, A. and Rice, C. (2016). Recovering Bodies: The Production of the Recoverable Subject in Eating Disorder Treatment Regimes. In J. Coffey, S. Budgeon and H. Cahill (eds), *Learning Bodies: The Body in Youth and Childhood Studies*. New York: Springer.

Rose, N. (1996). *Inventing Our Selves: Psychology, Power and Personhood*. Cambridge: Cambridge University Press.

Tait, S. (2007). Television and the Domestication of Cosmetic Surgery. *Feminist Media Studies*, 7(2), 119–135.

Wacquant, L. J. D. (1995). Review Article: Why Men Desire Muscles. *Body and Society*, 1(1), 163–179. doi: 10.1177/1357034x95001001010

Wiegers, Y. (1998). Male Bodybuilding: The Social Construction of a Masculine Identity. *Journal of Popular Culture*, 32(2), 147–161. doi: 10.1111/j.0022–3840.1998.00147.x

7 Conclusion: embodying youth studies

Introduction

This book has aimed to develop an embodied approach to youth sociology. A focus on embodiment entails a specific intention to place the body – and embodied experience – at the forefront of analysis. This approach also aims to highlight the active relations which produce bodies and the world. This focus on a body's potential and lived experience can assist in moving beyond previous approaches in which the body is invisible or rendered inferior to the mind in a binary logic. More than this, beginning to 'think through the body' can open up a way of exploring the ways the body is implicated in the complexities and tensions in young people's lives. I have argued that a focus on the dynamics of embodiment can assist in developing a new dimension of analysis, adding to existing critiques of reductive understandings of youth as well as expanded understandings of the dynamics of health and gender. Foregrounding embodiment can also be seen as a way of pursuing understandings which embrace complexity and ambivalence as a strategy of resistance to the homogenising influences of neo-liberalism, for example (Kelly 2015).

The concept of body work captures the current context of bodily concern while highlighting dynamic processes by which bodies and societies shape each other. This concept is developed from feminist sociological approaches to the body drawn from Deleuze, Guattari and Spinoza as an active, productive force which operates in relation to broader socio-historical–cultural contexts. Throughout this book, body work was explored through a focus on *body work practices* as a way of studying how the body is lived and produced in relation to gender, image, health and appearance. It speaks to an active conceptualisation of the body as assembling through connections.

The body as process of connections

Feminist–Deleuzo-Guattarian understandings of bodies highlight processes and relations as crucial, and argue that studying these dimensions shows the contingent and often unpredictable ways in which bodies and other

144 *Conclusion: embodying youth studies*

assemblages are produced. This perspective is also used in an effort to move beyond dualist understandings of the body's formation. It entails a shift from understanding the body as a bounded entity, effect of culture or a cultural object, to instead see the body and mind as parallel, inseparable from each other and focusing on the capacities of bodies (Deleuze 1988: 18). The affects and capacities of bodies cannot be known in advance, and thus we cannot presume to know the outcomes or intra-actions that may occur (such as the results of particular forms of body work practices, for example). The potential for generation and change is a central tenet of the ontology of Deleuzian theory, which has particular implications for how human and other bodies are conceptualised. The promise of a feminist Deleuzian perspective of the body lies in the attention it affords to the complexities and nuances of social life to enable fuller understandings of how gender, health and other key social arrangements assemble.

First in this chapter, I consider two central implications that result from this specific approach to the body, and what these can contribute to youth studies and sociological accounts of the body more broadly. These include embracing complexity to disrupt reductive understandings of youth, health and gender and the denaturalisation of bodily inequalities. Following this, I return to the key concepts used throughout the book and what they bring to our understandings of gender and health in relation to the body. I then discuss some of the current developments in feminist approaches aiming to 'embody' theory and methods including new materialist and post-human perspectives drawn from Barad and Braidotti, and the potential for feminist politics and critique. The chapter concludes with a reflection on what these concepts and perspectives can contribute to embodying youth studies.

Embracing complexity

A focus on the body can contribute to creating a rich and detailed picture of young embodiments in studying the diverse and complex dynamics between young people's lives and the social. It can also be useful in disrupting and critiquing dominant knowledge 'about' youth, for example, in concerns around 'risky' practices which often implicitly centre on the body. Adding the body to the story complicates media risk discourses which dominate discussions of sexting (as shown in Ringrose and Harvey 2015). A focus on the body highlights the affective and embodied processes which underpin the currency of images and the 'cultural sexism that normalises the coercive, unauthorised showing and distribution of images of girls' body parts' (Ringrose *et al.* 2013: 307).

A focus on the body can contribute to producing more nuanced understandings of the interrelationships between the macro and micro processes of social practices such as those relating to education and work patterns for contemporary youth across a range of different contexts and locales. There has similarly been over-emphasis on cerebral aspects of subcultures at the

Conclusion: embodying youth studies 145

expense of the body in youth cultures research (Driver 2011), and increased attention to the body could enhance understandings of the dynamics between embodied experience and broader patterns of youth cultural practices.

As both Woodman and Wyn (2015) and France and Roberts (2014) argue, it is crucial give due attention to both the macro and micro processes which shape the lives and experiences of young people. The body is one specific dimension of focus that could add much to understandings of the inter-relationships between the macro and micro processes of social practices.

A focus on the body in youth studies can assist in a range of other critical ways; for example, in unsettling the dominance of the focus on the 'adolescent developing brain' – or 'brain in a jar' as Kelly describes it (2015). It also is useful in disrupting accounts of young people's bodies as primarily sites of risks or problems to be individually managed by young people themselves (Coffey and Watson 2015). It contributes a way of locating young people themselves (as bodies) in social context, and provides a way of understanding the dynamics of social life and the active ways in which bodies are both shaped and involved in shaping the social.

Denaturalising inequalities

A Deleuzo-Guattarian approach understands a body as produced through encounters, relations, forces and practices. This approach moves beyond 'human nature' as the prime ontological category of analysis to also explore the ways in which matter, affect, biology, technology, politics and other forces are crucial in 'assembling' what we understand as human and natural (Rose 2007).

The body is centrally implicated in the feminist critique of gendered inequalities because of the ways in which such inequalities have been said to be *naturalised* by the body. If women are 'naturally' inferior, so the logic goes, then so too are gendered (and raced, and classed) inequalities and nothing can or should be done to change this. Decades of feminist theory and activism have challenged this argument, and have set about 'wresting notions of corporeality away from the constraints which have polarized and opposed it to mind, the mental or the conceptual, not to mention away from the confines of a biology that is considered universal, innate, fundamentally nonhistorical' (Grosz 1994: 187). Contemporary feminist philosophy and theory, through frameworks of embodiment and a focus on materiality, worked to unhook the body from naturalistic, dualistic and binaristic frameworks (Budgeon 2003).

Disconnecting the body from binaries which have aided in the perpetuation of inequalities has implications for a range of issues intersecting with gender, including sexualities, race, class and disabilities, all of which implicate the body. This perspective of the body contributes to showing yet another way in which the inequalities which were once understood as located in the body are not; there is no 'essence' or natural foundation which forms the basis for inequalities and hierarchies between human bodies. This point can be used as

146　*Conclusion: embodying youth studies*

further ammunition for dismantling understandings of inequalities as 'natural', demonstrating the ways in which inequalities emerge through social processes and hierarchies rather than based on any foundational 'essence'. This perspective will also be useful for those wanting to move beyond the political and ontological issues associated with constructionist arguments relating to the body and inequality. This enables a specific focus on the dynamics of minoritarian bodies, such as in the growing research showing the fluidity and non-bodily-binary nature of sexualities in relation to queer and transgender bodies. This clearly has numerous political implications, which are considered further in relation to micro-politics later in this chapter.

What does this approach to the body do?

Gender and health were explored as key themes central to young people's practices and experiences of bodies and body work. Gender and health were theorised as complex relational assemblages which produced the body, illustrated through examples of young people's body work practices.

Gender

Gender can be understood as a complex relational assemblage produced through affects, relations and 'doings'. It has been explored in examples in this book as a tension negotiated between forces of territorialisation and the openness inherent in the production of bodies. The body is produced by normative territorialisations of gender such as through the 'ideal' physical bodies participants describe, but not only by binary territorialisations. A multitude of other affects, relations, objects, ideas and experiences also produce the body. From this perspective, gendered embodiments are not simply the reproductions of dualist gender formations; rather, gender is engaged, negotiated and produced continually through affects and relations. This enables the ambiguities and complexities of gender to be explored, as well as binary categories and hierarchies. These forces together contribute a fuller picture of the dynamics by which gender assembles.

In Chapter 4, numerous examples which could be read as constitutive of (re)producing molar gendered identities were discussed, for example, through participants' discussions of 'ideal' male and female bodies, and the dynamics of 'spectacular' gendered bodies which garner 'respect', visibility and desirability on the street (in Adam's example) or the shopping mall (in Sara's and Isabelle's examples). This analysis aimed to show the micro-relations and affects which occur between bodies, spaces, norms, discourses and matter which produce these specific gendered assemblages (or territorialisations). In paying attention to the ways in which bodies 'assemble' through gender I have argued this highlights the non-essential and contingent nature of these engagements, while also enabling analysis of the potential force of these engagements which can be difficult to change. The study of these micro-relations

Conclusion: embodying youth studies 147

and how they link with the broader socio-historical context has been termed 'micro-politics' (Fox 2014). The point is not to show that gender is endlessly fluid or loose, but rather that it is actively produced in ways that can be read as more or less restrictive or creative. Movements between deterritorialisation and reterritorialisation are commonplace, 'part of the daily fabric of existence' because they are produced through a person's dynamic relations with their environment (Fox 2002: 354).

This focus assists therefore in making sense of those participants' experiences and descriptions which fell outside what is usually called 'dominant discourses' of gender and bodily appearance, such as in Kate's and Kim's criticisms of the expectations of feminine beauty work ('I can't be bothered!) and Peter's and Stephen's unsettling of the masculine body ideal in the gym. A focus on the micro-politics of different situations, examples and assemblages is a way of both critiquing and exploring in fine detail how the current contexts come to assemble, while also recognising that there is inherent capacity for change in these arrangements. As Houle describes, the micro-political ontology of Deleuze and Guattari has capacity inherent within it: the insistence that things could be otherwise (Houle 2011: 110). It is important to pay attention to these complexities and nuances and the processes by which bodies and the social assemble to understand the conditions of possibility for gender and social change more broadly. It is important to disrupt the naturalisation of gendered physiques such as muscularity, for example, to unpack the specific and deliberate ways in which gender is produced socially, and produced through the body.

This analysis has implications too for sociological attention to the 'narrowing of a bodily norm' that is occurring for young women (McRobbie 2015), and young men. It can also help us to broaden our understandings of practices which aim to produce gendered appearances, such as in the increased focus on muscle-building and steroid use for young men (Keane 2005; Ravn and Coffey 2015). It is important to continue to critique the social conditions which play a large part in comprising the gendered assemblage, particularly as these conditions may be narrowing further in the context of increasing gendered body pressure in an image-focused culture.

Health

'Health' was assembled by participants through body work practices against the backdrop of the contemporary consumer and popular focus on the body's appearance. The increased focus on the body's functioning and appearance is associated with the significant rise of health, beauty and fitness industries in the past two decades and public health discourses which emphasise individual responsibility and management of the body in the context of a declining welfare state in Australia and the UK (Lupton 1995; Leahy 2014). As well as being strongly gendered (Moore 2010), health ideals were discussed as central in the increasing public emphasis on individual management and

148 *Conclusion: embodying youth studies*

responsibility of the body towards an image of 'health' ('everyone should make the time to be healthy', as Adam says). Health was worked towards by participants in the study through work on the body via muscularising and exercise practices, and eating and diet practices. Concepts of affect and assemblage were drawn on to explore the complex and contradictory ways health is understood and lived. Health was described throughout examples as an imperative that links with appearance (look good, feel good and vice versa). However, it was also described as something people can become 'addicted' to and as having the potential to 'become dangerous' through practices which are undertaken too intensively or in the wrong 'dose', as in Clare's description of a school friend who suffered anorexia as 'becoming too healthy'.

Ideas about health, happiness and appearance were entangled and complicated by a perspective of 'affect', as the way the body 'feels' in relation to health was shown to be profoundly contingent and complex. Steph, Anna and others imagined that undertaking a larger range of 'healthy practices' such as toning exercises and a careful diet would enable them to feel 'happier and more confident' in their bodies. However, participants like Gillian and Jason who undertook regulative exercise and diet practices in this way described being 'locked in' to their routines as crucial to maintaining an acceptable sense of self. Rather than being enabling or 'liberating', through these examples the body's affects were shown to be restricted or closed down through having to 'keep up' this work. This was shown to have particularly difficult implications for sense of self if body work was interrupted by injury or illness. A focus on affect and assemblage understands 'health' as arranged through the contingent processes of engagement between bodies and other assemblages. A key focus here was on 'health affects' as composing 'what a body can do'. This perspective of health as a complex relational assemblage informing the body's capacities was also used in Chapter 6 to analyse the more intensive or 'extreme' practices of body work such as intensive weights training, cosmetic surgical procedures and recovering from anorexia. Cosmetic surgery and relations with food are other body work practices which involve affects similar to those discussed in relation to exercise and lifting weights, in that they entail particularly intensive affects which are meaningful for the ways the body is lived.

This perspective of health as an assemblage assists understandings of 'everyday health' practices as well as more 'extreme practices' beyond the dominant framings of risk and pathology. Isabelle's and Kate's cosmetic surgery examples are shown to be *more than* the simple territorialising effects of dominant feminine beauty standards. Their cosmetic surgery is not simply caused by poor body image or pathology such as body dysmorphic disorder. The model of bodies drawn upon in these examples also enables a more complex reading than cause-and-effect explanations. It focuses instead on the ways affects influence practices and intensities of body work form the self in non-deterministic – ways, such as Kate and Isabelle having different

Conclusion: embodying youth studies 149

'outcomes' related to breast implant surgery that will take them in different directions. Similarly, in Beth's example, recovering from anorexia was explored through affects and relations. 'Recovering' was shown to be possible through changing the affects related to food from 'shame and guilt' which had stopped her from eating. The examples in this final chapter intended to show that Deleuze and Guattari's (1987) concepts of the body can assist in building a more detailed understanding 'extreme' practices of body work such as of anorexia and other 'deadly practices of the self' such as drug addiction, alcoholism and masochism. In earlier chapters, it also intended to show that these concepts can also be comprehended and used as tools in analysing more 'everyday' practices related to 'health', including diet and exercise, showing how 'what a body can do' is negotiated through the ongoing relations and affects of bodies. This perspective can be useful for broadening understandings of practices typically analysed in the context of 'risk' and pathology such as eating disorders, body image and body dysmorphic disorder and steroid use.

Embodying research methodologies

There are a range of methodological tensions and issues which need to be further developed alongside efforts to 'bring the body in' to research. Numerous feminist scholars working from a post-structuralist or post-human approach have critiqued the 'rational, conscious, stable, unified, knowing individual' subject of humanism (St Pierre and Pillow 2000; Ryan-Flood and Gill 2010: 6; Braidotti 2013) that often continues to underpin research methodologies. Situated knowledge, or the 'view from a body' as Haraway (1988) calls it, emphasises the necessarily embodied and contextual production of all knowledge and experience, in which there are no 'innocent' or omniscient perspectives from which to theorise or do research. This may mean rethinking not only methods such as interviewing, but as St Pierre has suggested, the very foundations of research. St Pierre (2011: 618) argues that qualitative research methods have stemmed from rationalist, humanist foundations and the 'principle of individuation', in which the human subject is 'separate from everything else and usually master of the universe', and from which binary assumptions of subject/object, knower/known flow. St Pierre argues that this ontological and epistemological perspective has underpinned positivist as well as qualitative research methods, as concepts in social science are based on that 'I' – individuation: the researcher, participant, data, identity, reflexivity, experience, analysis (2011: 619).

> If we no longer believe in a disentangled humanist self, individual, person, we have to rethink qualitative methods (interviewing and observation) grounded in that human being as well as humanist representation.
>
> (St Pierre 2011: 620)

150　*Conclusion: embodying youth studies*

Deleuzian and other postmodern concepts aim to de-individualise, 'to disrupt individuations we believe are real' (St Pierre 2011: 618). Concepts such as 'events' (in the place of 'individuals' or 'subjects'), or becoming relate to instability and the entangled, processual qualities of all things; *and* rather than is. As St Pierre says, 'the implications of entanglement are staggering', as it involves no longer thinking of oneself as 'I' but as entangled with everyone, everything else. This focus on processes of entanglement and de-individualisation has been taken up by feminist researchers working from Deleuzo-Guattarian, post-human and new materialist frameworks drawn from Karen Barad.

Entanglement, intra-action and diffraction: developments in feminist research

The question of how to better em-body theory and research has been central in recent developments in feminist materialist perspectives (Coleman 2013). Hierarchical, dualistic frameworks are a lasting legacy of feminist theorising of embodiment which new materialist perspectives seek to challenge through a focus on matter as productive (van der Tuin and Dolphijn 2010). New materialist perspectives highlight the importance of more-than-discursive aspects of experience which produce embodiments through processes of entanglement, engagement and negotiation. Feminist researchers in sociology, education and cultural studies in particular have been advancing postmodern and post-human approaches to qualitative research methodologies working with Deleuze, Guattari, Barad and others (MacLure 2011; Coleman and Ringrose 2013a; Taylor and Ivinson 2013; Fox and Alldred 2015).

Barad's theories of agential realism and the body aims to account for the ways that matter, and not only discourse, 'comes to matter' (Barad 2007: 191–2). Barad argues that 'bodies are material–discursive phenomena that materialize in intra-action with (and, by definition, are indissociable from) the particular apparatuses of bodily production through which they come to matter (in both senses of the word)' (2007: 209). Barad conceives of matter as a doing rather than a thing (2007: 210). Barad's concepts of intra-action and diffraction are key in her framework for understanding 'the entanglement of matter and meaning'. Ringrose and Renold (2014), among many others, have drawn on Barad's concepts of diffraction and intra-action to foreground the entanglements which comprise research assemblages. To undertake a 'diffractive reading' entails a 'respectful, detailed, ethical engagement' with 'data' and all aspects of the research assemblage (see Hickey-Moody 2015: 808). It is a way of foregrounding the researcher in the research assemblage, and acknowledging the researcher's role in terms of 'an ethico-political commitment where the production of knowledge is about making a difference in the world and understanding the what, where, when, how, and for whom differences matter (Barad, 2007)' (Ringrose and Renold 2014: 1–2).

Conclusion: embodying youth studies 151

Methods of 'rhizomatic' research (see St. Pierre 1997, 2002; Hultman and Lenz Taguchi 2010; Mazzei 2011; Merceica and Merceica 2010; Ringrose 2011) have similarly been taken up by numerous researchers following a Deleuzo-Guattarian approach. Rhizomatic methodologies aim to foreground the intensities, relations and affects between bodies, including bodies in the research encounter (such as between researcher and interviewee). The focus of such research is on becomings, changes and possibilities for newness; seeing the body as a group of forces and intensities that are continually changing and modulating. In a similar vein, methods of 'schizoanalysis' are a further development which aims to map different formations of assemblages (Renold and Ringrose 2008, 2011; Ringrose 2013) and 'experiment with revolutionary scope' to produce change (Ringrose 2015: 397).

These epistemological, ontological and methodological innovations present new and exciting ways of exploring the body in empirical research. They also speak to broader efforts to 'enable the happening of the social world – its ongoingness, relationality, contingency and sensuousness – to be investigated' (Lury and Wakeford 2012: 2). Such developments have highlighted the need for methodologies to both pay attention to the processes of change, stability and inequalities in the social world, but also the ways in which social science methods also play into the 'creation of the world' (Coleman and Ringrose 2013b: 1). The implications of new materialist and Deleuzo-Guattarian methodologies for qualitative research have been explored, for example, in relation to analysis of interview data (see for example Fox and Ward 2008; Renold and Ringrose 2008, 2011; Jackson 2010; Mazzei and McCoy 2010; Mazzei 2011; Hickey-Moody 2013; Mazzei 2014; Renold and Ivinson 2014) and visual data including creative, digital or online methods (Hultman and Lenz Taguchi 2010; Lorimer 2013; Pettinger and Lyon 2012; Renold and Mellor 2013; Ringrose and Harvey 2015).

Embodied, visual, arts-based and digital methodologies will continue to be developed in response to recent efforts to pursue non-representational methodologies (Vannini 2015). This is not necessarily in the space of getting 'beyond representation' in the sense of 'solving' or transcending the issues with representing data (as discussed in relation to St Pierre's work above). Rather, the success in these methods lies not in the degree to which they objectively 'represent' or reproduce a scenario, but rather for what the engagement (or research entanglement) produces. As Vannini argues, there is no one right way of 'doing' non-representational methodologies; rather, it is a sensibility or an orientation to data-drawn recent insights, critiques and developments in qualitative feminist methodologies such as those by St Pierre (1997, 2002, 2011), St Pierre and Pillow (2000) and Lather (2001, 2007), and numerous others. This orientation has informed how I have approached the research assemblage described in the book. These approaches will contribute to expanding the frameworks and possibilities for those designing the methods used to generate embodied methodologies and research encounters (see Coffey *et al.* 2016).

152 *Conclusion: embodying youth studies*

Feminist micro-politics

Alongside the epistemological and ontological issues considered above, the status of the material body and its interaction with other entities such as culture are being rethought (Coleman 2014; Budgeon 2015). Those working from a feminist ethico-political position and motivated by the approaches of new materialist, post-humanist and/or Deleuzo-Guattarian perspectives are engaging with the implications for decentring the humanist subject in research, politics and critique.

Some are unsure of the political potential available to be mobilised by feminist new materialist approaches because of the ways subjectivity is theorised (related to the decentring of the human in analysis). Schnabel (2104), for example, argues that when compared with feminist post-colonial science studies and queer ecologies, new feminist materialisms do not retain enough focus on patriarchy or other social inequalities and systems of hierarchy. As Hinton (2014: 101) argues, however, positioning and standpoint is an important focus in feminist new materialist approaches as 'a political gesture and an ethical imperative', though this approach decentres, delegitimises claims to universal, disembodied knowledge. Following Haraway (1988), this feminist new materialist approach aims to be accountable, located, situated in embodiment (Hinton 2014). Hinton draws on what Lorenz-Meyer terms 'socially responsible epistemic agency' as informing a responsible, ethical feminist politics of location (Hinton 2014: 101). Hinton advocates a perspective of feminist practice as produced through intra-actions between positionings and entanglements of ideas, scale (local, global) and time (past, present or future iterations of feminism) to allow for openness and newness in feminist work (Hinton 2014: 112). Grosz has similarly argued that the key problems for feminism do not involve increasing women's 'freedom', but rather 'how to expand the variety of activities, including the activities of knowledge-production, so that women and men may be able to act differently and open up activities to new interests, perspectives and frameworks hitherto not adequately explored or invented' (2010: 154).

As Coleman suggests, feminism might be better understood as something that is done 'immanently' as an 'ethics of worlding' rather than something that is progressing towards some specific predefined future:

> An understanding of inventive feminist theory would place emphasis on the performativity of our ways of observing, describing and intervening in the worlds we are part of. As Barad puts it, 'our intra-actions contribute to the differential mattering of the world … We are responsible for the cuts that we help enact not because we do the choosing (neither do we escape responsibility because "we" are "chosen" by them), but because we are an agential part of the material becoming of the universe' (2007: 178). The politics of inventive feminist theory here is thus understood as 'an ethics of worlding' (2007: 392) and my suggestion is that such an

Conclusion: embodying youth studies 153

inventive practice might be a way of continuing to ensure the animation of feminism's transformative nature.

(2014: 42–3)

Micro-politics is another mode of paying attention to 'the vitality of matter' (Edwards and Fenwick 2014). Deleuze and Guattari's ontology is referred to as 'micro-political' because of the 'vitality' and capacity inherent in their theorisation of matter, bodies and the world which comes with the 'insistence that things could be otherwise' (Houle 2011: 110). Micro-politics is 'a concept out of which a non-oppositional and non-negative force of politicality – a lived, enacted affirmative belief in another, better, yet unknown outcome – can happen' (Houle 2011: 114). A focus on micro-politics in research encounters, for example, can mean giving attention to the ways the micro-politics of a particular assemblage are linked to a broader socio-political context or politics. Fox gives the example of 'the obesity assemblage', in which he analyses how the micro-politics of this context 'are also the politics of a much broader field of relations linking bodies and desires to flows of money, things and ideas occurring way beyond their immediate situations.' There are two potential implications or directions that a focus on micro-politics can take. One is in the mapping of the social, outlining micro-relations of encounters and assemblages in our research, and making visible the aspects that would usually go unnoticed or be written out of the research process. This micro-analysis has micro-political implications, through enabling the possibilities of becoming otherwise to be detected. Renold and Ivinson argue that for them, 'recovering and recognising queer affects ... is a pressing ethico-political priority' (2014: 371). The second implication relates to research or activities which aim to actively *change* the micro-politics or micro-relations of a given context. Fox (2014) for example suggests ways for altering the micro-politics of the obesity-assemblage, related to critical challenge:

To change the micropolitics of the obesity-assemblage requires a critical challenge to the marketisation and industrialisation of food production, processing and consumption, challenges that Alkon (2013: 2) argues can be underpinned by the principles of localism, justice and equality within the food sovereignty movement (Wittman, 2011).

In this example, the role of critique is highlighted as crucial in efforts to change the relations (and by extension, the micro-politics) of an assemblage. From a Baradian (2007) perspective, an alternative term for critique is 'diffractive analysis'. The concept of transversality also links with a focus on bringing about change in feminist intra-activist research through producing the variations and openness in relations which can produce new possibilities for feminist political engagement *produce* different assemblages through research practice (Coffey and Ringrose forthcoming). A focus on micro-politics, whether in highlighting the 'becoming-otherwise' that is already occurring, or

154 *Conclusion: embodying youth studies*

in actively working to produce micro-political change to assemblages via critique or transversal practices, is another way that developments in feminist post-human perspectives can engage with opening new possibilities and potential for feminist politics in research.

Conclusion: embodying youth studies

Youth sociology has at many points embraced feminist theoretical and methodological developments. The key points throughout this book can be perhaps seen an extension of the feminist tradition of 'demanding that the unseen and unacknowledged be made visible and heard' (Ryan-Flood and Gill 2010: 1) in the context of youth studies. Because of 'the body's' complex history in terms of philosophy, it brings significant 'baggage' that needs to be addressed and acknowledged if we are to understand its current significance in sociological theory and research. Critiques of humanism are particularly relevant to the study of the body and how the body has been conceptualised historically – as other to theory and as *the* natural or essential object upon which society and culture inscribes meanings. The sociology of youth can contribute to efforts to 'bring the body to theory' (Bordo 1997: 3), as well as continuing the post-structural feminist undertaking of troubling the subject of humanism (St Pierre and Pillow 2000: 6). Further sociological work is required to build methodologies and methods beyond humanism. Colebrook argues that we must see Deleuze's work as 'an active response to a host of problems in diverse areas, not just within philosophy' (2002: 7). In my work, I have used Deleuze and Guattari's concepts in providing a response to a range of theoretical problems in sociological and feminist empirical work, including the negotiation of dualisms, in which the body is centrally bound. It is because of the dualisms which have for so long surrounded and constrained research on the body that it is necessary to turn to other ways of conceptualising the body, such as through the philosophies of Deleuze, Guattari and Spinoza, and I have aimed to show the utility and promise of these concepts for empirical feminist youth research.

The challenges to humanist thought thrown down by post-humanist and new materialist perspectives raise a number of questions for the field which will need to be further considered. For example, what are the implications associated with understanding matter as 'vital' and productive for our analyses of youth and the conditions of experience for young people? What might the perspectives of Deleuze and Guattari, Barad and others produce in the way of previously unthought questions, practices and knowledge in the sociology of youth? A focus on micro-politics, through mapping the social or actively engaging with attempts to produce change through critique might provide a platform from which to begin for those unfamiliar with these approaches or sceptical of their utility. Beginning from a perspective of micro-politics holds that it will be crucial to continue to mobilise the critical perspectives of gender, class, race, place, sexuality and ability that have been so

Conclusion: embodying youth studies   155

useful in illuminating the conditions of inequality shaping young people's lives. Doing this alongside post-human or new materialist perspectives and the non-oppositional, embodied, fine-grained analytic tools they bring will enable new potential for an embodied youth studies.

References

Barad, K. (2007). *Meeting the Universe Halfway: Quantum Physics and the Entanglement of Matter and Meaning*. Durham and London: Duke University Press.

Bordo, S. (1997). Bringing Body to Theory. In D. Welton (ed.), *Body and Flesh: A Philosophical Reader*. London: Blackwell.

Braidotti, R. (2013). *The Posthuman*. New York: Wiley.

Budgeon, S. (2003). Identity as an Embodied Event. *Body and Society*, 9(1), 35–55.

Budgeon, S. (2015). Theorizing Subjectivity and Feminine Embodiment: Feminist Approaches and Debates. In J. Wyn and H. Cahill (eds), *Handbook of Youth and Childhood Studies* (pp. 243–256). New York: Springer.

Coffey, J., Budgeon, S. and Cahill, H. (2016). Learning Bodies: Towards Embodied Theories, Methodologies and Pedagogies. In J. Coffey, S. Budgeon and H. Cahill (eds), *Learning Bodies: The Body in Youth and Childhood Studies*. New York: Springer.

Coffey, J. and Ringrose, J. (forthcoming). Boobs, Barbie and Transversal Relations: Feminist Deleuzo-Guattarian Inspired Perspectives on Practice. In J. Lynch, J. Rowlands, T. Gale and A. Skourdoumbis (eds), *Diffractive Readings in Practice: Trajectories in Theory, Fields and Professions*. London: Routledge.

Coffey, J. and Watson, J. (2015). Bodies: Corporeality and Embodiment in Childhood and Youth Studies. In J. Wyn and H. Cahill (eds), *Handbook of Children and Youth Studies*. New York: Springer.

Colebrook, C. (2002). *Gilles Deleuze*. London: Routledge.

Coleman, R. (2013). Sociology and the Virtual: Interactive Mirrors, Representational Thinking and Intensive Power. *Sociological Review*, 61(1), 1–20. doi: 10.1111/1467-954x.12002

Coleman, R. (2014). Inventive Feminist Theory: Representation, Materiality and Intensive Time. *Women: A Cultural Review*, 25(1), 27–45.

Coleman, R. and Ringrose, J. (2013a). *Deleuze and Research Methodologies*. Edinburgh: Edinburgh University Press.

Coleman, R. and Ringrose, J. (2013b). Introduction: Deleuze and Research Methodologies. In R. Coleman and J. Ringrose (eds), *Deleuze and Research Methodologies*. Edinburgh: Edinburgh University Press.

Deleuze, G. (1988). *Spinoza: Practical Philosophy* (R. Hurley, trans.). San Francisco, CA: City Lights Books.

Deleuze, G. and Guattari, F. (1987). *A Thousand Plateaus: Capitalism and Schizophrenia* (B. Massumi, trans.). Edinburgh: Edinburgh University Press.

Driver, C. (2011). Embodying Hardcore: Rethinking 'Subcultural' Authenticities. *Journal of Youth Studies, 14*(8), 975–990. doi: 10.1080/13676261.2011.617733

Edwards, R. and Fenwick, T. (2014). Critique and Politics: A Sociomaterialist Intervention. *Educational Philosophy and Theory*, 1–20.

Fox, N. J. (2002). Refracting 'Health': Deleuze, Guattari and Body-Self. *Health*, 6(3), 347–363. doi: 10.1177/136345930200600306

156   *Conclusion: embodying youth studies*

Fox, N. J. (2014). The micropolitics of obesity: materialism, neoliberalism and food sovereignty. Paper presented at the British Sociological Association Medical Sociology Annual Conference, Birmingham.

Fox, N. J. and Alldred, P. (2015). Inside the research-assemblage: New materialism and the micropolitics of social inquiry. *Sociological Research Online*, 20(2), 6.

Fox, N. J. and Ward, K. J. (2008). What Are Health Identities and How May We Study Them? *Sociology of Health and Illness*, 30(7), 1007–21.

France, A. and Roberts, S. (2014). The Problem of Social Generations: A Critique of the New Emerging Orthodoxy in Youth Studies. *Journal of Youth Studies*, 18(2), 215–30. doi: 10.1080/13676261.2014.944122

Grosz, E. (1994). *Volatile Bodies: Towards a Corporeal Feminism*. St Leonards: Allen & Unwin.

Grosz, E. (2010). Feminism, Materialism and Freedom. In D. Coole, S. Frost, J. Bennett, P. Cheah, M. A. Orlie and E. Grosz (eds), *New Materialisms: Ontology, Agency, and Politics*. Durham and London: Duke University Press.

Haraway, D. (1988). Situated Knowledges: The Science Question in Feminism and the Privilege of Partial Perspective. *Feminist Studies*, 14(3), 575–599.

Hickey-Moody, A. (2013). Affect as Method: Feelings, Aesthetics and Affective Pedagogy. In R. Coleman and J. Ringrose (eds), *Deleuze and Research Methodologies*. Edinburgh: Edinburgh University Press.

Hickey-Moody, A. (2015). Beside Ourselves: Worlds beyond People. *British Journal of Sociology of Education*, 36(5), 802–813. doi: 10.1080/01425692.2015.1043187

Hinton, P. (2014). 'Situated Knowledges' and New Materialism(s): Rethinking a Politics of Location. *Women: A Cultural Review*, 25(1), 99–113. doi: 10.1080/09574042.2014.901104

Houle, K. (2011). Micropolitics. In C. J. Stivale (ed.), *Key Concepts: Gilles Deleuze: Key Concepts (2nd Edition)*. Durham: Acumen.

Hultman, K. and Lenz Taguchi, H. (2010). Challenging Anthropocentric Analysis of Visual Data: A Relational Materialist Methodological Approach to Educational Research. *International Journal of Qualitative Studies in Education*, 23(5), 525–542. doi: 10.1080/09518398.2010.500628

Jackson, A. Y. (2010). Deleuze and the girl. *International Journal of Qualitative Studies in Education (QSE)*, 23(5), 579–587.

Keane, H. (2005). Diagnosing the Male Steroid User: Drug Use, Body Image and Disordered Masculinity. *Health*, 9(2), 189–208. doi: 10.1177/1363459305050585

Kelly, P. (2015). Zygmunt Bauman's Challenge for Critical Youth Studies. In P. Kelly and A. Kamp (eds), *A Critical Youth Studies for the 21st Century*. Leiden and Boston, MA: Brill.

Lather, P. (2001). Postbook: Working the Ruins of Feminist Ethnography. *Signs*, 27(1), 199–227.

Lather, P. (2007). *Getting Lost: Feminist Efforts toward a Double(D) Science*. Albany, NY: State University of New York Press.

Leahy, D. (2014). Assembling a Health [y] Subject: Risky and Shameful Pedagogies in Health Education. *Critical Public Health*, 24(2), 171–181.

Lorimer, J. (2013). More-than-Human Visual Analysis. In R. Coleman and J. Ringrose (eds), *Deleuze and Research Methodologies*. Edinburgh: Edinburgh University Press.

Lupton, D. (1995). *The Imperative of Health: Public Health and the Regulated Body*. London: Sage.

Conclusion: embodying youth studies 157

Lury, C. and Wakeford, N. (2012). Introduction: A Perpetual Inventory. In C. Lury and N. Wakeford (eds), *Inventive Methods: The Happening of the Social*. New York and London: Routledge.

MacLure, M. (2011). Qualitative Inquiry: Where Are the Ruins? *Qualitative Inquiry*, 17(10), 997–1005. doi: 10.1177/1077800411423198

Mazzei, L. A. (2011). Thinking Data with Deleuze. *International Journal of Qualitative Studies in Education*, 23(5), 511–523. doi: 10.1080/09518398.2010.497176

Mazzei, L. A. (2014). Beyond an Easy Sense: A Diffractive Analysis. *Qualitative Inquiry*, 20(6), 742–746. doi: 10.1177/1077800414530257

Mazzei, L. A. and McCoy, K. (2010). Thinking with Deleuze in Qualitative Research. *International Journal of Qualitative Studies in Education*, 23(5), 503–509. doi: 10.1080/09518398.2010.500634

McRobbie, A. (2015). Notes on the Perfect. *Australian Feminist Studies*, 30(83), 3–20. doi: 10.1080/08164649.2015.1011485

Merceica, D. and Merceica, D. (2010). Opening Research to Intensities: Rethinking Disability Research with Deleuze and Guattari. *Journal of Philosophy of Education*, 44(1), 80–92.

Moore, S. (2010). Is the Healthy Body Gendered? Toward a Feminist Critique of the New Paradigm of Health. *Body and Society*, 16(2), 95–118.

Pettinger, L. and Lyon, D. (2012). No Way to Make a Living. Net: Exploring the Possibilities of the Web for Visual and Sensory Sociologies of Work. *Sociological Research Online*, 17(2), 18.

Ravn, S. and Coffey, J. (2015). 'Steroids, It's So Much an Identity Thing!' Perceptions of Steroid Use, Risk and Masculine Body Image. *Journal of Youth Studies*. doi: 10.1080/13676261.2015.1052051

Renold, E. and Ivinson, G. (2014). Horse-Girl Assemblages: Towards a Post-Human Cartography of Girls' Desire in an Ex-Mining Valleys Community. *Discourse: Studies in the Cultural Politics of Education*, 35(3), 361–76. doi: 10.1080/01596306.2014.888841

Renold, E. and Mellor, D. (2013). Deleuze and Guattari in the Nursery. In R. Coleman and J. Ringrose (eds), *Deleuze and Research Methodologies*. Edinburgh: Edinburgh University Press.

Renold, E. and Ringrose, J. (2008). Regulation and Rupture: Mapping Tween and Teenage Girls' Resistance to the Heterosexual Matrix. *Feminist Theory*, 9, 314–39.

Renold, E. and Ringrose, J. (2011). Schizoid Subjectivities? Re-theorizing Teen Girls' Sexual Cultures in an Era of 'Sexualization'. *Journal of Sociology*, 47(4), 389–409.

Ringrose, J. (2011). Beyond Discourse? Using Deleuze and Guattari's Schizoanalysis to Explore Affective Assemblages, Heterosexually Striated Space, and Lines of Flight Online and at School. *Educational Philosophy and Theory*, 43(6), 598–618.

Ringrose, J. (2013). *Postfeminist Education?: Girls and the Sexual Politics of Schooling*. New York: Routledge.

Ringrose, J. (2015). Schizo-Feminist Educational Research Cartographies. *Deleuze Studies*, 9(3), 393–409. doi: doi:10.3366/dls.2015.0194

Ringrose, J. and Harvey, L. (2015). Boobs, Back-off, and Small Bits: Mediated Body Parts, Sexual Reward and Gendered Shame in Teens' Networked Images. *Continuum: Journal of Media and Cultural Studies*, 29.

Ringrose, J., Harvey, L., Gill, R. and Livingstone, S. (2013). Teen Girls, Sexual Double Standards and 'Sexting': Gendered Value in Digital Image Exchange. *Feminist Theory*, 14(3), 305–23. doi: 10.1177/1464700113499853

158 *Conclusion: embodying youth studies*

Ringrose, J., and Renold, E. (2014). 'F**k Rape!': Exploring Affective Intensities in a Feminist Research Assemblage. *Qualitative Inquiry*, 20(6), 772–780. doi: 10.1177/ 1077800414530261

Rose, N. (2007). *The Politics of Life Itself: Biomedicine, Power, and Subjectivity in the Twenty-First Century.* Princeton, NJ: Princeton University Press.

Ryan-Flood, R. and Gill, R. (2010). *Secrecy and Silence in the Research Process: Feminist Reflections.* New York: Routledge.

St Pierre, E. A. (1997). Methodology in the Fold and the Irruption of Transgressive Data. *International Journal of Qualitative Studies in Education*, 10(2), 175–89.

St Pierre, E. (2002). Circling the Text: Nomadic Writing Practices. In N. K. Denzin and Y. S. Lincoln (eds), *Qualitative Inquiry Reader.* Thousand Oaks, CA: Sage.

St Pierre, E. (2011). Post Qualitative Research: The Critique and the Coming After. In N. K. Denzin and Y. S. Lincoln (eds), *The Sage Handbook of Qualitative Research.* California: Thousand Oaks.

St Pierre, E. and Pillow, W. (eds) (2000). *Working the Ruins: Feminist Poststructural Theory and Methods in Education.* New York: Routledge.

Schnabel, L. (2014). The Question of Subjectivity in Three Emerging Feminist Science Studies Frameworks: Feminist Postcolonial Science Studies, New Feminist Materialisms, and Queer Ecologies. *Women's Studies International Forum*, 44(0), 10–16. doi: http://dx.doi.org/10.1016/j.wsif.2014.02.011

Taylor, C. A. and Ivinson, G. (2013). Material Feminisms: New Directions for Education. *Gender and Education*, 25(6), 665–670. doi: 10.1080/09540253.2013.834617

van der Tuin, I. and Dolphijn, R. (2010). The Transversality of New Materialism. *Women: A Cultural Review*, 21(2), 153–171. doi: 10.1080/09574042.2010.488377

Vannini, P. (2015). Non Representational Research Methodologies: An Introduction. In P. Vannini (ed.), *Non-Representational Methodologies: Re-envisioning Research.* New York: Routledge.

Woodman, D. and Wyn, J. (2015). *Youth and Generation: Rethinking Change and Inequality in the Lives of Young People.* London: Sage.

Index

absent presence 1–2, 18, 42
addiction 105–6, 121–27, 138–39,
　148–49
affect theory 28–33, 55–60, 81–3, 87–8,
　92–4, 99–101, 107–11, 114–17,
　126–35, 139–40
agency 19, 22–8, 34–8, 50–2, 133–34
analysis 28, 33, 35–7, 50–4, 74, 143–51
appearance 4–5, 8–11, 29, 47, 76–81,
　83–6, 101–4, 106–16, 123–24, 130–36,
　147–49
arts-based methods 151
assemblage 10–13, 28–37, 53–5, 73–9,
　86–90, 93–4, 99–101, 113–21, 133–35,
　139, 144–54

Barad, K. 26, 31, 38, 144, 150–54
beauty work 48, 51–2, 89, 147
Beck, U. 7, 19
Butler, J. 22, 25, 32
Bourdieu, P. 19–20, 25, 35
Braidotti, R. 27, 34
binaries 10, 23, 83, 145
biological determinism 2
body dysmorphic disorder 8, 127–28,
　133–35, 140, 148–49
body ideals 76–86, 98, 124, 134, 147
body image 1, 6–11, 72, 75, 83–4,
　131–35, 140; psychological
　understandings of 24, 126–29;
　see also body dysmorphic disorder
body pressure 79–81, 89–95, 124, 147
body theory 17–31, 35–8
body work 1, 4–5, 10, 47–57, 72–3,
　75–81, 83–6, 89–92, 103–11, 113–17,
　121–36, 147–49
body work practices 4–5, 47–50, 55–7,
　72–81, 98–101, 104–7, 114–17,
　122–31

body project 4–5, 48, 93
bodily difference 2, 12, 22, 78
brain development 5, 145
breast implants 10, 130–32
buff culture 121–28

Cartesian binaries 3, 23; see also dualism
class 2, 5, 44, 61–2
consumer culture 8–11, 48–9, 79–84, 93,
　98–99, 123–27
cosmetic surgery 75, 98, 128–35
change 17, 20, 25, 28–33, 35, 38, 88, 99,
　115, 137–38

Deleuze, G. 26–37, 52–4, 73–5, 99–100,
　115–17, 139, 151–55
diffraction 150; diffractive analysis
　153
disability 29, 47, 92
discourse 20–22, 25, 30–3, 78–9, 101–6,
　134, 147
dualism 3, 23–4, 34–5, 154
Durkheim, E. 18, 24–5

epistemology 24, 117, 128
eating disorders 75, 135, 139–40
embodiment 2–6, 18, 22, 43–4, 98–100,
　112–15, 143–46; embodied research
　59–61, 149–55; embodied sensations
　see sensations
ethnicity 6, 44, 66, 74
exercise 48–50, 56, 75–6, 101–8, 110–13,
　122–23, 128, 139, 148–49

Facebook 55, 99
fat 75, 78, 84, 101–3
feminism 2–3, 19–24, 50–7, 129, 143–46,
　150–55; feminist critique of Deleuze
　33–5

160   *Index*

feminist activism 22–4, 145–46; feminist politics 152–54 *see also* politics
femininities 44–6, 79–81
football 125–26; footballer's body 84–7, 93
fitness 8–10, 48–50, 72, 98, 104–11
folding 26
Foucault, M. 21, 48

Gender 8–11, 20–5, 31–5, 44, 47–8, 72–9, 83–8, 146–7; gender ideals 89–93, 114, 123–9
Grosz, E. 21–3, 152
Guattari, F. 4, 25, 27–35, 52, 73–4, 154
gym 8, 48–9, 56, 75, 84–7, 90–1, 128; gym culture 73, 90, 91, 123

health 6–11, 35–7, 48–50, 54, 99–100, 121–23, 147–49; health as happiness 107–115; health as moral responsibility 101–06; health practices 56, 75
health ideals 1, 4, 9, 57, 84–6, 101, 147
heterosexuality (heteronormativity) 46, 57, 78–9, 82–3, 88, 124

identity 4–5, 25, 43–5, 53–4, 86–7 *see also* self
images 24, 51–3, 147; digital images 45–7; ideal images 7–11, 80–1, 92–3, 101, 127–28
interviews (method) 55–8
inequalities 2–3, 7, 18–24, 38, 44, 78, 86, 145–46
intensity 26, 29–30, 134

materiality 22, 24, 34, 145
materiality/representation 23–4, 30
masculinities 44, 46, 58, 90, 92
media images 24, 52–3; *see* ideal images
mental illness 6
methodology 42, 55, 57–61, 149–51, 154
micro-politics 90, 94, 147, 152–54
molar 31–2, 86–8
molecular 31–2, 53–4, 88, 90, 92
muscular ideal 49, 77, 84–6, 91, 106, 147; muscles 123–26

natural 2, 18, 21–3, 78, 86, 145–46; nature-culture 37
neoliberalism 48–50, 100, 107

new materialism: theory 11–12, 14, 37, 154; data analysis 81, 144, 150–52

obesity 6, 153 *see also* overweight, fat
ontology 26, 30–1, 38, 94, 117, 128, 144
overweight 75, 78, 102–03, 107, 111, 122

performativity 32, 82–3, 86–7, 152
post-feminism 45, 54, 83, 129–31
post-structural theory 3, 21–3, 25, 149
power 20–1, 74
photovoice 58–9
politics 143–46, 152–53
potentialty *see* change
psychosocial development 5–8, 42

qualitative research methods 58–9, 149–51
queer 43, 146, 152

race 2, 44, 145
recovering 136–39, 148–9
reflexivity 59, 149
regulation 7, 10, 44–6, 48–9, 88, 104, 114–15
representation 24, 51–2, 98
resistance 19, 34, 51, 94, 143
rhizomatic research 59, 151
risk 6–7, 44–7, 107, 144–45; risk society 6–7
risk discourses 6, 46–7, 144

schizoanalysis 151
self 4–5, 72, 100, 110–14, 125–27, 135; self-responsibility 9, 100–4
sensation 36, 60, 75, 99–102, 108–11, 114
sex 21–3, 34, 45–7
sex/gender binary 20, 22–4, 31–2, 74, 145–46
sexism 46–7, 78, 93
sexting 19, 45–7
sexuality 44–7, 79–80, 83, 87–8, 124
sexualisation 45–7
sexuality education 45–6
slenderness 48, 51, 77, 83, 112
Spinoza, B. 1, 4, 10, 26, 29, 136, 143, 154
social change 2, 17, 19, 34, 38, 43, 94
social media 9, 19, 46–7, 98
social theory 2–3, 17–31, 37–8, 143–45

Index 161

sport 49, 75, 86
structure/agency 19–20, 25–6, 38, 51–2
subject/object – 23, 52, 54, 149
subjectivity 20, 25, 54, 58, 152

territorialisation 13, 73–4, 78, 83, 146
thin ideal *see* slenderness

visual culture 45, 51, 85, 93
visual methods 58–9, 151

wellbeing 7, 9, 13

youth transitions 6, 42–3, 61
youth cultures 43–5, 58
youth 5–8, 19, 42–47, 72–3, 98–9, 144
youth studies 1, 5–11, 19, 42–3, 47, 58, 143–50, 154–55; youth sociology 1–4, 19, 42, 143, 154

Zyzz 123

eBooks
from Taylor & Francis
Helping you to choose the right eBooks for your Library

Add to your library's digital collection today with Taylor & Francis eBooks. We have over 50,000 eBooks in the Humanities, Social Sciences, Behavioural Sciences, Built Environment and Law, from leading imprints, including Routledge, Focal Press and Psychology Press.

Choose from a range of subject packages or create your own!

Benefits for you
- Free MARC records
- COUNTER-compliant usage statistics
- Flexible purchase and pricing options
- 70% approx of our eBooks are now DRM-free.

Benefits for your user
- Off-site, anytime access via Athens or referring URL
- Print or copy pages or chapters
- Full content search
- Bookmark, highlight and annotate text
- Access to thousands of pages of quality research at the click of a button.

Free Trials Available

We offer free trials to qualifying academic, corporate and government customers.

eCollections
Choose from 20 different subject eCollections, including:
- Asian Studies
- Economics
- Health Studies
- Law
- Middle East Studies

eFocus
We have 16 cutting-edge interdisciplinary collections, including:
- Development Studies
- The Environment
- Islam
- Korea
- Urban Studies

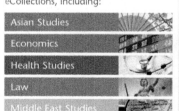

For more information, pricing enquiries or to order a free trial, please contact your local sales team:

UK/Rest of World: **online.sales@tandf.co.uk**
USA/Canada/Latin America: **e-reference@taylorandfrancis.com**
East/Southeast Asia: **martin.jack@tandf.com.sg**
India: **journalsales@tandfindia.com**

www.tandfebooks.com